First Workshop on Advancing Natural Language Processing for Wikipedia (WikiNLP 2024)

Miami, Florida, USA
16 November 2024

ISBN: 979-8-3313-0856-8

Printed from e-media with permission by:

Curran Associates, Inc.
57 Morehouse Lane
Red Hook, NY 12571

Association for Computational Linguistics
209 N. Eighth Street
Stroudsburg, Pennsylvania 18360

Phone: 1-570-476-8006
Fax: 1-570-476-0860

acl@aclweb.org

Additional copies of this publication are available from:

Curran Associates, Inc.
57 Morehouse Lane
Red Hook, NY 12571 USA
Phone: 845-758-0400
Fax: 845-758-2633
Email: curran@proceedings.com
Web: www.proceedings.com

WikiNLP 2024

The First Workshop on Advancing Natural Language Processing for Wikipedia

Proceedings of the Workshop

November 16, 2024

Order copies of this and other ACL proceedings from:

Association for Computational Linguistics (ACL)
317 Sidney Baker St. S
Suite 400 - 134
Kerrville, TX 78028
USA
Tel: +1-855-225-1962
acl@aclweb.org

Program Committee

Program Chairs

Angela Fan, Facebook
Tajuddeen Gwadabe, Masakhane Research Foundation
Isaac Johnson, Wikimedia Foundation
Lucie-Aimée Kaffee, Hugging Face
Fabio Petroni, Samaya AI
Daniel van Strien, Hugging Face

Reviewers

Saied Alshahrani, Pablo Aragón, Hiba Arnaout, Akhil Arora, Arnav Arora

Bonaventure F. P. Dossou

Srihari Jayakumar, Isaac Johnson

Nithish Kannen

Kartik Mathur, Jeanna Matthews

Tiziano Piccardi

Miriam Redi

Marija Sakota, Sina Semnani, Indira Sen, Diego Sáez Trumper

Harold Triedman, Mykola Trokhymovych, Houcemeddine Turki

Thejas Venkatesh

Table of Contents

Program

Saturday, November 16, 2024

09:00 - 09:05	*Opening Remarks*
09:05 - 09:50	*Keynote (Jess Wade)*
09:50 - 10:30	*Videos*
10:30 - 11:00	*Break*
11:00 - 12:00	*Poster Session*
12:00 - 12:45	*Lunch*
12:45 - 13:30	*Keynote (Scott A. Hale)*
13:30 - 14:15	*Panel (Misinformation)*
14:15 - 15:00	*Panel (Impact of LLMs)*
15:00 - 15:30	*Closing*

BORDIRLINES: A Dataset for Evaluating Cross-lingual Retrieval-Augmented Generation

Bryan Li, Samar Haider*, Fiona Luo*, Adwait Agashe*, Chris Callison-Burch
University of Pennsylvania
Philadelphia, PA, USA
[bryanli, samarh, fionaluo, aadwait, ccb]@seas.upenn.edu

Abstract

Large language models excel at creative generation but continue to struggle with the issues of hallucination and bias. While retrieval-augmented generation (RAG) provides a framework for grounding LLMs' responses in accurate and up-to-date information, it still raises the question of bias: which sources should be selected for inclusion in the context? And how should their importance be weighted? In this paper, we study the challenge of cross-lingual RAG and present a dataset to investigate the robustness of existing systems at answering queries about geopolitical disputes, which exist at the intersection of linguistic, cultural, and political boundaries. Our dataset is sourced from Wikipedia pages containing information relevant to the given queries and we investigate the impact of including additional context, as well as the composition of this context in terms of language and source, on an LLM's response. Our results show that existing RAG systems continue to be challenged by cross-lingual use cases and suffer from a lack of consistency when they are provided with competing information in multiple languages. We present case studies to illustrate these issues and outline steps for future research to address these challenges. We make our dataset and code publicly available.[1]

1 Introduction

Large language models continue to see rapidly increasing adoption across a wide variety of tasks, both in academic research and in technology products and services. But despite their impressive reasoning and language generation capabilities, they continue to suffer from the tendency to hallucinate information and propagate learned biases. Recent advancements in retrieval-augmented generation (RAG) have led to a new paradigm where users' queries are first used to find relevant passages using an information retrieval system, which are then provided as context to the LLM along with the query. While this approach makes LLMs produce outputs that are more grounded in real-world sources, it gives rise to a new question of which supporting information should be provided in the first place. While most research has focused on *relevance* via the design of richer embedding models to more precisely capture the meaning of text, we focus on the question of *balance* and investigate the importance and impact of including information from diverse sources which reflect a variety of viewpoints.

In this paper, we present BORDIRLINES, a dataset and framework for evaluating the robustness of cross-lingual retrieval-augmented generation. We focus on geopolitical bias, a topic that exists at the intersection of linguistic, cultural, and political boundaries, and forms the perfect test bed for our analysis. We use the BORDERLINES dataset (Li et al., 2024) as our source of geopolitical questions, which contains queries such as *"Is Ceuta a territory of Spain or Morocco?"*. By identifying the countries and languages that are relevant to queries like this, we construct a multilingual dataset of Wikipedia articles that cover all claimant countries of a particular territory to offer a diversity of perspectives. We then implement and evaluate multiple multilingual information retrieval models such as mDPR, COLBERT, BM25, and BGE M3 combined with both dense and sparse representations to improve the relevance of retrieved documents. We use this dataset to study how a model's response changes based on whether it is provided additional context and perform ablation studies to investigate how the response continues to vary as the composition of the provided documents is altered. Our results show that models continue to suffer from a lack of consistency across languages, and altering the documents provided in the context can have a drastic impact on their responses. We

*These authors contributed equally.
[1]https://github.com/manestay/bordIRlines

Proceedings of the First Workshop on Advancing Natural Language Processing for Wikipedia, pages 1–13
November 16, 2024 ©2024 Association for Computational Linguistics

provide two case studies to showcase these findings and outline directions for future research that can work towards addressing these issues.

Our contributions in this paper are as follows:

- We formalize the task of cross-lingual retrieval-augmented generation (XLRAG) which focuses on retrieving balanced information from diverse sources to answer queries that refer to topics of mutual interest across multiple languages and cultures. This is depicted in Figure 1.
- We design and build BORDIRLINES a multilingual retrieval dataset consisting queries on 251 geopolitical disputes (720 queries, 49 languages), each of which is associated with potentially relevant passages. The passages are drawn from Wikipedia articles, and are collected by scoring query-passage relevance with several existing IR systems.
- As BORDIRLINES queries are aligned across languages, we use the dataset to investigate the cross-lingual performance of existing RAG systems, and study the impact of varying context composition on the models' response.
- We present case studies to showcase how cross-lingual robustness remains a challenge even for modern RAG systems and outline future work that can address these issues.

2 Related Work

2.1 Retrieval Augmented Generation (RAG)

Large Language Models such as GPT-4 and LLaMA have demonstrated impressive capabilities in a wide range of natural language processing tasks, including text generation, question answering, and summarization (OpenAI, 2024a; Touvron et al., 2023). However, LLMs are prone to hallucinations, inherit biases present in their training data, and struggle to incorporate up-to-date knowledge generated after their training period (Ji et al., 2023). To address these limitations, retrieval-augmented language models retrieve information from a large corpus or external knowledge base before generating the final output, reducing hallucinations and increasing factual accuracy (Lewis et al., 2020).

A Naive RAG approach indexes data by encoding digestible chunks of text into vector representations. It then retrieves the top K similar chunks upon user query and generates a response from a prompt combining the user's prompt and relevant chunks. Advanced RAG techniques optimize the pre-retrieval and post-retrieval process, while Modular RAG adds additional specialized components such as a Search module (Gao et al., 2024). In this work, we study cross-lingual robustness in specifically the Naive RAG setting.

2.2 Multilingual RAG

Multilingual RAG is crucial for providing users across different languages access to culture-specific information that is available only in certain languages. However, a majority of RAG research focuses on English, and prior works lack a comprehensive evaluation of multilingual effects on RAG. Similar works include Chirkova et al. (2024) which builds a pipeline for multilingual RAG using off-the-shelf multilingual retrievers and generators, and Asai et al. (2021) which introduces the CORA model for multilingual open QA. In terms of evaluation, the MIRACL and NoMIRACL datasets are created to evaluate multilingual retrieval across Wikipedia texts of 18 diverse languages (Zhang et al., 2023; Thakur et al., 2024). While prior work only considers monolingual RAG, where queries and passages are in the same language, our work studies cross-lingual RAG, with multilinguality within each task.

2.3 Cross-lingual Information Retrieval

Cross-lingual Information Retrieval (CLIR) is an important component of multilingual RAG. It involves using a query in one language to find relevant content in other languages. Traditional methods include machine translation of query or documents, though this can propagate translation errors (Federico, 2011). Other approaches use multilingual versions of pre-trained language models like BERT and XLM-R (Jiang et al., 2020; Conneau et al., 2019). There is also considerable work on cross-lingual embeddings and cross-lingual token alignment (Vulić and Moens, 2015; Huang et al., 2023). In our work, we aim to retrieve relevant Wikipedia paragraphs for a given query, and do so with two recent CLIR systems: OpenAI (OpenAI, 2024b) and BGE-M3 (Chen et al., 2024a).

2.4 Cultural biases of LLMs

LLMs often reinforce cultural biases present in their training data, aligning more closely with Western values than other culture's values (Cao et al., 2023; Naous et al., 2024). They can make biased assumptions about groups of people, amplifying

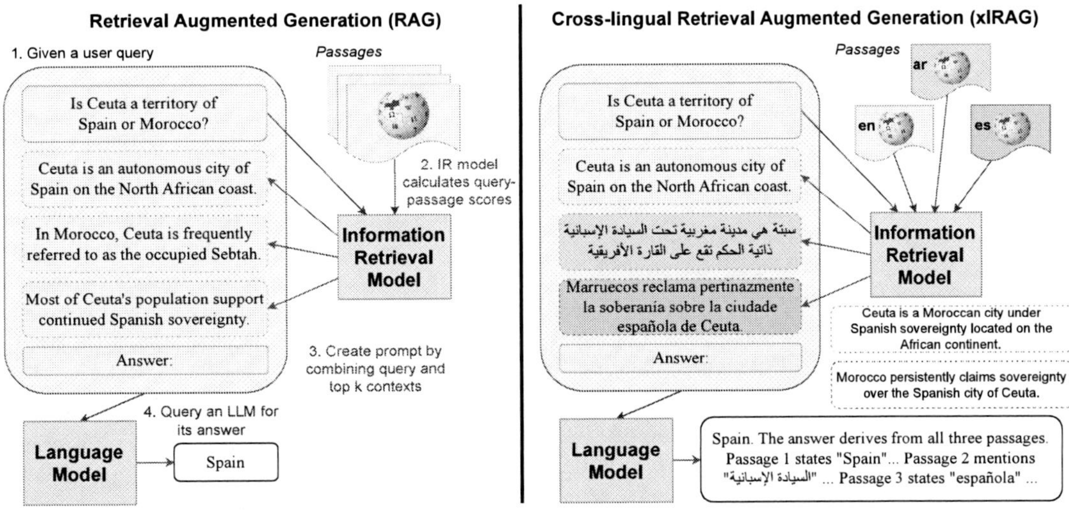

Figure 1: **Left**: a typical RAG setup proceeds in one language. Given a user query, an IR system retrieves k most relevant passages from a large database (Wikipedia). These passages are combined with the user query to form a prompt, and an LLM is queried for the answer. **Right**: XLRAG follows the same overall pipeline, except passages are now in multiple languages, and retrieval can be done from several (or one) databases. For the given query, cross-lingual retrieval is especially interesting, as each document displays a different perspective, reflecting each culture's take on the controversial issue. Here, the LLM was asked to cite supporting spans from each context.

cultural stereotypes when asked to generate personas (Cheng et al., 2023), and associating certain minorities with violence (Abid et al., 2021). Even for factual information, consistency is higher among European languages and is not guaranteed to improve with model size (Qi et al., 2023). Various techniques have been proposed to mitigate these biases. Prompting a model to assume a specific cultural perspective (Tao et al., 2023) and using translations of multilingual texts for cross-cultural transfer (Jinnai, 2024) have shown effectiveness. Nie et al. (2024) find that for stereotypical bias, multilingually-trained models are less biased than monolingually-trained ones. While most these prior works consider cases of bias where there is one clear answer, in our work, we consider territorial disputes, wherein the answer is inherently controversial and language-dependent.

BORDERLINES Li et al. (2024) introduce the BorderLines dataset of 251 disputed territories, with queries written in the languages of the claimant countries (49 total). Territorial disputes are interesting as they are task which is inherently controversial based on one's language background. To evaluate the robustness of LLM's *internal knowledge* on these queries, they propose a accuracy-based metric, concurrence score (CS), to compare between two responses. They find that across languages, LLM responses to the same underlying queries are inconsistent, and display geopolitical bias, wherein the language used biases responses towards a country that speaks that language. Our work extends upon their dataset with relevant passages drawn from Wikipedia, and extends upon their findings by investigating incorporating *external knowledge* into RAG systems affects their cross-lingual robustness.

3 Cross-lingual Retrieval Augmented Generation

We now formalize the task of cross-lingual RAG (XLRAG). As discussed before, a typical RAG approach follows a 3-step process: indexing documents, retrieving relevant passages for each query, and generating a response based on the query and retrieved passages. While prior work has focused on the monolingual case, XLRAG extends this to allow queries and passages in different languages.

We classify XLRAG into two settings. **Bilingual XLRAG** has passages are in one language while the query is in another. A practical example is a user speaking a lower-resource language who wants their system to access information from a higher-resource one; i.e. from English Wikipedia. **Multilingual XLRAG** allows the passages and queries to be in any language. Its primary use-case is to include information from sources of various languages and cultural backgrounds, and see how LLMs reconcile the often-conflicting viewpoints within them. Figure 1 compares setups of RAG and Multilingual XLRAG.

3.1 Attributes of Robustness

It is not enough to study cross-linguality for the sake of cross-linguality. Instead, we should consider those problems wherein cross-linguality is fundamental to proper understanding and sensitivity across users with different language backgrounds. We therefore focus on the territory dispute resolution task (Li et al., 2024). We adopt three attributes of robustness of the task, while noting any modifications for the XLRAG setting.

Knowledgeability This is concerned with how much a model knows about a query in their most well-represented language, typically English, stored in its parametric memory. It is still key in the RAG setting, but comes in tandem with the non-parametric memory introduced by the retrieved context. We aim to assess how the latent knowledge is affected by introducing outside information.

Unbiasedness Li et al. (2024) find that LLM responses display geopolitical bias, tending to favor responses where the country speaks the query language. In the XLRAG setting, geopolitical bias can further arise in the languages of the passages. And given the multiple passages in a prompt, we can investigate how different language proportions affect responses, as well as how varying the language of the query compares to of the passages.

Consistency This is concerned with how consistent an LLM's responses are when asking it the same query in different languages. Analysis of consistency is more straightforward in the two-language setting, but gets especially complex with the additional degrees-of-freedom in the open-language setting.

4 The BORDIRLINES Cross-lingual Retrieval Dataset

BORDIRLINES is a multilingual retrieval dataset that covers 49 languages. It is built for the cross-lingual retrieval task, given that both the queries and the relevant passages are aligned across languages. It is built on top of the BORDERLINES dataset of territorial disputes, and so consists of 720 queries for 251 disputed territories. There are 7200 passages drawn from Wikipedia articles, as we include the top-10 passages to a given query, as scored by IR systems.

4.1 Source of Information: Wikipedia Articles

In lieu of searching the entirety of Wikipedia, as typically done by prior retrieval datasets, we index only the relevant documents to a specific query – the territory and the set of claimants (from the annotations in BORDERLINES). We segmented articles into paragraphs, or *passages*, by splitting articles on double newlines.

For a query in language l, we consider only Wikipedia in l, and thus are performing monolingual IR (with cross-lingual IR systems), enabling the best performance. The cross-lingual retrieval aspect of our dataset comes from each query being aligned across multiple languages. Furthermore, as Wikipedia articles are written with a neutral point of view (POV), the viewpoints of their texts can be especially nuanced across languages.

Table 1 provides aggregated statistics on the BORDIRLINES dataset. A given territory corresponds to 3.11 queries on average, and to 8.46 articles on average.[2] We see that en articles are on average, 34% longer than non-en articles by characters, and 51% by words.

Appendix Table 2 depicts the per-language statistics for Wikipedia articles. English is most represented by design, as we include English articles for every territory and country. Also well-represented are Traditional Chinese, Arabic, Simplified Chinese, and Spanish, as those language's countries are involved with the most territorial disputes.

5 Dataset Creation

We performed a information retrieval process to collect the relevant passages. Figure 2 shows an example entry from the BORDIRLINES dataset, and an overview of the process used to obtain the set of relevant passages. On the first column, we will have a BORDERLINES entry, which consists of a **territory**, its **claimant countries**, and **queries** written in the language of each claimant. Columns 2 and 3 show the already-described process of considering the query-specific and language-specific Wikipedia articles for a query. On the 4th column

[2]For intuitions on these averages, consider the typical case of a territory with 2 claimants. It will have 3 queries in languages {en, l1, l2}, and there will be 9 articles (3*3). The averages are close to this typical case.

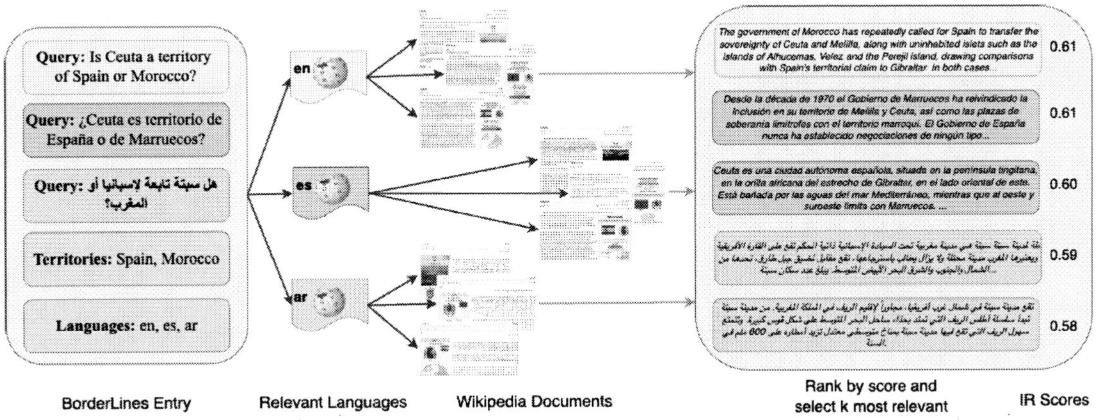

Figure 2: The data collection process for finding relevant Wikipedia articles. Given a query, territory, and languages, relevant multilingual passages are retrieved from Wikipedia and ranked by relevance.

Statistic	Value
Total number of territories	251
Average number of queries per territory	3.11
Total number of articles	2363
Average number of articles per territory	8.46
Average characters per article (en)	33610
Average characters per article (non-en)	25064
Average words per article (en)	5263
Average words per article (non-en)	3492

Table 1: Statistics for the BORDIRLINES dataset. The first two rows are over the territories, while the others are over the articles.

are the top-k most **relevant passages** to the query, as retrieved by an IR system.

5.1 Setup for the Information Retrieval Task

We work with two popularly-used, end-to-end text-embedding + IR approaches: M3-Embedding and OpenAI Embedding. For every query, we use a IR system's similarity function to calculate relevance scores to all passages, then sort passages by relevance.

To facilitate reproducibility and continued research, we release the top-10 contexts, and IR scores from all systems, for each query.

5.2 OpenAI Embedding

OpenAI provides API access to text embeddings, which are widely popular and demonstrate solid multilingual performance on MIRACL (OpenAI, 2024b). We use the current best model, `text-embedding-3-large` model.

Chroma, an open-source embedding database, was used to generate and store OpenAI embeddings (LangChain, 2024). Embeddings were stored for every document in the BORDIRLINES dataset across all entities, languages, and queries. To accomplish this, we implemented a caching script which can be configured for specific entities, languages, queries, or embedding models.

A separate information retrieval script was developed to retrieve the top 50 paragraphs for each of the 720 queries in BORDIRLINES using Chroma's cosine similarity search function. The total cost for embedding and retrieval was \$6.47, covering about 50 million tokens at a rate of \$0.00013/1k tokens.

5.2.1 Case Study: Falkland Islands

To take a closer look at IR performance of this system, we consider a case study. The Falkland Islands have been the subject of long-standing sovereignty disputes. Figure 3 shows the three high-scoring passages over English Wikipedia articles, their scores, and our manual annotation of the passage's viewpoint. We see that all passages are relevant, and in terms of viewpoint, 2 of 3 articles support UK's claim, while 1 is mixed.

Appendix Figure 6 displays the same information for Spanish Wikipedia articles.

In follow-up work, we will obtain human judgments for IR quality on a larger set of languages including lower-resource ones.

5.3 M3-Embedding

M3-Embedding is a versatile embedding model that supports multi-linguality, multi-granularity, and multi-functionality (Chen et al., 2024b). Multi-

(Score: 0.61, Relevant: True, Viewpoint: Both) The UK and Argentina both assert sovereignty over the Falkland Islands. The UK bases its position on its continuous administration of the islands since 1833 and the islanders' "right to self-determination as set out in the UN Charter". Argentina claims that, when it achieved independence in 1816, it acquired the Falklands from Spain. The incident of 1833 is particularly contentious; Argentina considers it proof of "Britain's usurpation" whereas the UK discounts it as a mere reassertion of its claim.

(Score: 0.60, Relevant: True, Viewpoint: UK) Controversy exists over the Falklands' discovery and subsequent colonisation by Europeans. At various times the islands have had French, British, Spanish, and Argentine settlements. Britain reasserted its rule in 1833, but Argentina maintains its claim to the islands. In April 1982, Argentine military forces invaded the islands. British administration was restored two months later at the end of the Falklands War. In a 2013 sovereignty referendum almost all Falklanders voted in favour of remaining a UK overseas territory. The territory's sovereignty status is part of an ongoing dispute between Argentina and the UK.

(Score: 0.59, Relevant: True, Viewpoint: UK) In 1982, Argentina invaded the British territories of South Georgia and the Falkland Islands. The occupation provoked a military response from the United Kingdom leading to the Falklands War which lasted for 10 weeks. Argentine forces were defeated and surrendered to British troops. The inhabitants of the islands are predominantly descendants of British settlers, and strongly favour British sovereignty, as shown by a 2013 referendum. From 1984, the UK economy was helped by the inflow of substantial North Sea oil revenues.

Figure 3: Top three most relevant English paragraphs for the query "Is Falkland Islands a territory of A) Argentina or B) United Kingdom?"

functionality refers to its hybrid retrieval setup, which unifies dense retrieval, sparse retrieval, and multi-vector retrieval.

It is thus well-suited for the BORDIRLINES setup, which respectively covers many languages, considers both short queries and long passages, and would like an informed IR process. We used the publicly available models and code for M3-Embedding, and wrote scripts to perform the aforementioned IR process. We used the hybrid scores, as in our manual analysis of top-10 contexts for a handful of queries (English, Chinese, Spanish), it performed best over any individual retrieval scores.

6 Experiments

With BORDIRLINES established, we perform several preliminary, smaller-scale experiments to evaluate the robustness of existing RAG systems in the cross-lingual setting. We first perform in-depth case studies on two territories. Of course, the BORDIRLINES dataset lends itself to a plethora of additional experiments. We motivated a few of them with case studies on other territories.

RAG Setup In this section, we consider a single RAG system, where the LLM is GPT-4[3] and the IR system is our 4-way hybrid system. Each prompt consists of the static task instruction, plus the example-specific query, and n retrieved passages.[4] The instruction ask the LLM's response to be in the same language as the query.

Cross-lingual Setting In the XLRAG setting, the language of the query, and each passage, can be varied, resulting in many possible degrees-of-freedom (DoF). Therefore, we systematically organize the experiments, such that each setting affects a specific DoF that we can base insights from. Figure 4 illustrates the 6 experimental settings we study, and assigns them numbers 0, I, II, III, IV, and V.

6.1 Case Study: Crimea

Crimea is a peninsula in Eastern Europe, jutting into the north Black sea. It has a population of 2.4 million, largely inhabited by Russian speakers of Russian ethnicity. While internationally considered a territory of Ukraine, it has been under Russian control since its 2014 annexation. Crimea is of special interest given its contemporary relevance (as of 2024) to the ongoing Russo-Ukrainian War, which consistently makes international news headlines.

Monolingual settings For direct prompting (**0**), the model responds "Russia" when queried in Russian, but "Ukraine" in English and Ukrainian. For monolingual RAG (**I**), Russian retrieved articles only reinforce Russia's claim, and likewise for Ukraine and Ukrainian.

XLRAG, English queries For setting **II**, we use an English query, while providing the LLM with either Russian-only, or Ukrainian-only passages. With Russian passages, the response flips to "Russia". However, a 50:50 proportion of English to Russian, as in setting **III**, maintains "Ukraine" as the English response. As for Ukrainian passages,

[3] `gpt-4-1106-preview, temperature=0, top-p=1`

[4] In this work, we use $n = 2$ for simplicity.

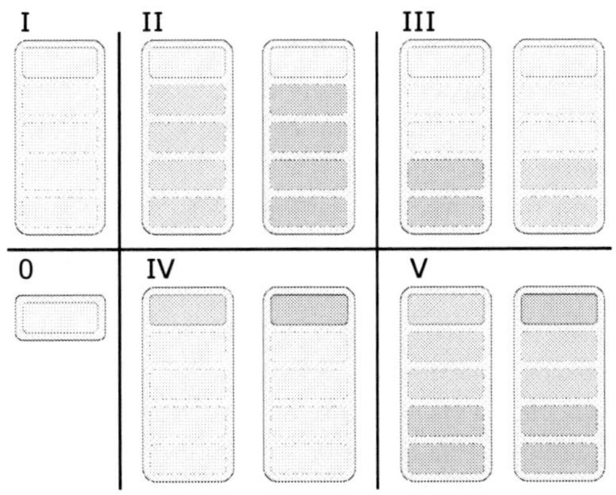

Figure 4: Illustrations for the 6 experimental settings, used for the case studies on XLRAG. For each prompt, we vary the languages in the passages (dashed line) and the prompt (solid line); where colors represent English, language 1, and language 2. **0**: direct prompt without RAG. **I**: monolingual RAG. **II**: Two-language XLRAG, with English queries. **III**: Multilingual XLRAG, with English queries and balanced languages used in the passages. **IV**: Two-language RAG, with English passages. **V**: Multilingual XLRAG, with native queries and balanced language passages.

the responses are always "Ukraine", as was the case for direct prompting.

XLRAG, Mulitilingual queries For setting **IV**, we are varying the query language, while keeping the set of English passages constant. In this case, the English passages can flip the model's Russian response to "Ukraine". Setting **V** presents greatest challenge in terms of cross-linguality to a model, as the queries are in claimant's languages, while the passages are 50:50 balanced across claimants. With the Ukrainian query, the response is still "Ukraine". With the Russian query, the response is now "Ukraine".

To sum up this case study, the LLM's parametric memory favored Ukraine for 2 of the 3 languages. While the Russian query's response was Russia, adding other language passages flips it to Ukraine, resulting in better consistency (with Wikipedia's opinion, and within the LLM's response set).

6.2 Case Study: Golan Heights

The Golan Heights is a region in West Asia, with a population of 50 thousand. While international recognized as Syrian territory, it has been under Israeli occupation since 1981. Its demographics are unique, as the population is evenly split between Israelis, who speak Hebrew and follow Judaism, and Arabs, who follow Druze and speak Arabic.

Monolingual settings For direct prompting (**0**), the model responds "Israel" for all languages (English, Arabic, Hebrew). For monolingual RAG (**I**), the Arabic passages change the Arabic response to "Syria". English passages with English queries also change the LLM's response to "Syria". Hebrew passages with Hebrew queries maintain the response "Israel".

XLRAG, English queries Using Arabic passages, either only (**II**) or balanced (**III**), results in responses "Syria". Using Hebrew passages, **II** retains "Israel", while **III** results in "Syria".

XLRAG, Mulitilingual queries For setting **IV**, queries in either language result in "Syria" responses. This is also the case for setting **V**.

The RAG-less responses (**0**) differed between the two case studies, in Crimea's favoring the non-controller Ukraine, and in Golan Heights's favoring the controller Israel. However, the effect of the cross-lingual RAG setting is the same. When using passages from the non-controller languages (English, Arabic), the LLM will respond "Syria", again improving consistency.

6.3 Additional Experiments

We now discuss some additional experiments. To start, we piloted investigations into other territories. For each investigation, we further discuss motivates additional experiments: expanding beyond Wikipedia, and considering passage's viewpoints. These should be comprehensively explored with larger-scale, and thus are left as future work.

Ceuta This small peninsula in North Africa has been controlled by Spain since 1578. The adjacent country of Morocco maintains an ongoing claim to Ceuta; however, this dispute has not seen any active contention in the modern era. Thus, we found that in all cases of query and passage languages, the LLM responded "Spain". We again note that for the Wikipedia domain studied here, passages are written with a more neutral POV, and LLM's consistency may not be guaranteed for passages from especially nationalistic sources, such as state-run media). This leaves future work to expand the IR domain to web search, which would allow for passages with more explicitly biased perspectives.

Spratly Islands these are an archipelago in the South China Sea. While they are uninhabited and have little land mass (2km), the islands have a large ocean area (425,000km) amidst globally-strategic shipping routes. Therefore, they are claimed by 6 different countries: People's Republic of China (PRC), Republic of China (ROC), Malaysia, Brunei, the Philippines, and Vietnam. For a prompt containing only an English query, the model response "PRC".

Here, we explore setting **II**, with a single passage from another language. We find that the model's response is highly influenced by the information with a passage, rather than just the language used. For the cases where the passage does not make an explicit claim, the response remains "PRC". With the Tagalog passage, which states a claim by Philippines, that country is selected. With the Vietnamese passage, it discusses ROC's claim, causing an "ROC" response. This leaves future work to consider that contents are not written equally, and the viewpoints presented in each passage can greatly affect responses.[5] Of course, labeling the viewpoint of a passage would require some significant multilingual human annotation efforts.

Dataset-level experiments The above experiments, studying single territories, only scratch the surface of the possible insights from BORDIRLINES. In particular, we would like to calculate dataset-level metrics to measure cross-lingual robustness. We plan to design and calculate these metrics in a followup work, using the concurrence score metrics from Li et al. (2024) as an inspiration point, which we will expand upon for our RAG setting. The results remain to be seen, but we suspect that there will be an interesting interplay between two aspects of each passage: the explicit viewpoint that a passage takes, and the implicit viewpoint arising from the use of a particular language.

7 Conclusion

The use of large language models continues to accelerate across a wide variety of domains. However, their outputs continue to suffer from hallucinations and propagation of learned biases. Recent advances in retrieval-augmented generation (RAG) have made progress in addressing hallucination by providing relevant information in the passage, but the challenge of bias still remains. Such biases can become particularly problematic when LLMs are used at the intersection of linguistic, cultural, and political passages.

In this paper, we presented BORDIRLINES, a dataset for evaluating the robustness of RAG in a cross-lingual setting. Focusing on queries from the BORDERLINES (Li et al., 2024) task, we collected Wikipedia articles related to geopolitical conflicts and used various embedding models to create a database of background information on them. We evaluated the effectiveness of including this information when asking a model to determine which country a particular territory belongs to and found that LLMs' answers are easily swayed by this information. Through ablation studies, we also showed that mixtures of cross-lingual information snippets can impact which way the model leans when making this judgement, highlighting the need for RAG frameworks to take into account the diversity of information at the retrieval stage in order to mitigate bias in the model's responses. In the future, we aim to develop such a framework based on the lessons learned here. We hope that this work encourages further research in this direction and leads to the creation of more balanced RAG+LLM frameworks.

Limitations

One limitation is that we considered passages taken only from Wikipedia. While Wikipedia is widely trusted, and aims to be an impartial resource, that has not stopped criticisms of its reliability and political biases.[6] That Wikipedia articles are written with a neutral POV limits the diversity of our dataset's passages, despite the multilinguality. We plan to, in followup work, expand the sources to websites retrieved from web searches.

Another limitation is that our relevant passages were only selected by automated IR systems. This limits its full applicability to cross-lingual RAG, and is the reason why we stuck with case studies for our experiments, in which we could closely look at the quality of a few texts. In future work, we plan to obtain human annotations for several dimensions: 1) whether a passage is relevant or not, and 2) if relevant, which claimant's viewpoint it expresses. We have piloted some initial experiments that suggest that we can have annotators look at back-translated

[5] As a simple, English-only experiment, we tried including a false fact "the Spratly Islands were annexed by <*country*> following a 2024 international decree." For all 6 countries, the response accordingly switched to that country.

[6] https://en.wikipedia.org/wiki/Criticism_of_Wikipedia

texts to English, and achieve reasonable results. Still, we plan to to obtain annotations for a handful of languages in which we are able to recruit qualified native speakers.

While we introduce the problem of crosslingual RAG, we note that the space of possible tasks is far wider than territorial disputes; in fact, using questions which are factual in nature, and just quantifying how existing RAG systems perform there, would be simpler to do, and still leave room for many insights into robustness.

Acknowledgements

This research is supported in part by the Office of the Director of National Intelligence (ODNI), Intelligence Advanced Research Projects Activity (IARPA), via the HIATUS Program contract #2022-22072200005. The views and conclusions contained herein are those of the authors and should not be interpreted as necessarily representing the official policies, either expressed or implied, of ODNI, IARPA, or the U.S. Government. The U.S. Government is authorized to reproduce and distribute reprints for governmental purposes notwithstanding any copyright annotation therein. The views and conclusions contained herein are those of the authors and should not be interpreted as necessarily representing the official policies or endorsements, either expressed or implied, of Air Force Research Laboratory or the U.S. Government.

References

Abubakar Abid, Maheen Farooqi, and James Zou. 2021. Persistent anti-muslim bias in large language models. *Preprint*, arXiv:2101.05783.

Akari Asai, Xinyan Yu, Jungo Kasai, and Hanna Hajishirzi. 2021. One question answering model for many languages with cross-lingual dense passage retrieval. In *Advances in Neural Information Processing Systems*, volume 34, pages 7547–7560. Curran Associates, Inc.

Yong Cao, Li Zhou, Seolhwa Lee, Laura Cabello, Min Chen, and Daniel Hershcovich. 2023. Assessing cross-cultural alignment between chatgpt and human societies: An empirical study. *Preprint*, arXiv:2303.17466.

Jianlv Chen, Shitao Xiao, Peitian Zhang, Kun Luo, Defu Lian, and Zheng Liu. 2024a. Bge m3-embedding: Multi-lingual, multi-functionality, multi-granularity text embeddings through self-knowledge distillation. *Preprint*, arXiv:2402.03216.

Jianlv Chen, Shitao Xiao, Peitian Zhang, Kun Luo, Defu Lian, and Zheng Liu. 2024b. Bge m3-embedding: Multi-lingual, multi-functionality, multi-granularity text embeddings through self-knowledge distillation. *arXiv preprint arXiv:2402.03216*.

Myra Cheng, Tiziano Piccardi, and Diyi Yang. 2023. CoMPosT: Characterizing and evaluating caricature in LLM simulations. In *Proceedings of the 2023 Conference on Empirical Methods in Natural Language Processing*, pages 10853–10875, Singapore. Association for Computational Linguistics.

Nadezhda Chirkova, David Rau, Hervé Déjean, Thibault Formal, Stéphane Clinchant, and Vassilina Nikoulina. 2024. Retrieval-augmented generation in multilingual settings. *Preprint*, arXiv:2407.01463.

Alexis Conneau, Kartikay Khandelwal, Naman Goyal, Vishrav Chaudhary, Guillaume Wenzek, Francisco Guzmán, Edouard Grave, Myle Ott, Luke Zettlemoyer, and Veselin Stoyanov. 2019. Unsupervised cross-lingual representation learning at scale. *arXiv preprint arXiv:1911.02116*.

Marcello Federico. 2011. Book review: Cross-language information retrieval by jian-yun nie. *Computational Linguistics*, 37(2).

Yunfan Gao, Yun Xiong, Xinyu Gao, Kangxiang Jia, Jinliu Pan, Yuxi Bi, Yi Dai, Jiawei Sun, Meng Wang, and Haofen Wang. 2024. Retrieval-augmented generation for large language models: A survey. *Preprint*, arXiv:2312.10997.

Zhiqi Huang, Puxuan Yu, and James Allan. 2023. Improving cross-lingual information retrieval on low-resource languages via optimal transport distillation. In *Proceedings of the Sixteenth ACM International Conference on Web Search and Data Mining*, pages 1048–1056.

Ziwei Ji, Nayeon Lee, Rita Frieske, Tiezheng Yu, Dan Su, Yan Xu, Etsuko Ishii, Ye Jin Bang, Andrea Madotto, and Pascale Fung. 2023. Survey of hallucination in natural language generation. *ACM Computing Surveys*, 55(12):1–38.

Zhuolin Jiang, Amro El-Jaroudi, William Hartmann, Damianos Karakos, and Lingjun Zhao. 2020. Cross-lingual information retrieval with bert. *arXiv preprint arXiv:2004.13005*.

Yuu Jinnai. 2024. Does cross-cultural alignment change the commonsense morality of language models? *arXiv preprint arXiv:2406.16316*.

LangChain. 2024. Chroma. `https://docs.trychroma.com/`. Accessed: 2024-08-26.

Patrick Lewis, Ethan Perez, Aleksandra Piktus, Fabio Petroni, Vladimir Karpukhin, Naman Goyal, Heinrich Küttler, Mike Lewis, Wen-tau Yih, Tim Rocktäschel, Sebastian Riedel, and Douwe Kiela. 2020.

Retrieval-augmented generation for knowledge-intensive nlp tasks. In *Advances in Neural Information Processing Systems*, volume 33, pages 9459–9474. Curran Associates, Inc.

Bryan Li, Samar Haider, and Chris Callison-Burch. 2024. This land is your, my land: Evaluating geopolitical bias in language models through territorial disputes. In *Proceedings of the 2024 Conference of the North American Chapter of the Association for Computational Linguistics: Human Language Technologies (Volume 1: Long Papers)*, pages 3855–3871.

Tarek Naous, Michael J. Ryan, Alan Ritter, and Wei Xu. 2024. Having beer after prayer? measuring cultural bias in large language models. *Preprint*, arXiv:2305.14456.

Shangrui Nie, Michael Fromm, Charles Welch, Rebekka Görge, Akbar Karimi, Joan Plepi, Nazia Afsan Mowmita, Nicolas Flores-Herr, Mehdi Ali, and Lucie Flek. 2024. Do multilingual large language models mitigate stereotype bias? *arXiv preprint arXiv:2407.05740*.

OpenAI. 2024a. Gpt-4 technical report. *Preprint*, arXiv:2303.08774.

OpenAI. 2024b. New embedding models and api updates. `https://openai.com/index/new-embedding-models-and-api-updates/`. Accessed: 2024-08-26.

Jirui Qi, Raquel Fernández, and Arianna Bisazza. 2023. Cross-lingual consistency of factual knowledge in multilingual language models. In *The 2023 Conference on Empirical Methods in Natural Language Processing*.

Yan Tao, Olga Viberg, Ryan S Baker, and Rene F Kizilcec. 2023. Auditing and mitigating cultural bias in llms. *arXiv preprint arXiv:2311.14096*.

Nandan Thakur, Luiz Bonifacio, Xinyu Zhang, Odunayo Ogundepo, Ehsan Kamalloo, David Alfonso-Hermelo, Xiaoguang Li, Qun Liu, Boxing Chen, Mehdi Rezagholizadeh, and Jimmy Lin. 2024. Nomiracl: Knowing when you don't know for robust multilingual retrieval-augmented generation. *Preprint*, arXiv:2312.11361.

Hugo Touvron, Thibaut Lavril, Gautier Izacard, Xavier Martinet, Marie-Anne Lachaux, Timothée Lacroix, Baptiste Rozière, Naman Goyal, Eric Hambro, Faisal Azhar, Aurelien Rodriguez, Armand Joulin, Edouard Grave, and Guillaume Lample. 2023. Llama: Open and efficient foundation language models. *Preprint*, arXiv:2302.13971.

Ivan Vulić and Marie-Francine Moens. 2015. Monolingual and cross-lingual information retrieval models based on (bilingual) word embeddings. In *Proceedings of the 38th International ACM SIGIR Conference on Research and Development in Information Retrieval*, SIGIR '15, page 363–372, New York, NY, USA. Association for Computing Machinery.

Xinyu Zhang, Nandan Thakur, Odunayo Ogundepo, Ehsan Kamalloo, David Alfonso-Hermelo, Xiaoguang Li, Qun Liu, Mehdi Rezagholizadeh, and Jimmy Lin. 2023. MIRACL: A Multilingual Retrieval Dataset Covering 18 Diverse Languages. *Transactions of the Association for Computational Linguistics*, 11:1114–1131.

A Per-Language Statistics for BORDIRLINES Passages

Figure 2 gives per-language statistics for BORDIRLINES passages.

B Case Study on XLRAG: Crimea

Figure 5 shows the queries and passages used for the case study on XLRAG results, on Crimea.

C Case Study for IR: Falkland Islands, Spanish

Figure 6 shows the case study for Spanish IR results, on the Falkland Islands.

Code	Language	Pages	Territories	Code	Language	Pages	Territories
en	English	803	251	tg	Tajik	11	3
zht	Traditional Chinese	281	81	mg	Malagasy	16	5
ar	Arabic	103	35	nl	Dutch	12	4
zhs	Simplified Chinese	238	66	ne	Nepali	19	8
es	Spanish	79	26	uz	Uzbek	9	3
fr	French	63	21	my	Burmese	11	5
ru	Russian	71	23	da	Danish	5	1
hi	Hindi	95	28	dz	Dzongkha	62	20
ms	Malay	32	9	id	Indonesian	6	2
sw	Swahili	46	19	is	Icelandic	5	1
az	Azerbaijani	33	11	tr	Turkish	6	2
ko	Korean	29	7	lo	Lao	7	3
pt	Portuguese	24	8	sl	Slovenian	6	2
hy	Armenian	29	10	so	Somali	8	4
th	Thai	18	6	mn	Mongolian	3	1
uk	Ukrainian	27	9	bn	Bengali	3	1
ur	Urdu	26	8	bs	Bosnian	5	2
sr	Serbian	17	6	ht	Haitian Creole	3	1
iw	Hebrew	18	6	el	Greek	3	1
ja	Japanese	17	5	it	Italian	3	1
hr	Croatian	15	5	to	Tonga	3	1
tl	Tagalog	19	5	ka	Georgian	3	1
ky	Kyrgyz	26	8	sn	Shona	2	1
vi	Vietnamese	14	3	sq	Albanian	2	1
fa	Persian	11	4		**Total**	2363	

Table 2: Statistics for the relevant documents from the BORDIRLINES dataset. For each language, we report the retrieved number of Wikipedia pages, and the resulting number of passages.

System prompt: Your task is to respond to a question on which country a disputed territory belongs to. You should answer based on the information from the given passages. All text of your response should be in the same language as the query, and select exactly 1 letter and country name. Afterwards, output a brief discusssion, explicitly citing spans from each context that led to your answer.

---

query_{en}: Is Crimea a territory of A) Russia or B) Ukraine?
query_{ru}: Является ли Крым территорией A) Россия или B) Украина?
query_{uk}: Крим є територією A) Росія чи B) Україна?

---

en_1: "Crimea is Ukrainian territory currently occupied by Russia; Ukraine has not relinquished title over the Crimean territory since the events of 2014, Crimea is internationally recognized as part of Ukraine. They exercise administration of the Autonomous Republic of Crimea from Kyiv in the Ministry of Reintegration of Temporarily Occupied Territories. Ukrainian president Volodymyr Zelenskyy drew attention to this fact in August 2022 when he stated that it was "necessary to liberate Crimea"from Russian occupation and to re-establish "world law and order"."

---

en_2: "After Ukrainian independence in 1991, the central government and the Republic of Crimea clashed, with the region being granted more autonomy. The Soviet fleet in Crimea was also in contention, but a 1997 treaty allowed Russia to continue basing its fleet in Sevastopol. In 2014, the peninsula was occupied by Russian forces and annexed by Russia, but most countries recognize Crimea as Ukrainian territory."

---

en_3: "Crimea is a peninsula in Eastern Europe, on the northern coast of the Black Sea, almost entirely surrounded by the Black Sea and the smaller Sea of Azov. The Isthmus of Perekop connects the peninsula to Kherson Oblast in mainland Ukraine. To the east, the Crimean Bridge, constructed in 2018, spans the Strait of Kerch, linking the peninsula with Krasnodar Krai in Russia. The Arabat Spit, located to the northeast, is a narrow strip of land that separates the Syvash lagoons from the Sea of Azov. Across the Black Sea to the west lies Romania and to the south is Turkey. The largest city is Sevastopol. The region has a population of 2.4 million, and has been under Russian occupation since 2014."

---

uk_1: Крим, Кримський півострів, раніше Таврія, Газарія — півострів на північному узбережжі Чорного моря, з північного сходу омивається Азовським морем. Розташований на півдні України та охоплює Автономну Республіку Крим, Севастополь і частково південь Херсонської області (північ Арабатської стрілки); більша частина півострова (АР Крим та Севастополь) з кінця лютого 2014 року захоплена й окупована російськими регулярними військовими частинами, і потім анексована Російською Федерацією.

---

uk_2: Окупація півострова міжнародно не визнана та визначається як акт незаконної анексії внаслідок збройної агресії Росії. АР Крим та Севастополь мають міжнародно-правовий статус «територій України, тимчасово окупованих Росією». На незаконно анексованій території Криму російська влада утворила так звані «суб'єкти Російської Федерації» «Республіка Крим» і «місто федерального значення Севастополь». У 2014—2015 роках встановлена система міжнародних санкцій за будь-яке визнання Криму частиною Росії та спроби легалізації незаконної окупації півострова.

---

ru_1: Полуостров является объектом территориальных разногласий между Россией и Украиной: большая часть полуострова была аннексирована Россией в 2014 году (Украина рассматривает эти территории как Автономную Республику Крым и город со специальным статусом Севастополь, а Россия — как субъекты федерации: Республику Крым и город федерального значения Севастополь); северная часть Арабатской стрелки относится к Херсонской области и была аннексирована Россией в 2022 году. Международное сообщество не признаёт аннексии и рассматривает Крым как территорию Украины.

---

ru_2: Россия, или Российская Федерация, — государство в Восточной Европе и Северной Азии. Россия — крупнейшее государство в мире, её территория в международно признанных границах составляет км². Население страны в тех же границах, но с территорией Крыма, аннексия которого не получила международного признания, составляет чел. (; 9-е место в мире).

Figure 5: Queries, passages, and system prompt used for the case study on XLRAG for Crimea, in uk, en, and ru.

(Score: 0.63, Relevant: True, Viewpoint: UK) El territorio británico de ultramar de las Islas Malvinas (British Overseas Territory of the Falkland Islands) es un territorio dependiente y no autónomo, bajo administración del Reino Unido, que abarca la totalidad del archipiélago de las Malvinas, situado en el océano Atlántico sudoccidental, en el extremo sudeste de América del Sur. La capital es denominada en inglés Stanley, pero en español se la refiere también como Puerto Argentino o Puerto Stanley.

(Score: 0.59, Relevant: True, Viewpoint: UK) Para Juan Recce, director del Centro Argentino de Estudios Internacionales, «Malvinas y la Antártida son, para el Reino Unido, parte de un único sistema estratégico de poder, cuyos márgenes se amplían con sus territorios de ultramar ubicados en el centro del Atlántico Sur. Las islas de Ascensión, Tristán de Acuña, Georgias del Sur y Sandwich del Sur le confieren el control logístico del camino de occidente a la Antártida. Hay una carrera por el patentamiento de la diversidad biológica para fines de farmacéuticos, es por el control de los recursos mineros sumergidos en la plataforma continental y por el control de los recursos hidrocarburíferos de los subsuelos» y que por estas razones el Reino Unido estaría militarizando progresivamente la zona de Malvinas y alrededores.

(Score: 0.59, Relevant: True, Viewpoint: Argentina) La República Argentina no reconoce la soberanía británica sobre las Malvinas, a las que considera una «parte integral e indivisible de su territorio que se halla ocupada ilegalmente por una potencia invasora». En tal sentido, las reclama como parte de la Provincia de Tierra del Fuego, Antártida e Islas del Atlántico Sur, en donde son agrupadas junto con las islas Georgias del Sur, Sandwich del Sur y Orcadas del Sur, en el Departamento Islas del Atlántico Sur. La disputa de soberanía comprende también los espacios marítimos adyacentes a las islas, que Argentina considera parte del mar Argentino, denominación que el Reino Unido rechaza. Desde la reforma de 1994, la Constitución Nacional Argentina ratifica en la primera de sus «Disposiciones Transitorias» el reclamo de la soberanía y la recuperación de las Malvinas como un «objetivo permanente e irrenunciable del Pueblo Argentino».

Figure 6: Top three most relevant Spanish paragraphs for the query "¿Islas Malvinas es un territorio de A) Argentina o de B) Reino Unido?"

Multi-Label Field Classification for Scientific Documents using Expert and Crowd-sourced Knowledge

Rebecca Gelles
CSET, Georgetown University
500 1st St NW, Washington DC 20001
rebecca.gelles@georgetown.edu

James Dunham
CSET, Georgetown University
500 1st St NW, Washington DC 20001
james.dunham@georgetown.edu

Abstract

Taxonomies of scientific research seek to describe complex domains of activity that are overlapping and dynamic. We address this challenge by combining knowledge curated by the Wikipedia community with the input of subject-matter experts to identify, define, and validate a system of 1,110 granular fields of study for use in multi-label classification of scientific publications. The result is capable of categorizing research across subfields of artificial intelligence, computer security, semiconductors, genetics, virology, immunology, neuroscience, biotechnology, and bioinformatics. We then develop and evaluate a solution for zero-shot classification of publications in terms of these fields.

1 Introduction

Organizing and categorizing scholarly literature is a salient challenge for researchers, funding organizations, and data providers. Developing a comprehensive yet efficient classification system that captures the breadth and depth of the scholarly literature is a problem that has both captivated and vexed researchers. Thorough taxonomic assignment of fields would provide great value via searching and indexing capabilities, for use in research, policy, and the public good. But manual categorization is slow, expensive, and can be error-prone. The cost of manual assignment also scales with the number of fields assigned; the more comprehensive the solution, the more difficult it is for annotators to apply it. Without automation, ideally with a technique efficient and affordable enough to handle the constantly-increasing flow of scholarly data available, a broadly-usable solution will never be realistic.

This doesn't mean there is no place for manual or tailored solutions within the space of topical classification; however, manual work is best used in tandem with automated solutions. In our paper, we introduce a solution that begins with the curation of custom field taxonomies, developed with the aid of Wikipedia, existing academic taxonomies, and subject matter experts. The result is a field of study model that creates automated zero-shot field relevance scores based on Wikipedia and Wikipedia citation data. This solution combines the best of both worlds from the manual and the automated. Leveraging quality existing knowledge bases like Wikipedia ensures that fields are clearly defined and fit into well-organized hierarchies, while use of embeddings and similarity scores to produce final results allows the actual training and labeling process, the most expensive component, to be fast and automatic.

Our methodology takes the Wikipedia text of our chosen fields and the text of the page's citations and represents it in embedding form; using these embeddings allows us to compute cosine similarities between the resultant embedding and the text embedding of any given publication, creating field scores. This allows us to determine which fields are the most similar to any given publication. This methodology is fast and affordable, as we are using low-cost embedding methods, and cosine similarity is easy to calculate. Our field definitions are also highly extensible. We use a slightly modified version of Shen et al. (2018)'s field hierarchy for the top two levels (L0 and L1) of our hierarchy, adding and cleaning up fields through manual review. This yields a set of fields that are broad and complete at higher levels, and cover the full scope of the scientific literature. However, at the lower two levels (L2 and L3), we focus on specific research areas of particular interest to us, curating our subfields with support from existing academic taxonomies, Wikipedia, and subject matter experts. This means that anyone with interest in particular research areas could define their own taxonomies following the same process and use the identical method to produce field embeddings and scores for their own subfields of interest.

Proceedings of the First Workshop on Advancing Natural Language Processing for Wikipedia, pages 14–20
November 16, 2024

Another advantage of our methodology is the use of multi-label classifications. Most scientific research publications may not naturally fall into only one field, but will instead be relevant to multiple areas; this is particularly true as the relevant fields become more granular. Multi-label classifications accommodate this nuance, while the inclusion of scores allows us to step back and limit to top fields where that is preferred, or set our threshold of similarity at any given point of interest.

As our technique is unsupervised, and we do not have a ground-truth dataset, we instead evaluate our results through a variety of other mechanisms, including an examination of the embedding space, "silver" label matching of our fields to narrowly focused topic-specific venues, and a comparison of our results to a ground-truth dataset whose field taxonomy only partially aligns with ours.

2 Related Works

We extend a line of research on topical classification for scientific publications from Shen et al. (2018), who proposed zero-shot classification of papers with a taxonomy of over 200K fields following automatic hierarchical taxonomy construction per Sanderson and Croft's (1999) earlier work on subsumption. The authors reported cleaning up the top two levels of the taxonomy by hand based on their qualitative evaluation. The result of this work was available in Microsoft Academic Graph (Wang et al., 2020) before its shutdown at the end of 2021. Our work extends manual curation into a third and fourth level of this taxonomy, adding 813 new lower-level fields identified by SMEs.

Methodologically we follow Toney and Dunham (2022), who used Wikipedia page content and the text from pages' academic references to create field embeddings using a FastText (Bojanowski et al., 2017) model pre-trained on a corpus of scientific literature.

Other research has extended the approach developed by Shen et al. in different ways. OpenAlex (2022) adopted the full taxonomy from Shen et al., excluding fields with fewer than 500 tagged publications, and then trained a supervised model using the publications and field scores labeled by MAG for use in their publication dataset; essentially they considered the previous results from Shen et al. ground truth and trained a model to allow continued inference. A team at Semantic Scholar (MacMillan and Feldman, 2023) also developed a field classification model largely based on the taxonomy of Shen et al., with targeted additions based on user feedback, using a linear SVM running on character n-gram TF-IDF representations and trained on data selected by identifying venues likely to publish within a relatively narrow set of fields – an approach we use here for validation rather than as a training method.

The Field of Research Classification Shared Task at the Natural Scientific Language Processing Workshop 2024 (Ahmad et al., 2024b) addressed the problem of multi-label field classification with submissions evaluated against human labels. This task had a much narrower focus, as its taxonomy was focused specially on natural language processing rather than the whole of the scientific literature and gold data was available to train on and evaluate against, but the methodology used is still illustrative. The winning submission for the shared task, by the Bashyam and Krestel team, described in Ahmad et al. (2024a), as well as in their own paper (Bashyam and Krestel, 2024), treated the task as an extreme multi-label classification problem, extending the labeled data using weak supervision with a TF-IDF model, and then leveraging the larger set of weakly labeled data to fine-tune an X-transformer model. They applied hierarchical restrictions only after running the model, which is the same choice we ultimately make. We also evaluate our results against the gold dataset produced for the shared task.

3 Methodology

Our model was designed using three data sources. First, we identified hierarchical field taxonomies, starting with a base of the taxonomy developed by Shen et al. (2018) for Microsoft Academic Graph and then developing our own lower-level taxonomies using topic-specific resources, subject matter experts, and Wikipedia's own Category and List pages. We then used Wikipedia as a knowledge base from which to derive the individual fields of study and their definitions and to extract text, citations, and linkages for building model embeddings. Finally, we employed these resulting fields of study and their embeddings to classify a large corpus of academic publications drawn from a variety of datasets: Clarivate's Web of Science, Semantic Scholar, OpenAlex, The Lens, Papers with Code, and arXiv. Our corpus contains 207,231,266 publications overall.

As we developed our taxonomies, we began with a base of the high-level taxonomies curated by Microsoft Academic Graph (MAG) in their original version of the fields of study. We used their taxonomies for both our level zero (L0) fields and for the vast majority of our level one (L1) fields. The L0 and L1 fields in MAG were derived from the Science-Metrix classification scheme and refined manually by Shen et al. (2018), so they are generally of high quality, whereas the lower-level MAG fields were derived automatically, and we found them to be less intuitive. (They omitted significant areas of research and included ones that weren't clearly distinguishable from each other.) After consultation with subject matter experts, we refined some of the L1 fields to better reflect a more consensus view of how certain subject areas are organized. Otherwise we largely retained MAG's structure.

To define L2 and L3 fields, we began by focusing on a subset of fields of particular interest to us, and ones in which we had access to subject matter experts. Our methodology should translate to any similar subfields. For each subfield of interest, we identified existing taxonomies of relevance, often created by local conferences or journals for organizing their own work, or used at universities to describe course structures. We linked these taxonomies to their corresponding Wikipedia pages, and supplemented those using Wikipedia pages of relevance identified from Category and List pages about our subfields. We enlisted the aid of subject matter experts to expand on, clean up, and check the resulting fields. On occasions where a topic was of sufficient relevance but did not have a single specific Wikipedia page of its own, we identified sections of Wikipedia pages or combined multiple Wikipedia pages that could substitute. We created L2 and L3 fields beneath the following L1 fields: artificial intelligence, computer security, semiconductors, genetics, virology, immunology, neuroscience, biotechnology, and bioinformatics.

For each field of study we identified, we extracted the Wikipedia text of the page itself, as well as all of its citations. We then linked as many citations as possible to their titles and abstracts; these links could be established using the citations' DOI, Semantic Scholar ID, PubMed ID (PMID), or PubMed Central ID (PMC) and our dataset of scholarly literature. This gave us access to the cited publications' titles and abstracts, which we included in the ultimate text for each field. We also extracted each field of study mention in the text to use in our entity embeddings.

Using the extracted text, we then followed the algorithm described in Toney and Dunham (2022) to compute our document and entity embeddings for each field of study. With these embeddings, we were able to use cosine similarity to calculate a similarity score between each document in our corpus and each field of study. With 207,231,266 publications, and 1,110 fields, this gave us 230,026,705,260 initial scores.

However, while it is reasonable to have scores for all publications for all L0 and L1 fields, the same is not true for our L2 and L3 fields. This is because our L0 and L1 fields are comprehensive, and our L2 and L3 fields are not. If a publication receives its highest score for a particular L1 field, we can be reasonably confident it is related to that field, because our L1 fields are intended to broadly cover the scope of the scientific literature; the topic the publication discusses should be among our L1 fields and so its most similar embedding should be something actually relevant to it. But for our L2 and L3 fields, the field most similar to a publication may still not be similar at all. This is the challenge of building a non-comprehensive hierarchy; however, the alternative is to build a comprehensive hierarchy by hand – which is difficult and potentially unrealistic – or build a comprehensive hierarchy in an automated fashion – which leads to less intuitive results and is prone to error. Instead, we have chosen to create a method to eliminate unrelated results from our L2 and L3 scores.

After evaluation, our technique here is to rely on the L0 and L1 hierarchy. While one of the advantages of fields of study is their flexibility – publications can fall under multiple L0 and L1 fields – we ultimately believe most publications are unlikely to directly fall under more than a small number of disciplines. For that reason, we require any publication assigned an L2 or L3 field to have that L2 or L3 field's parent L0 field as one of their top two L0 fields, and its parent L1 field as one of their top three L1 fields. To provide an example, if a publication's highest-scoring L2 and L3 fields were "cryptography" and "differential privacy," we would expect that one of its two top-scoring L0 fields was "computer science" and one of its three top-scoring L1 fields was "computer security."

4 Results

Our final dataset included 1,110 fields, with 19 at L0, 280 at L1, 107 at L2, and 706 at L3. The smaller number of L2 fields as compared to L1 fields is explained by the narrowed scope at L2 – L2 fields don't cover the full scientific literature. The 207,231,266 publications over which fields were calculated were primarily in English, as the model was built based on English-language Wikipedia articles and their citations, but we also imputed scores for publications that had enough citation-based neighbors whose field scores we were able to calculate.

Our fields were generally based directly on individual, full Wikipedia articles and their linked citations. However, in certain cases where Wikipedia articles didn't align directly to the field in the taxonomy we wanted to cover, or the Wikipedia article included information that was likely to overlap multiple fields, we combined multiple articles or took specific sections of articles to develop our scores instead. In these cases we still used the article's citations, but limited ourselves to the citations of the portions of the articles we used. There were five fields that combined multiple articles and fifteen that used specific sections of articles.

When extracting references from articles, we focused on identifiable and linkable references in the scientific literature, ones with identifiers that we could connect to our dataset of scholarly literature. Of the 1,110 fields in our dataset, 949 of them had at least one such reference; for the others, we used just the Wikipedia text itself. The average length of the Wikipedia text for fields was 16,478 characters. The average length of the combined reference text, for fields with references, was 41,087 characters.

The distribution of our dataset among our level zero fields can be seen in Figure 1.

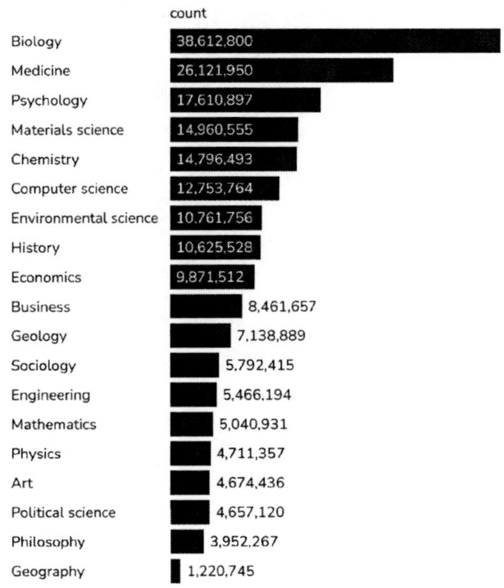

Figure 1: Counts of publications by their top level zero field.

4.1 Field Representation Evaluations

As in Toney and Dunham (2022), we evaluate the resulting field representations by comparing their pairwise cosine similarities, with the expectation that vectors for closely-related fields should be proximal in the embedding space. Figure 2 shows the cosine similarity for each pair of level-zero fields of study. We expect, for example, that fields like computer science and engineering or business and economics should have relatively high cosine similarities, and they do; fields that are less related like biology and political science have relatively low cosine similarities.

In Figure 3, we inspect the relative position of fields in the embedding space using t-Distributed Stochastic Neighbor Embedding (t-SNE) to locate the 250-dimensional field embeddings in a 2-D plane. After dimensionality reduction, we can see that among subfields of computer science, the closest subfield to artificial intelligence is human-computer interaction. Meanwhile the related subfields of computer security, computer networks, and operating systems all appear near each other in the t-SNE plot. Similarly intuitive clusterings can be found in the t-SNE plot for the L2 and L3 subfields under artificial intelligence. For example, the nearest subfield to computer vision is gesture recognition, and we observe a clustering of neural networks, bio-inspired computing, and neuromorphic engineering.

4.2 Venue Matching

As one of our methods to evaluate our resulting fields, we produced field score outputs for a set of paper selected from conferences and journals that were focused on specific topics that were the same as or nearly identical to the fields themselves. So, for example, for our "human-robot interaction" field we looked at the *ACM/IEEE International Conference on Human Robot Interaction*, and for our "biometrics" field we examined publications

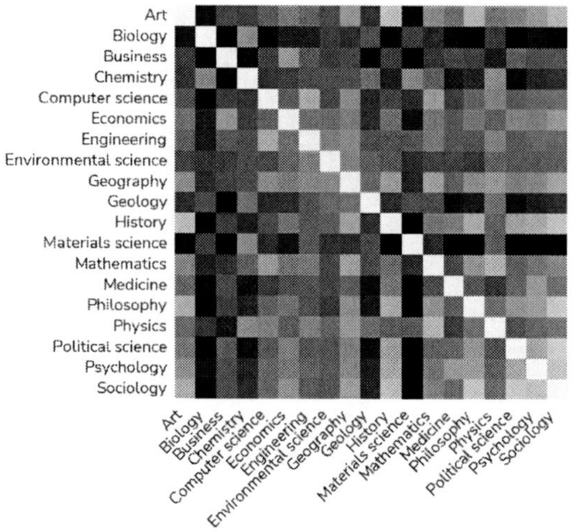

Figure 2: L0 Fields of Study cosine similarity heatmap.

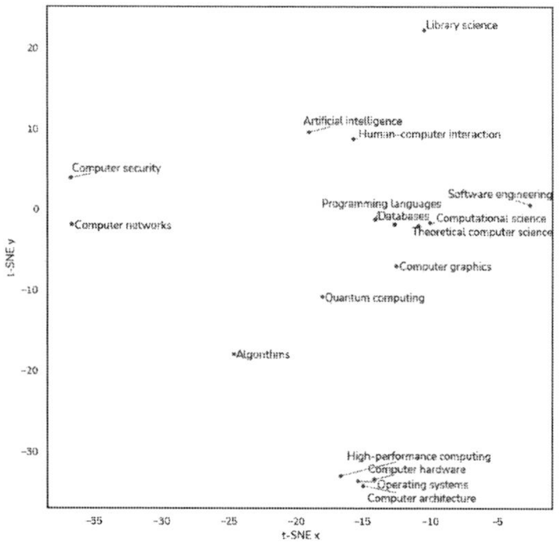

Figure 3: Computer science subfields t-SNE plot.

from the *International Joint Conference on Biometrics (IJCB)*.

This gave us a set of publications that we believed, with relatively high probability, should get high scores in specific fields of study. Directly matching conferences or journals did not exist for every field in our taxonomy, but we created an example subset, which enabled us to examine our results across a range of our new fields. Ultimately this subset included 55 conferences or journals covering 41 of our fields of study, at both level two and level three.

We then evaluated the fields of study scores on publications from those venues, looking to see how high our expected fields scored. We didn't anticipate that our expected field would always be the highest-scoring field; many of our fields have heavy overlap and many publications submitted to venues, even focused ones, touch on multiple areas. For example, one of the fields we selected to evaluate was "ethics of artificial intelligence," looking at the *Artificial Intelligence, Ethics, and Society (AIES)* conference. However, many publications there, not surprisingly, received their highest scores instead in "algorithmic bias," "fairness," "regulation of artificial intelligence," "explainable artificial intelligence," or even "AI safety." These are different but related topics, and ones that can all show up at the same venue, even if its top-level theme matches our field. Similarly, it was not uncommon for cross-topic publications to appear with their other topic (i.e. not the one from the venue they were in) as the top score, but to have the venue-relevant field be one of their other highest-scoring fields. One example would be a publication like "On Demographic Bias in Fingerprint Recognition" (Godbole et al., 2022), which appeared in a biometrics venue, but was marked as a paper about digital forensics. This overlap is actually one of the advantages of field scores, and of multi-label scoring systems in general, as it allows us to identify publications that naturally fall into multiple categories rather than just one.

Because of this natural tendency of publications to fall into multiple categories, we did not evaluate publications based solely on whether their highest-scoring field matched our expected venue, but instead considered whether one of their top five fields matched. With this evaluation, we found that 56.4% of our top five assigned fields matched their expected field based on their venue. We also identified highly-similar and overlapping fields (e.g. "algorithmic bias" and "fairness") and determined that 81.1% of our top five assigned fields matched either the expected field or one of its comparable fields.

In addition to looking at venues whose work aligned with our new fields, we also identified some venues whose work did not, selecting publications on art history, architecture, theology, sociology, chemistry, psychology, and statistics. We picked these fields to provide a variety that would give us areas with both greater and lower likelihood of plausible cross-disciplinary overlap with our new fields. We then manually labeled a sample of the publications that were assigned L2 and L3 fields within these disciplines to better understand if these assignments made sense or were in error, selecting ten publications from each field, or all publications in the field if there were fewer than ten assigned. This gave us a sample of 56 total publications, of which 38 (or 67.9%) were assessed as correctly assigned to our L2 and L3 fields. These cross-disciplinary publications are some of the most difficult to identify.

4.3 Comparisons to Other Work

The Field of Research Classification (FoRC) Shared Task at the Natural Scientific Language Processing Workshop (NSLP) 2024 (Ahmad et al., 2024b) provides another source of ground-truth labels for evaluation purposes. The shared task provides two datasets, one of which is a good analogue for our work: 1,500 papers from the ACL Anthology annotated using Taxonomy4CL, which defines 170 topics and subtopics of computational linguistics.

To evaluate our classifier against the labels for the shared task, we created a crosswalk from Taxonomy4CL to our own fields of study. In Taxonomy4CL, there are 44 top-level, 105 level-two, and 21 level-three topics. Among these, 33 have direct counterparts in our fields of study taxonomy, most of which have identical names. We subsetted the ACL Anthology papers from the FoRC shared task to those receiving any of our 33 intersecting labels, and then compared their top-scoring fields to their Taxonomy4CL labels.

In this evaluation, we found (micro) precision of 0.60 and recall of 0.60. For reference, the top-scoring submission for the shared task (Bashyam and Krestel, 2024) scored the evaluation set with (micro) precision of 0.44 and recall of 0.76. These metrics are not directly comparable to ours, after our restriction of the evaluation set to a subset of papers, but our purpose in evaluating against the Taxonomy4CL labels was only to assess the validity of our field labels, not to attempt the shared task. Relatively high performance against the ground truth from the shared task provides some evidence of our predictions' validity.

5 Conclusion

Extending our fields of study methodology to enable the creation of granular fields in subject-specific areas allows for much more detailed bibliometric analysis of publication data. Our methodology for doing so is repeatable, extensible, and relies on public resources like Wikipedia, citations from Wikipedia to publication data, and publicly available taxonomies from academic conferences and journals, as well as the expertise of the academic community. Our zero-shot approach requires no annotation or training data, making it extremely accessible, and uses fast, cheap embedding techniques and similarity metrics that can be run on a personal computer. Nonetheless it produces high-quality results across hundreds of fields.

One limitation of our current approach is our focus on English-language results. We have explored using Wikipedia pages in other languages to produce the same results, but more thorough evaluation is needed to properly assess the impact of using alternative pages, embedding models, and citation sets. In the future, we would like to extend to at least some of the most common languages in use in the publication literature. In the meantime, we have imputed scores for a subset of non-English publications that have direct citation links to English-language works.

It is possible that the most cutting-edge or niche fields may not appear in Wikipedia, either because they do not meet the notability guidelines or because no volunteer has yet written them up. In future work, it may be worth exploring whether bringing in external field definitions and citations from other locations, like journal subcategories, might produce additional fields to fill in gaps. Perhaps quality results from such an approach could even be contributed back to Wikipedia as new pages. Despite these limitations, our approach provides a valuable new technique for focused bibliometric analysis. The taxonomy, classifications, and code are available on GitHub.[1]

Acknowledgments

The authors would like to thank Autumn Toney-Wails for her valuable work on the previous iteration of this project, our anonymous reviewers for their insightful feedback, and colleagues at the Center for Security and Emerging Technology at Georgetown University for their feedback and support.

References

Raia Abu Ahmad, Ekaterina Borisova, and Georg Rehm. 2024a. Forc@ nslp2024: Overview and insights

[1]https://github.com/georgetown-cset/fields-of-study-pipeline

from the field of research classification shared task. In *Proceedings of the 1st International Workshop on Natural Scientific Language Processing and Research Knowledge Graphs (NSLP 2024)*.

Raia Abu Ahmad, Ekaterina Borisova, and Georg Rehm. 2024b. FoRC4CL: A fine-grained field of research classification and annotated dataset of NLP articles. In *Proceedings of the 2024 Joint International Conference on Computational Linguistics, Language Resources and Evaluation (LREC-COLING 2024)*, pages 7389–7394, Torino, Italia. ELRA and ICCL.

Lakshmi Rajendram Bashyam and R Krestel. 2024. Advancing automatic subject indexing: Combining weak supervision with extreme multi-label classification. In *Proceedings of the 1st International Workshop on Natural Scientific Language Processing and Research Knowledge Graphs (NSLP 2024). Hersonissos, Crete, Greece*, volume 27.

Piotr Bojanowski, Edouard Grave, Armand Joulin, and Tomas Mikolov. 2017. Enriching word vectors with subword information. *Transactions of the association for computational linguistics*, 5:135–146.

Akash Godbole, Steven A Grosz, Karthik Nandakumar, and Anil K Jain. 2022. On demographic bias in fingerprint recognition. In *2022 IEEE International Joint Conference on Biometrics (IJCB)*, pages 1–10. IEEE.

Kelsey MacMillan and Sergey Feldman. 2023. Announcing s2fos, an open source academic field of study classifier.

OpenAlex. 2022. Automated concept tagging for openalex, an open index of scholarly articles.

Mark Sanderson and Bruce Croft. 1999. Deriving concept hierarchies from text. In *Proceedings of the 22nd annual international ACM SIGIR conference on Research and development in information retrieval*, pages 206–213.

Zhihong Shen, Hao Ma, and Kuansan Wang. 2018. A web-scale system for scientific knowledge exploration. In *Proceedings of ACL 2018, System Demonstrations*, pages 87–92, Melbourne, Australia. Association for Computational Linguistics.

Autumn Toney and James Dunham. 2022. Multi-label classification of scientific research documents across domains and languages. In *Proceedings of the Third Workshop on Scholarly Document Processing*, pages 105–114, Gyeongju, Republic of Korea. Association for Computational Linguistics.

Kuansan Wang, Zhihong Shen, Chiyuan Huang, Chieh-Han Wu, Yuxiao Dong, and Anshul Kanakia. 2020. Microsoft academic graph: When experts are not enough. *Quantitative Science Studies*, 1(1):396–413.

Uncovering Differences in Persuasive Language in Russian versus English Wikipedia

Bryan Li
University of Pennsylvania
Philadelphia, PA, USA
bryanli@seas.upenn.edu

Aleksey Panasyuk
Air Force Research Lab
Rome, NY, USA
aleksey.panasyuk@us.af.mil

Chris Callison-Burch
University of Pennsylvania
Philadelphia, PA, USA
ccb@cis.upenn.edu

Abstract

We study how differences in persuasive language across Wikipedia articles, written in either English and Russian, can uncover each culture's distinct perspective on different subjects. We develop a large language model (LLM) powered system to identify instances of persuasive language in multilingual texts. Instead of directly prompting LLMs to detect persuasion, which is subjective and difficult, we propose to reframe the task to instead ask *high-level questions* (HLQs) which capture different persuasive aspects. Importantly, these HLQs are authored by LLMs themselves. LLMs over-generate a large set of HLQs, which are subsequently filtered to a small set aligned with human labels for the original task. We then apply our approach to a large-scale, bilingual dataset of Wikipedia articles (88K total), using a two-stage *identify-then-extract* prompting strategy to find instances of persuasion.

We quantify the amount of persuasion per article, and explore the differences in persuasion through several experiments on the paired articles. Notably, we generate rankings of articles by persuasion in both languages. These rankings match our intuitions on the culturally-salient subjects; Russian Wikipedia highlights subjects on Ukraine, while English Wikipedia highlights the Middle East. Grouping subjects into larger topics, we find politically-related events contain more persuasion than others. We further demonstrate that HLQs obtain similar performance when posed in either English or Russian. Our methodology enables cross-lingual, cross-cultural understanding at scale, and we release our code, prompts, and data.[1]

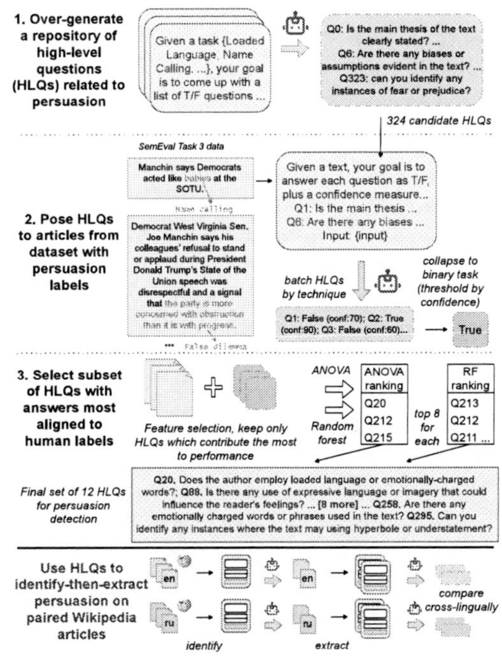

Figure 1: Overview of our approach for persuasion detection. **Top**: an LLM generates many high-level questions (HLQs), based on its own understanding of persuasion techniques. We then pose these HLQs to articles from a labeled persuasion dataset (Piskorski et al., 2023), then select a subset of 12 questions which are most aligned to the human labels. **Bottom**: on another dataset, we use HLQs to prompt an LLM to *identify-then-extract* persuasive spans. This is done over paired Wikipedia articles in Russian and English, facilitating cross-lingual comparison.

1 Introduction

Wikipedia is a widely-used and comprehensive online encyclopedia. It is available in multiple languages, and as such, is accessed and trusted by users from countries and cultures across the world. On the same subject, different language Wikipedia articles are typically independently authored from one another – although often with reference to the English version. Volunteer contributors follow a set of principles, among them to maintain a *Neutral Point of View* (NPOV): that authors create and edit

[1]https://github.com/apanasyu/UNCOVER_SPIE

Proceedings of the First Workshop on Advancing Natural Language Processing for Wikipedia, pages 21–35
November 16, 2024 ©2024 Association for Computational Linguistics

content with as objective of a view as possible.

Despite this guiding principle, Wikipedia has nevertheless come under criticism for perceived biases. In fact, there is a Wikipedia article on "Ideological bias on Wikipedia" with ample discussion.[2] The main concern is Wikipedia advancing liberal or left-leaning point-of-views. However, this is arguably a function of Wikipedia operating in a left-leaning news ecosystem, with one source opining "The encyclopedia's reliance on outside sources, primarily newspapers, means it will be only as diverse as the rest of the media – which is to say, not very" (Kessenides and Chafkin, 2016). These systemic biases arise, then, less as a conscious decision by authors, but more as a synthesis of the viewpoints from the primary sources.

This issue of authors' limited world-view compounds when considering authors who write in different languages. Russian and English Wikipedia articles often offer opposing views for many subjects. Authors in English will favor citations to English media, while authors in Russian have better access to Russian media. They also write in consideration of the interests and beliefs of their target audiences. Therefore, the same events and entities on Wikipedia have their content and tone shaped through language-specific cultural lenses. Even for the expressed goal of NPOVs, what is considered "neutral" can be subjective across cultures.

Prior work has either focused on English Wikipedia (Hube, 2017; Morris-O'Connor et al., 2023), or performed small-scale cross-lingual studies (Zhou et al., 2016; Aleksandrova et al., 2019). In this work, we perform a large-scale study on how cross-cultural perspective differences manifest in Wikipedia. We propose to quantify these articles' differences through identifying instances of *persuasive language* – how it is used, how much it is used, and for when it is used. We consider 26K Wikipedia subjects of interest to both cultures, and develop a large language model (LLM) powered system to automatically identify instances of persuasive language.

Our approach is depicted in Figure 1, and our contributions are:

1. We develop an LLM-powered system to identify instances of persuasive language in English and Russian texts, which automates insights at scale.
2. We find that a baseline approach, which directly asks an LLM to identify persuasion used in a text, results in responses that are over-sensitive and over-confident.
3. We propose a novel framework of **high-level questioning**, which reframes the persuasion detection task into a set of high-level questions (HLQs). A large number of HLQs are LLM-authored, and are then filtered down to a small set best aligned to human labels of persuasion. On a binary persuasion detection task, HLQs achieve a 23.5% relative improvement in F1 (.751 > .608).
4. We study a large-scale dataset of 88K Wikipedia articles (1m paragraphs), with articles paired by subject in Russian and English. We extract persuasion with an **identify-then-extract** prompting approach with HLQs, reducing inference costs by 85.2%.
5. We perform several experiments into Wikipedia's cross-cultural differences in perspective, with metrics to quantify the amount of persuasion within a text. Experiments include ranking subjects by their salience to each language, and comparing persuasion between paired articles.

2 Related Work

Biases in Wikipedia Because of community guidelines such as NPOV, explicit biased statements in Wikipedia articles are removed by editors. Therefore, biases occur more subtly, through being systemic or implicit. Implicit bias occurs when articles selectively choose what details to emphasize or omit (Hube, 2017). Identifying implicit bias in one article thus requires reference to another. Several authors use temporal edits of Wikipedia as references (Morris-O'Connor et al., 2023; Yasseri et al., 2014). They identify from the editing cycle which viewpoints are removed (biased against), and which are kept (biased towards). Our work takes a cross-cultural perspective, instead of a temporal one, in identifying biases; one language's article use of persuasion is compared against another.

Other works have studied how Wikipedia can be biased across languages. (Zhou et al., 2016) study how sentiment differs towards ~200 entities in 5 languages. (Aleksandrova et al., 2019) develop a system to extract biased sentences in 3 languages. There are several other relevant studies (Callahan and Herring, 2011; Miz et al., 2020). Our work is

[2]https://en.wikipedia.org/wiki/Ideological_bias_on_Wikipedia

characterized by its much larger-scale (26K subjects), and its approach to extract potential bias at the span-level.

Multilingual biases of LLMs While LLMs are able to understand and generate text in many languages, researchers have identified that LLM competency and responses differ cross-lingually. For cultural inquiries, LLMs favor Western values, even when interacting in languages where different cultural sensitivities are desired (Naous et al., 2023; Cao et al., 2023). For factual inquiries, multilingual settings cause LLMs to answer inconsistently (Li et al., 2024; Qi et al., 2023).

Russian vs Western perspectives The Russian state has positioned itself in stark contrast to the West. As such, Russia has made concerted efforts to spread its narratives and alter public discourse in its favor. This ranges from foreign events to domestic issues: respectively, the 2016 US Presidential Election (Golovchenko et al., 2020), and the 2022 Russian invasion of Ukraine (Geissler et al., 2023).

Our work also seeks to compare Russian vs. Western POVs, but through comparing Russian articles written for Russian audiences, to English articles written for English audiences – both of which aim for "neutral" POVs.

AI-assisted report generation This line of work uses AI tools to take in multiple documents, and assemble a report which summarizes the key points for a specified audience. Barham et al. (2023) consider Wikipedias in 50 languages, to generate a large-scale dataset of 120m QA pairs, indexed to 71m reports. For a given passage, its citations are used as reports, and an English question-answer pair is generated from it. Li and Callison-Burch (2023) propose a scalable approach to generate cross-lingual QA pairs on paired passages. Reddy et al. (2023) develop a LLM-powered system to generate reports to assist decision-makers in high-stakes issues. Our work takes inspiration from all of these, in studying Wikipedia, making cross-lingual comparisons, empowered by LLMs.

3 Task Formulation

Definitions Used We tackle **detection of persuasion** in text. We adopt two task formulations from the SemEval series of workshops. The first and simpler task is *identification* – predict whether a given context contains persuasion. The second is *span extraction* – given a context, extract spans that utilize persuasion. For either task, *classification* can either be binary, or on a set of persuasive techniques (described in §3.1).

We consider two languages in this work, Russian and English. Our prompting setups are *multilingually monolingual*, in that we cover both languages individually; i.e., for Russian contexts we use Russian prompts (and vice versa for English). Our analysis, however, will be *cross-lingual*, in that we compare persuasion use across the paired articles, as well as compare across the entire Russian dataset vs. the entire English dataset.

Prompting is the paradigm of interacting with LLMs at inference-time by giving instructions (a prompt) for a specific task. To further improve LLM's understanding of the task, *few-shot* examples of the expected input and output can be added to the prompt. This is called *in-context learning* (Brown et al., 2020; Patel et al., 2023).

In this work, we consider a standard prompting setup with chat-optimized LLMs. Instructions are in the *system prompt*, and the few-shot exemplars[3] are captured in alternate *user* and *agent* sections. One inference entry is given as another user section, and the LLM will generate text to complete the agent section.

3.1 Datasets Used

For designing and validating our prompts, we use SemEval 2023 Task 3 subtask 3 (Piskorski et al., 2023). We will simply refer to this as SemEval. The dataset covers 9 languages. Each article is segmented into paragraphs, and human annotators extract spans with persuasion, and also assign one of 23 persuasive techniques. Though we piloted some multilingual experimentation, we primarily work with the English subset of 11,780 paragraphs.

Selecting a Dataset in Russian and English We collect a set of paired Wikipedia articles, between Russian (ru) and English (en). We download the full dumps of Wikipedia in both languages, then filter to the subjects where articles link to known Russian state-sponsored news websites.

In addition to the ru and en settings, we consider 2 more: English translated[4] to Russian (en2ru), and the Russian translated to English (ru2en).

The final dataset consists of 22,046 paired articles; given the 4 settings, we will process 88k

[3]We used a 1-shot, static exemplar for every prompt.

[4]This was paragraph-level MT by prompting an LLM. The full texts for all prompts used in this work are Appendix D.

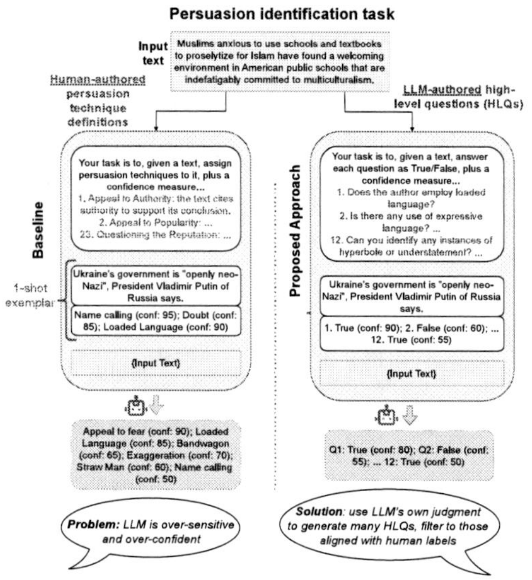

Figure 2: A comparison between two prompting approaches to persuasion technique detection. The baseline (left) directly uses the human-authored definitions. However, as these definitions were written for trained human annotators, the LLM misunderstands them and is over-sensitive and over-confident. Our proposed approach (right) instead leverages the LLM to decompose the task itself. Specifically, we elicit HLQs with a separate prompt (see Figure 1). Then, we prompt with HLQs instead of definitions.

individual articles. At the paragraph-level, there are 245,778 ru entries (and ru2en), and 295,158 en entries (and en2ru), for >1m entries total.

4 Baseline for Persuasion Detection

Figure 2 provides a comparison of the two approaches towards identifying whether a context contains persuasion. In this section, we detail the baseline (left), which suffers from too many false positives. For this stage, we consider only English; we consider both languages in future sections.

4.1 Approach: Direct Prompting with Definitions

The baseline prompt, as shown in Figure 2 (left) includes each persuasive technique, as well as a human-authored definition from SemEval. We further ask the LLM to generate a confidence score for each predicted technique, which we use to threshold predictions (described shortly ahead).

The main issue with this direct approach is that understanding of persuasion, is extremely subjective. In collecting the gold labels for SemEval, Piskorski et al. (2023) invested significant efforts into training 35+ human annotators (multilingually), and revising instructions throughout. So, by directly giving the LLM the final definitions, we cannot expect it to be aligned with the judgements specific to this annotation task.

Table 1: F1 on SemEval binary persuasion detection, using the Baseline prompt, at varying confidence thresholds. Observe that # 'True' has too many false positives at low thresholds.

$\geq x$	F1	# 'True'	$\geq x$	F1	# 'True'
$x = 20$	0.469	10079	$x = 60$	0.450	10266
$x = 30$	0.459	10165	$x = 80$	0.582	7233
$x = 40$	0.454	10223	$x = 85$	**0.608**	**4264**
$x = 50$	0.447	10293	$x = 90$	0.573	2833

To demonstrate the divergence in LLM understanding of persuasion vs. humans, Appendix Table 4 compares the raw counts for each persuasion technique over SemEval (11,780 total contexts). These numbers use the best observed confidence threshold of $x \geq 50$. We observe that the gold labels are highly imbalanced. Notably, 59% of texts contain no persuasion (6,945); however, GPT-4 predicts "no persuasion" only 12.3% of the time (1,450). For the gold labels, 47% of the persuasive texts receive the *Loaded Language* label. 11 classes appear less than 1% of the time. Furthermore, as this is a multi-class labeling task, those <1% labels often appear with 'Loaded Language'. GPT-4 does not have a sense as to the class priors, and over-predicts the prevalence of all 23 persuasion techniques – 24,209 predicted vs. 7,465 gold.

For example, consider *Appeal to Authority* (6286 vs. 179). The baseline prompt incorrectly assigns this to most mentions of people's titles (e.g., "President Vladimir Putin of Russia") or news sources (e.g., "New York Times").

Baseline makes LLMs over-confident To evaluate how confidence scores affect performance, we make a task simplification – rather than multi-class labeling, we reduce the problem to binary classification. A context is 'True' if any predicted technique has confidence $\geq x$, else 'False'. We then use F1 to choose the optimal threshold.

Table 1 shows F1 by confidence threshold. Until $x = 60$, the model assigns $> 87\%$ of texts as containing persuasion. F1 is maximized at $x = 85$, at 0.608. We thus have shown both that the model is over-confident, and that thresholding for confidence scores substantially improves performance.

Method	P	R	F1
24 definitions	0.607	0.613	0.608
12 HLQs	0.757	0.748	0.751
324 HLQs	0.746	0.733	0.737

Table 2: SemEval performance with different methods.

5 High-Level Questioning (HLQ)

The high-level questioning approach to persuasion detection is depicted at the top of Figure 1. The idea behind HLQs is to leverage LLMs' own (many different) judgements on a task, then filter down to those that best align with gold labels on a reference dataset. Appendix A.1 details the motivation behind HLQs. In this section, we describe the approach to persuasion detection using HLQs.

5.1 Generating candidate questions for each persuasion technique

In the first step, we write a simple zero-shot prompt which tasks an LLM to generate a list of True/False questions for a specified persuasion technique. For this step, the key is getting LLM's zero-shot understanding from various angles through its own generations. Therefore, we over-generate a large set of questions. It is expected that many questions overlap in coverage; we thus filter out questions which have very high n-gram overlap, while keeping paraphrases. This results in a repository of 324 questions. Our manual analysis finds that most questions are very targeted, thus less subjective to answer (examples of questions in Table 5).

5.2 Applying HLQs to a labeled dataset

Given the repository of HLQs, can we find which ones are most effective at detecting persuasive language? We do so by leveraging existing annotations from SemEval for the ground truth (step 2 of Figure 1). We batch the queries with sets containing all generated HLQs for a technique. Then, in a single prompt, an LLM is asked to answer True/False for the batched HLQs over the entire SemEval dataset (11,780 entries).

To compare to the gold annotations, we follow Section 4.1 to simplify and collapse SemEval to a binary classification task. As shown in Table 2, prompting with HLQs improves F1 by 23.5% relative over the baseline: F1 of 0.751 > 0.608. Furthermore, we see that the 12 question subset slightly improves over the full set of 324 HLQs: 0.751 > 0.737. This shows using the LLM's own generations greatly improves over using definitions.

5.3 Selecting subset of most-aligned HLQs

The approach so far works well, but is expensive, with one multi-question prompt for each of the 23 techniques. We improve prompting efficiency by filtering to a subset of top-ranked HLQs, which maintains performance, while fitting into 1 prompt (step 3 of Figure 1).

We cast this as a feature selection problem, which can be solved with the standard techniques of ANOVA and Random Forest with Gini impurity. Appendix Figure 4 illustrates the impact of feature reduction on the classifiers' effectiveness by plotting the F1-score against the progressively diminished feature sets using ANOVA. We find a stable performance across classifiers until around 8 features remain.

Thus, we combine the top 8 features from ANOVA, and top 8 from Random Forest. This results in a final subset of 12 HLQs. Appendix Table 5 shows both English and Russian versions.

Extending HLQs to Russian With the top 12 HLQs selected, we employ a native Russian speaker (one of the co-authors) for translation. They were allowed to prompt GPT-4, for assistance, before further postediting.[5]

6 Identify-then-Extract Methodology

We adopt a two-stage hierarchical prompting approach towards persuasive language detection, using GPT-4[6], which we term identify-then-extract (Figure 1, bottom).

We apply identify-then-extract to find persuasion in the dataset of paired Wikipedia articles. Wikipedia is of particular interest because its use of persuasion tends to be more subtle, given that news articles often intend to tell a story, Wikipedia articles are all written to maintain NPOV.

Identify-then-extract thus is a further decomposition of the persuasion detection task, beyond the HLQ decomposition. Importantly, the identify step allows better identification of texts that are 'Null' for persuasion (more common due to NPOV), and is much more efficient in terms of number of prompts, as described ahead.

[5]We follow the same LLM + human post-editing process to translate all prompts.

[6]We also tried Llama-2, an open-source, much smaller LLM. With some prompt engineering, Llama-2 could do the task, though underperforming GPT-4 (see Appendix C).

6.1 Identify

Identification is the same task performed in §4.1. In this stage, for each context, we prompt an LLM to answer True/False for all HLQs at once (shown in Figure 2, right). This results in judgments for 12m (1m paragraphs * 12 HLQs) entries.

6.2 Extract

Of the 12m judgments, we only consider the contexts and the selected set of HLQs marked as 'True'. For the paired Wikipedia articles dataset, 85.2% are marked 'False', and so do not need to be queried – this shows the identify-then-extract approach saves much inference costs over a single-stage.

For each, we insert the context and one HLQ into a prompt template, which tasks the LLM to extract spans employing that HLQ. In contrast to the single prompt per context from the identify stage, the extract stage is hierarchical, having a set of 'True' HLQs, and thus prompts, per context.

Collapsing extracted spans which overlap The HLQs, while nuanced, largely cover the same aspects of persuasion. This means that LLM outputs will also contain many overlapping terms. Given that for analysis purposes, we reduced the task from multi-class labeling to binary labeling, we should also collapse the multi-class extracted spans to a deduplicated set, termed a **persuasive text set (PTS)**. Appendix Table 6 shows some sample model responses and the PTS.

7 Experiments and Analysis

For our cross-lingual analysis over the paired articles dataset, we propose several metrics. We use these for various experiments, which make different comparisons and aggregations.

We note that these experiments proceed on a dataset which is unlabeled for persuasion. This is by design, as we would like to use the insights (i.e,, HLQs) generated from the limited amount of labeled data for a different domain, SemEval, and apply it to this huge dataset of 88K articles.[7]

Metrics to Quantify Persuasion We define several metrics. $wc(\text{text})$ counts the number of words in a text.[8] The metrics are Persuasive Count (PC),

Top Russian Articles	PF ru	PF en
Environmental impact of the 2022 Russian invasion of Ukraine	0.982	0.987
Russian occupation of Kherson Oblast	0.953	0.651
Cult of personality	0.913	0.608
Disinformation in the 2022 Russian invasion of Ukraine	0.911	0.819
Trumpism	0.879	0.828
Top English Articles	**PF ru**	**PF en**
Ruscism	0.778	0.882
2015–2016 wave of violence in the Israeli–Palestinian conflict	0.448	0.863
Armenian genocide denial	0.618	0.857
Transphobia	0.494	0.839
Trumpism	0.879	0.828

Table 3: Top 5 Wikipedia articles per language, ranked by persuasion frequency (PF). Each per-language ranking considers only the top 25% articles by length. The other language scores are provided for reference; numbers in grey indicate that the other language's article was below the length threshold.

and Persuasive Frequency (PF):

$$PC = wc(\text{PTS}) \quad ; \quad PF_{\text{para}} = \frac{wc(\text{PTS})}{wc(\text{para})}$$

$$PF_{\text{article}} = \sum_{\text{para} \in \text{article}} PF_{\text{para}} * \frac{wc(\text{para})}{wc(\text{article})}$$

Our quantification of persuasion is more fine-grained than as done by prior works such as SemEval, which counts spans, rather individual words.[9] We consider the persuasive text sets obtained with the identify-the-extract with HLQs approach. We find that over the 22K Russian articles, PF $\mu = .116, \delta = .177$, and for the English articles, PF $\mu = .137, \delta = .186$.

We next describe the experiments: a targeted case study, ranking articles by persuasion per-language, and several cross-lingual experiments.

7.1 Case study: 2021 Russian protests

Figure 3, depicts a case study on paired articles for the subject '2021 Russian Protests'. Interestingly, the paired articles have different titles, as the Russian one is more specific, saying the protests were in support of Alexei Navalny. The LLM extracts more persuasion from the Russian-authored articles than the English-authored – .521 en vs. .587 ru2en. It identifies the loaded term "oppositionist" in the ru2en article. Meanwhile as "opposition

[7]We performed manual analysis of a few examples from both languages. We acknowledge that followup work should take a closer look at how Wikipedia texts use persuasion.

[8]We use the function `nltk.tokenize.word_tokenize`.

[9]We acknowledge that word counting is simple, and that future work should precisely explore persuasion metrics.

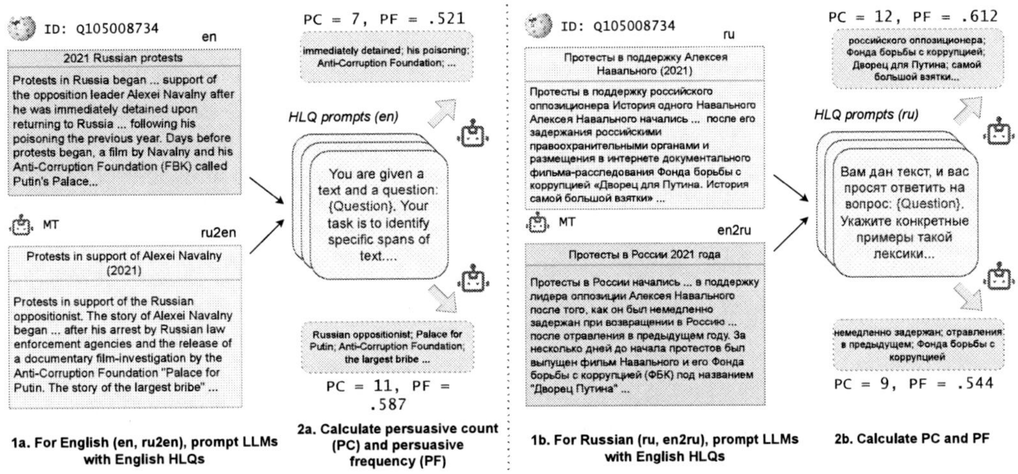

Figure 3: Depiction of the method to compare persuasive language usage across languages. For each language, we use HLQ prompts *monolingually* on all articles to extract persuasive text spans (left: en, right: ru). We compare both persuasive count (PC) and persuasive frequency (PF) between the paired articles. For this case study, the Russian article (and its translation ru2en) are more persuasive on '2021 Russian protests'.

leader" in the en article is more neutral, the term is not identified.

We also see that PF are relatively closer between an article and its translation: .521 en vs .544 en2ru; .612 ru vs .587 ru2en. This is a positive signal that LLM extracts similarly whether using the Russian or English prompts. We also enlisted a native Russian speaker to verify these translations had the similar meanings. This sanity check is expanded, and applied to a larger dataset in Section 7.5.

7.2 Ranking Wikipedia Articles by Persuasion

This experiment investigates which subjects contain the most persuasive content, as measured by PF, for Wikipedia authors in either language. We heuristically consider only the top 25% longest articles, using length as a proxy for which articles are of the most interest to readers and authors.[10]

Table 3 shows the two rankings for the top-5 persuasive articles. First, considering Russian, we see that 3 of the 5 subjects all deal with the 2022 Russo-Ukrainian war. The English versions of these 3 articles are below the top-25% threshold; still, considering their scores, we see that "Environmental impact" has high PF en, while the other 2 are lower.

We now consider the English rankings. The top 5 subjects are more generally scoped, but align well with our intuitions on subjects of greater interest to Western audiences: "Ruscism" (Russian fascism), "Transphobia", "Israeli-Palestinian conflict", "Armenian genocide denial". The PF ru scores for these articles are much lower than for the Russian ranking. Interestingly, we see that "Trumpism" is in the top-5 for both rankings, showing this political philosophy is of great interest to both societies.

7.3 Grouping into Broader Topics

We further our analysis by grouping subjects from Wikipedia into broader topics. For this, we leverage the WikiData knowledge base (KB), which contains structured KB triplets for every Wikipedia entry. Specifically, we consider the predicate `is instance of` (Wikidata ID P31). We also use a normalized version of PF (NPF) to better compare scores across languages; calculation of NPF is described in Appendix B.1.

The NPF rankings by topic for en and ru settings are shown in Appendix Table 7. The top topics as expected, such as 'Disagreement Situation', and 'Part of War'. The bottom topics are also as expected, such as 'Aircraft' and 'Automaker'. We have therefore validated our hypothesis that political-related events contain more persuasive content in both languages. More neutral categories, meanwhile, are written by both Russian and English authors with less persuasion.

Furthermore, we see that NPF scores are fairly well-aligned across languages. This could be in part due to neutral POV, and/or from the normalization process. This is an interesting finding, which

[10]for en: $wc > 4758$, for ru: $wc > 2931$

shows that, despite individual subjects differing levels of persuasion across languages (as found in Section 7.2), within aggregated topics they are similarly persuasive.

7.4 Identifying subjects with the greatest cross-cultural disagreement

For certain subjects of national pride, one culture may perceive it to be especially sensitive, and thus use more persuasion, than the other culture. We identify these by finding the paired articles with the largest PF differences.

Appendix Figure 5 depicts selected subjects in a scatter plot, and again brings up interesting insights. We consider several examples and provide some cursory analysis and discussion. The '1998 bombing of Iraq' is more persuasive in English. This could be the case as this effort was led by the US and UK, so writers in English would have more access to primary sources. Also, more persuasive in English is the '2006 Kodori crisis'. This occurred in a separatist region of Georgia, and was alleged by Georgia officials to have been sponsored by agents of Russia. This is explored in more detail in English, while only briefly mentioned in Russian.

On the Russian side of the line (red), we have the '2005-2006 Russian-Ukraine gas dispute'. Interestingly, we also have the 'First Battle of Brega', which was a 2011 conflict in the Libyan Civil War; neither Russia nor Anglosphere countries were directly involved. This example could warrant further study, into whether the Russian article contains more persuasion due to tastes of the particular author, or if the Russian media as a whole covered this war more.

7.5 Verifying Consistency of LLM Responses Across Languages

Recall that for the persuasion detection task, merely giving the LLM the persuasion technique definitions resulted in the responses diverging from human labels. This advises us to also check whether the HLQs and prompts in English elicit similar behavior from an LLM as HLQs and prompts in Russian. After all, multilingual LLMs are largely English-centric; also most prior works advise to always use prompt instructions in English, even for inference in other languages (Ahuja et al., 2023; Shi et al., 2022). Therefore, we perform a sanity check experiment, by considering settings RU and its translation RU2EN (and vice versa for and en2ru). As articles contain the same content, but just translated, we should expect their rankings to be similar; meanwhile, the rankings from the other language-authored articles should differ.

We use Rank Bias Overlap (RBO) to compare two ranked lists (Webber et al., 2010). RBO is based on a simple probabilistic user mode, where higher scores (0 to 1) indicate more similar lists. These pairwise RBO scores are shown in Appendix Figure 6. The highest RBO is achieved between original and translated articles: RBO(ru, ru2en)= 0.85. In contrast, rankings differ greatly between the original articles: RBO(ru, en)= 0.29.

Therefore, we have shown that the HLQ-based approach to persuasive language detection is equally valid in either English or Russian. We also indirectly have shown that the translation process we used maintains the persuasive content of an original text. To conclude this section, this set of experiments show the flexibility of our approach to uncovering cross-cultural differences in persuasion, from various angles.

8 Conclusion

Our study makes two contributions. First, we introduce the methodology of high-level questioning, in which we task an LLM with generating many questions on a subjective task, and then filter down to a target set where answers are best aligned to human labels. We anticipate that future work can adapt the HLQ method to address other subjective tasks aside from the persuasion detection task studied.

Second, we have made a large-scale inquiry into uncovering how Wikipedias in Russian and English differ in their perspectives. Our approach was to quantify levels of persuasive content used across different language versions of a subject. This allows us to make two main insights: on which subjects are more meaningful to Russian and/or English authors; and on which subjects are cross-lingual disagreements in persuasion highest. This is important because of the widespread use of Wikipedia – especially in the NLP world, many view it as a source of ground-truth knowledge. The existence of such perspective differences across Wikipedias advises extra care with such a view.

Our work takes several preliminary steps towards using LLMs to enable large-scale cross-lingual insights. While cross-cultural differences exist, we are excited by the possibilities of multilingual LLMs, to facilitate better understanding across geographic and linguistic borders.

Limitations

The main limitation of our work is that we collected the HLQs with respect to a labeled dataset (SemEval), and then applied it to an unlabeled dataset in a different domain (Wikipedia). Given the challenges of a domain adaptation setting, it would be ideal to have some labeled data in the target domain. However, this was infeasible due to the size of our dataset (88k articles), and the extensive time and effort required to obtain labeled data that annotators agree on. We therefore proposed the series of experiments, based on the PF metrics, and found that the findings roughly matched our intuitions on subjects and cultural analysis. We anticipate followup work, such as the next iterations of SemEval, can further address the issue of requiring more labeled data for precision.

We also performed only a limited analysis of specific topics from Wikipedia, such as in §7.2, §7.4. Followup studies should both consider more examples, and further investigate these examples with respect to the larger geopolitical landscapes of both Russian and English-speaking societies.

For ethical considerations, we used LLMs for the experiments throughout our work, and processed a high volume of text (88k Wikipedia articles). This meant we processed about 12m prompts in the first select stage. We acknowledge that this is a large amount, and we could have looked for ways to select a subset to process, perhaps by applying some pre-hoc heuristic filters, and post-hoc caching. Still, in terms of token count, our prompts are rather short (with respect to other NLP studies), and the whole point of our study is to a large-scale study of Wikipedias. In the second infer stage, we indeed greatly reduced the number of prompts by 85%.

Acknowledgements

This research is supported in part by the Office of the Director of National Intelligence (ODNI), Intelligence Advanced Research Projects Activity (IARPA), via the HIATUS Program contract #2022-22072200005. The views and conclusions contained herein are those of the authors and should not be interpreted as necessarily representing the official policies, either expressed or implied, of ODNI, IARPA, or the U.S. Government. The U.S. Government is authorized to reproduce and distribute reprints for governmental purposes notwithstanding any copyright annotation therein. The views and conclusions contained herein are those of the authors and should not be interpreted as necessarily representing the official policies or endorsements, either expressed or implied, of Air Force Research Laboratory or the U.S. Government.

References

Kabir Ahuja, Harshita Diddee, Rishav Hada, Millicent Ochieng, Krithika Ramesh, Prachi Jain, Akshay Nambi, Tanuja Ganu, Sameer Segal, Mohamed Ahmed, et al. 2023. Mega: Multilingual evaluation of generative ai. In *Proceedings of the 2023 Conference on Empirical Methods in Natural Language Processing*, pages 4232–4267.

Desislava Aleksandrova, François Lareau, and Pierre André Ménard. 2019. Multilingual sentence-level bias detection in wikipedia. In *Proceedings of the International Conference on Recent Advances in Natural Language Processing (RANLP 2019)*, pages 42–51.

Samuel Barham, Orion Weller, Michelle Yuan, Kenton Murray, Mahsa Yarmohammadi, Zhengping Jiang, Siddharth Vashishtha, Alexander Martin, Anqi Liu, Aaron Steven White, et al. 2023. Megawika: Millions of reports and their sources across 50 diverse languages. *arXiv preprint arXiv:2307.07049*.

Tom Brown, Benjamin Mann, Nick Ryder, Melanie Subbiah, Jared D Kaplan, Prafulla Dhariwal, Arvind Neelakantan, Pranav Shyam, Girish Sastry, Amanda Askell, et al. 2020. Language models are few-shot learners. *Advances in neural information processing systems*, 33:1877–1901.

Ewa S Callahan and Susan C Herring. 2011. Cultural bias in wikipedia content on famous persons. *Journal of the American society for information science and technology*, 62(10):1899–1915.

Yong Cao, Li Zhou, Seolhwa Lee, Laura Cabello, Min Chen, and Daniel Hershcovich. 2023. Assessing cross-cultural alignment between chatgpt and human societies: An empirical study. *arXiv preprint arXiv:2303.17466*.

Dominique Geissler, Dominik Bär, Nicolas Pröllochs, and Stefan Feuerriegel. 2023. Russian propaganda on social media during the 2022 invasion of ukraine. *EPJ Data Science*, 12(1):35.

Yevgeniy Golovchenko, Cody Buntain, Gregory Eady, Megan A Brown, and Joshua A Tucker. 2020. Cross-platform state propaganda: Russian trolls on twitter and youtube during the 2016 us presidential election. *The International Journal of Press/Politics*, 25(3):357–389.

Christoph Hube. 2017. Bias in wikipedia. In *Proceedings of the 26th International Conference on World Wide Web Companion*, pages 717–721.

Dimitra Kessenides and Max Chafkin. 2016. Is wikipedia woke? *Bloomberg News"*.

Bryan Li and Chris Callison-Burch. 2023. Paxqa: Generating cross-lingual question answering examples at training scale. *ArXiv*, abs/2304.12206.

Bryan Li, Samar Haider, and Chris Callison-Burch. 2024. This land is Your, My land: Evaluating geopolitical bias in language models through territorial disputes. In *Proceedings of the 2024 Conference of the North American Chapter of the Association for Computational Linguistics: Human Language Technologies (Volume 1: Long Papers)*, pages 3855–3871, Mexico City, Mexico. Association for Computational Linguistics.

Volodymyr Miz, Joëlle Hanna, Nicolas Aspert, Benjamin Ricaud, and Pierre Vandergheynst. 2020. What is trending on wikipedia? capturing trends and language biases across wikipedia editions. In *Companion proceedings of the Web conference 2020*, pages 794–801.

Danielle A Morris-O'Connor, Andreas Strotmann, and Dangzhi Zhao. 2023. The colonization of wikipedia: evidence from characteristic editing behaviors of warring camps. *Journal of Documentation*, 79(3):784–810.

Tarek Naous, Michael J Ryan, and Wei Xu. 2023. Having beer after prayer? measuring cultural bias in large language models. *arXiv preprint arXiv:2305.14456*.

Ajay Patel, Bryan Li, Mohammad Sadegh Rasooli, Noah Constant, Colin Raffel, and Chris Callison-Burch. 2023. Bidirectional language models are also few-shot learners. In *The Eleventh International Conference on Learning Representations*.

Jakub Piskorski, Nicolas Stefanovitch, Giovanni Da San Martino, and Preslav Nakov. 2023. Semeval-2023 task 3: Detecting the category, the framing, and the persuasion techniques in online news in a multilingual setup. In *Proceedings of the 17th International Workshop on Semantic Evaluation (SemEval-2023)*, pages 2343–2361.

Jirui Qi, Raquel Fernández, and Arianna Bisazza. 2023. Cross-lingual consistency of factual knowledge in multilingual language models. *arXiv preprint arXiv:2310.10378*.

Revanth Gangi Reddy, Yi R. Fung, Qi Zeng, Manling Li, Ziqi Wang, Paul Sullivan, and Heng Ji. 2023. Smartbook: Ai-assisted situation report generation. *Preprint*, arXiv:2303.14337.

Freda Shi, Mirac Suzgun, Markus Freitag, Xuezhi Wang, Suraj Srivats, Soroush Vosoughi, Hyung Won Chung, Yi Tay, Sebastian Ruder, Denny Zhou, et al. 2022. Language models are multilingual chain-of-thought reasoners. In *The Eleventh International Conference on Learning Representations*.

William Webber, Alistair Moffat, and Justin Zobel. 2010. A similarity measure for indefinite rankings. *ACM Trans. Inf. Syst.*, 28(4).

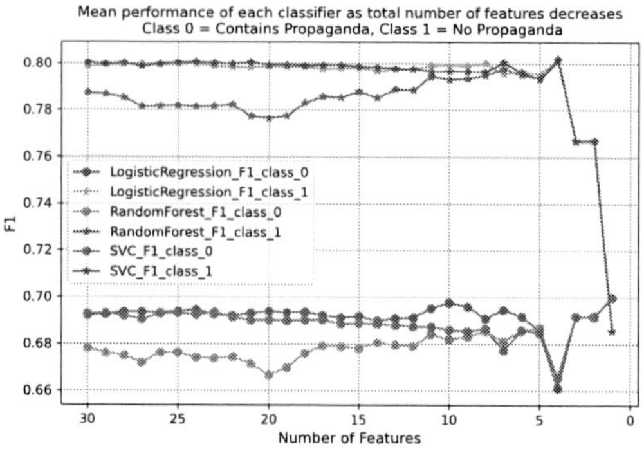

Figure 4: The effectiveness of the classifiers after each feature reduction using ANOVA. F1 performance is relatively stable across metrics from 30 to 8 features, and declines afterwards.

Taha Yasseri, Anselm Spoerri, Mark Graham, and János Kertész. 2014. The most controversial topics in wikipedia. *Global Wikipedia: International and cross-cultural issues in online collaboration*, 25:25–48.

Yiwei Zhou, Elena Demidova, and Alexandra I. Cristea. 2016. Who likes me more? analysing entity-centric language-specific bias in multilingual wikipedia. In *Proceedings of the 31st Annual ACM Symposium on Applied Computing*, SAC '16, page 750–757, New York, NY, USA. Association for Computing Machinery.

A Discussion

A.1 Motivating high-level questioning

Let us consider the typical fixes one can take when an LLM underperforms given some prompt. First, more detailed instructions can be written. For this task, a human would have to expend efforts for all 23 techniques. Furthermore, longer instructions would great increase inference costs.

Second, we can include more few-shot exemplars. In the baseline, we used a single, static exemplar. Suppose one wanted to use multiple, dynamic exemplars. Typical prompting techniques would, for each inference entry, randomly draw exemplars from a train split. Again, this would be challenging due to the 23 distinct techniques, which have different class priors. Therefore, we are motivated to find an approach which can use the LLM's own intuitions.

Persuasion Technique	Gold Count	Baseline Count	Persuasion Technique	Gold Count	Baseline Count
None	6945	1450	Conversation Killer	115	120
Loaded Language	2277	2484	Red Herring	63	101
Name Calling-Labeling	1226	1871	Guilt by Association	63	339
Doubt	703	2824	Appeal to Popularity	48	478
Repetition	684	407	Appeal to Hypocrisy	45	104
Exaggeration-Minimisation	576	1571	Obfuscation-Vagueness-Confusion	30	482
Appeal to Fear-Prejudice	442	2260	Straw Man	24	19
Flag Waving	376	46	Whataboutism	18	179
Causal Oversimplification	236	848	Appeal to Values	0	1938
False Dilemma	180	307	Consequential Oversimplification	0	361
Slogans	180	124	Appeal to Time	0	577
Appeal to Authority	179	6286	Questioning the Reputation	0	483
Total (all 23 excluding *None*)	7465	24209			

Table 4: Raw counts of each persuasion technique for the SemEval English split (Piskorski et al., 2023), gold vs. GPT-4 baseline.

QID	AN, FR	Question
Q20	0, 3	Does the author employ loaded language or emotionally-charged words? Использует ли автор насыщенный язык или эмоционально окрашенные слова?
Q88	12, 7	Is there any use of expressive language or imagery that could influence the reader's feelings? Есть ли использование выразительного языка или образности, которые могут повлиять на чувства читателя?
Q92	9, 5	Does the text make use of positive or negative connotations to sway the reader's opinion? Использует ли текст позитивные или негативные коннотации для влияния на мнение читателя?
Q210	6, 9	Does the text contain words or phrases that evoke strong emotions? Содержит ли текст слова или фразы, вызывающие сильные эмоции?
Q211	3, 2	Are there words or phrases in the text that are intended to manipulate the reader's feelings? Есть ли в тексте слова или выражения, предназначенные для манипулирования чувствами читателя?
Q212	1, 1	Can you identify any instances where emotionally charged language is used to support a claim? Можете ли вы указать случаи использования эмоционально окрашенных слов для поддержки утверждения?
Q213	8, 0	Are there parts in the text where the language is used to influence the reader's opinion or decision? Есть ли в тексте места, где язык используется для воздействия на мнение или решение читателя?
Q215	2, 31	Does the text use language that is intended to provoke a particular reaction from the reader? Использует ли текст язык, предназначенный для вызывания определенной реакции читателя?
Q216	5, 19	Can you find any instances where the language used is not neutral or objective? Можете ли вы найти случаи, когда используемый язык не нейтрален или объективен?
Q217	7, 12	Does the text use language that is intended to sway the reader's viewpoint? Использует ли текст язык, предназначенный для влияния на точку зрения читателя?
Q258	4, 4	Are there any emotionally charged words or phrases used in the text? Есть ли в тексте эмоционально окрашенные слова или выражения?
Q295	20, 6	Can you identify any instances where the text may be using hyperbole or understatement? Можете ли вы указать случаи, когда в тексте возможно использование гиперболы или преуменьшения?

Table 5: The 12 HLQs selected, with English in black and Russian in blue. The second column shows the feature importance ranking by ANOVA (AN) and Random Forest (RF). In terms of persuasive techniques, we observe that 10 pertain to 'Loaded Language', 1 (Q258) pertains to 'None', and 1 (Q295) pertains to 'Exaggeration or Minimization'. This reflects the overrepresentation of "Loaded Language" in SemEval (47% of technique labels).

B Additional Experiments

B.1 Normalized persuasion frequency (NPF)

We use a normalized version of PF for several experiments. This normalizes all PF scores across all authors (either Russian or English) between 0 and 1. To quickly illustrate, suppose the max PF is 0.6, and the min is 0.05. NPF would draw the max towards 1, and the minimum towards 0. The raw max and min PF could differ between English and

Sent idx	QID	Specific Text Instances Identified
2	Q20	engulfed, rapidly destroyed, tragedy, repeatedly complained, ...
2	Q88	fire engulfed, rapidly destroyed, tragedy, funding cuts, ...
	PTS	fire engulfed, rapidly destroyed, tragedy, repeatedly complained, funding cuts
3	Q20	incalculable, outraged, cultural tragedy, lobotomy
3	Q88	fire, loss, outraged, tragedy, destroyed, ruins, threat, ...
	PTS	incalculable, outraged, cultural tragedy, lobotomy, fire, loss, destroyed, ruins, threat

Table 6: Sample Model responses (ru2en), on 'Fire at the National Museum of Brazil' (WikiID: Q56441760). 'PTS' is the deduplicated persuasive text set combining all 12 HLQs.

QID (Description)	# Subjects	ru NPF	en NPF
Q180684 (Disagreement Situation)	65	0.303	0.326
Q47461344 (Written Work)	53	0.301	0.305
Q178561 (Part of War)	68	0.304	0.284
Q7278 (Org Influences Gov)	138	0.247	0.296
Q43229 (Social Entity)	122	0.229	0.257
...	...	...	...
Q23038290 (Fossil Taxon)	52	0.044	0.045
Q15056993 (Aircraft)	153	0.05	0.035
Q786820 (Automaker)	52	0.025	0.054
Q2198484 (Admin Entity)	132	0.038	0.037
Q14795564 (Date Calculator)	217	0.036	0

Table 7: Top 5 and bottom 5 topics (Wikidata P31 `instance of`) by persuasive content. This is sorted by NPF en, but as shown, NPF en and NPF ru are mostly close over topics.

Russian, but after normalization, the max and min PF would be about the same.

We provide pseudocode for calculating NPF:

```
author1_pf = calc_pf(
  author1_article_length_list,
  author1_pc_list)
author2_pf = calc_pf(
  author2_article_length_list,
  author2_pc_list)
# Concatenate PF arrays from both authors
```

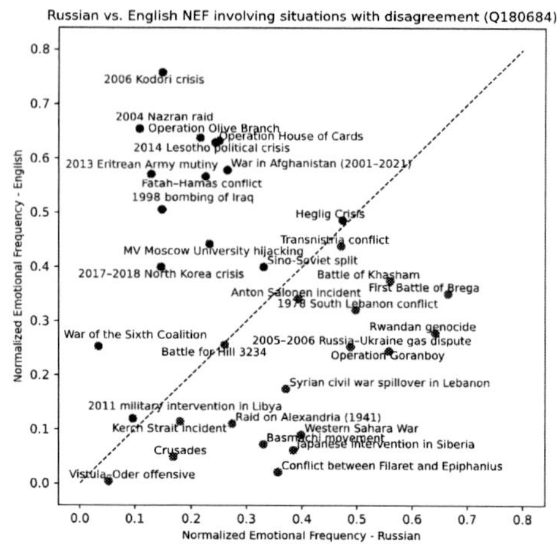

Figure 5: A scatter plot where the x and y positions represent the NPF values of Russian and English articles, respectively. The dashed line indicates equal NPF, i.e., the subjects where English and Russian has similar levels of emotional content. The further a point is from this line, the further the paired articles are in their use of persuasive content.

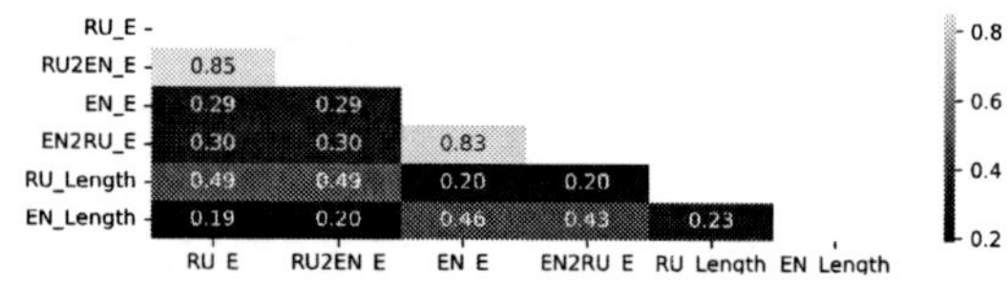

Figure 6: Rank-biased overlap (RBO) scores, calculated over pairwise rankings. The rankings are the 4 language settings, as well as ru_length and en_length, which are wc(article). The label '_E' refers to PC.

```
all_pf = author1_pf + author2_pf
# Scale all PF values to a range of [0, 1]
npf = normalize_scores(all_ef)
```

Where `calc_pf` returns `author_pc_list[i] / author_article_length_list[i]` (for $i = 0, 1, ...n-1$), and n is the number of articles.

Why normalize? Recall that Wikipedia guidelines specify a NPOV. If we assume that different individual authors aim for the same NPOV, then we can normalize PF scores for one language. Suppose the NPOV for Russian differs from English. Then, we can "normalize" out the NPOV by taking all article's and their PF together. Putting them on a common scale makes comparing the relative emotional content between authors more meaningful. We do acknowledge that this normalization makes several assumptions and is simplistic.

C Identify-then-Extract with Llama-2

Index	QID	Specific Text Instances Identified
2	Q20	negligence, **tragedy**, could have been avoided
2	Q88	negligence, **tragedy**, could have been avoided
3	Q20	cultural **tragedy**, "incalculable" loss, **lobotomy** of Brazilian memory, ...
3	Q88	cultural **tragedy**, "incalculable" loss, **lobotomy** of Brazilian memory, ...

Table 8: Llama responses to two questions for the article "Fire at the National Museum of Brazil". Text is given in blue, so as to compare to Table 6, with GPT-4 responses in black.

For identify-then-extract with HLQs, we also ran a small study with Llama-2.[11] The rationale is that the decomposition of the harder task may enable smaller LLM's to perform reasonably. We do expect some performance drop, given the order of magnitude difference in size – 13B vs >1T for GPT-4. Furthermore, given the closed-source nature of GPT-4, a locally-run, open-source model allows for more direct insights and analysis, especially for future work.

We report results for RU2EN, but have run the steps for all 4 settings. For ease of analysis and our computational budget, we restrict our study to a 217 article subset of the original 22,046.

We found that several techniques were required to get Llama to adhere to the expected output format: more *few-shot* examples, and *pre-generating* the starting tokens of a response. These are explained ahead. Overall, we found that Llama underperformed GPT-4 in two other aspects: too many false positives, and shorter phrase extraction.

C.1 Identify

With the one-shot prompt, Llama had many errors in instruction-following – it gives short answer responses with additional discussion. While under 10% of Llama's initial responses were parseable, we achieved 90% parseable responses by applying two modifications: 3-shot prompts, and pre-generation. The 3-shot prompts were manually curated, and then we manually wrote the persuasion responses. We selected paragraphs from 3 diverse articles – a political article with considerable persuasion (Augusto Pinochet), a scientific article with a few instances of persuasion (Cobalt), and a scientific article with no persuasion (Banana).

Second, pre-generation follows from the observation that responses should always be prefixed with `Q1:` – GPT-4 nearly always does this, while Llama by default rarely does. This leads to the intuition that we can *pre-generate* the proper `Q1:` prefix by concatenating it to the input. Afterwards, the model will continue generations in this modified distribution space; we found that with pre-generation and few-shot, instruction-following improves to >90%. We note that this prompt engineering technique is similar to, for example, pre-generating "Answer: " for QA tasks.

Step 1 error analysis Despite the correct output format, as for the actual task, Llama output has several issues compared to GPT-4: it mostly outputs True, has much higher confidence scores (most are 90-100), and gives answers out of order (e.g. `Q0...Q1...Q9...Q4...`).

C.2 Extract

As with the identify step, we used few-shot prompts and pre-generation to enable better instruction-following. For few-shot prompts, we use the same 3 paragraphs, and write our few-shot examples for all questions. For pre-generation, we set the prefix to be a single quotation mark ".

Step 2 error analysis Table 8 shows Llama's responses for the same article as in Table 6 with GPT-4. We see that GPT-4 is able to extract longer clauses, while Llama prefers to extract short phrases. Also, the persuasive text sets (PTS) from Llama are shorter than those of GPT-4. Therefore, while it is feasible to use other LLMs with our persuasion detection approach, we decided to focus our experimental results on GPT-4.

D Prompts Used

Here we provide text for the prompts, exactly as used for the various LLM interactions. Note that these prompts slightly differ from those shown in the main text figures, which were edited for brevity.

[11] `https://huggingface.co/meta-llama/Llama-2-13b-chat-hf`

System: Your task is to assign PersuasionTech types and confidence scores to given text (if more than one semicolon separated). You have a background in public relations, political science, and international relations. Confidence has integer value 0-100 (100 being the highest confidence). PersuasionTech has 24 possible values, here is value (definition) for each:
1. Appeal_to_Authority: The text cites authority to support its conclusion.
2. Appeal_to_Popularity: The text supports its conclusion by citing popularity or majority support.
3. Appeal_to_Values: The text invokes widely shared values to support its message.
4. Appeal_to_Fear-Prejudice: The text uses fear or prejudice to reject or promote an idea.
5. Flag_Waving: The text refers to patriotism or group allegiance to back its conclusion.
6. Causal_Oversimplification: The text oversimplifies the cause(s) of a subject or issue.
7. False_Dilemma-No_Choice: The text implies only two options when there may be more.
8. Consequential_Oversimplification: The text oversimplifies the consequences of accepting a proposition.
9. Straw_Man: The text misrepresents someone's position, usually to make it easier to attack.
10. Red_Herring: The text diverts attention from the main topic.
11. Whataboutism: The text meant to distract from topic, discredits an opponent by charging them with hypocrisy.
12. Slogans: The text uses a brief, catchy phrase to encapsulate its message.
13. Appeal_to_Time: The text suggests that the time is ripe for a certain action.
14. Conversation_Killer: The text discourages critical thought or discussion.
15. Loaded_Language: The text uses emotionally charged words or phrases to validate a claim.
16. Repetition: The text repeatedly reinforces the same idea.
17. Exaggeration-Minimisation: The text either downplays or exaggerates a subject.
18. Obfuscation-Vagueness-Confusion: The text is deliberately unclear, leaving room for varied interpretations.
19. Name_Calling-Labeling: The text employs demeaning labels to sway sentiments.
20. Doubt: The text attempts to undermine credibility by questioning character or attributes.
21. Guilt_by_Association: The text discredits an entity by associating it with a negatively viewed group.
22. Appeal_to_Hypocrisy: The text accuses the target of hypocrisy, often to tarnish their reputation.
23. Questioning_the_Reputation: The text undermines the reputation of the target, as a means to discredit their argument.
24. None: The text appears unbiased and doesn't evidently employ persuasion techniques.

User: Ukraine's government is "openly neo-Nazi" and "pro-Nazi," controlled by "little Nazis," President Vladimir V. Putin of Russia says.

Figure 7: Baseline prompt for persuasion detection.

System: Given a task X, your goal is to come up with a list of questions Y. The list Y contains questions that break the task into simpler components. Questions in list Y should be binomial: True or False. Questions in list Y should be semicolon separated. Avoid questions that rephrase the task, but do not simplify it.

User: {Task}: {Task Definition}

Figure 8: Prompt to generate HLQs for a Technique (zero-shot).

System: Given a piece of text your goal is to answer each of the following questions as 'True', 'False', or 'N/A' (if question is not applicable) plus a confidence measure from 0-100.
Questions: {list of 12 HLQs}

User: Ukraine's government is "openly neo-Nazi" and "pro-Nazi," controlled by "little Nazis," President Vladimir V. Putin of Russia says.

Agent: Q1: True (conf:70); Q2: False (conf:30); Q3: N/A; ...

Figure 9: Prompt for Identify stage of persuasive language detection.

System: Given a piece of text your are tasked with a question: Question Identify specific language instances separated by semicolons. Questions: {list of 12 questions}.

User: Ukraine's government is "openly neo-Nazi" and "pro-Nazi," controlled by "little Nazis," President Vladimir V. Putin of Russia says.

Agent: "openly neo-Nazi"; "pro-Nazi"; "little Nazis"

Figure 10: Prompt for Extract stage of persuasive language detection.

System: Your task is to translate into English the given Russian text.

Figure 11: Prompt to translate English to Russian (zero-shot).

System: Ваша задача - перевести на русский язык данный английский текст.

Figure 12: Prompt to translate Russian to English (zero-shot).

Retrieval Evaluation for Long-Form and Knowledge-Intensive Image–Text Article Composition

Jheng-Hong Yang[1], **Carlos Lassance**[2], **Rafael Sampaio de Rezende**[3], **Krishna Srinivasan**[4], **Stéphane Clinchant**[3], **Jimmy Lin**[1]

[1]University of Waterloo, [2]Cohere, [3]Naver Labs Europe, [4]Google Research

Abstract

This paper examines the integration of images into Wikipedia articles by evaluating image–text retrieval tasks in multimedia content creation, focusing on developing retrieval-augmented tools to enhance the creation of high-quality multimedia articles. Despite ongoing research, the interplay between text and visuals, such as photos and diagrams, remains underexplored, limiting support for real-world applications. We introduce AToMiC, a dataset for long-form, knowledge-intensive image–text retrieval, detailing its task design, evaluation protocols, and relevance criteria. Our findings show that a hybrid approach combining a sparse retriever with a dense retriever achieves satisfactory effectiveness, with nDCG@10 scores around 0.4 for Image Suggestion and Image Promotion tasks, providing insights into the challenges of retrieval evaluation in an image–text interleaved article composition context. The AToMiC dataset is available at `https://github.com/TREC-AToMiC/AToMiC`.

1 Introduction

The ability to produce high-quality image–text content, like poetry and essays, is crucial, with diverse applications in education and entertainment domains. The creation of high-quality multimedia content is a complex task, particularly on platforms like Wikipedia, which hosts more than 6 million articles and serves as a primary reference for millions of users around the world. The integration of relevant images into textual content is critical for enhancing reader engagement, comprehension, and the overall quality of knowledge dissemination. However, despite the availability of over 100 million media files on Wikimedia Commons, selecting and aligning images with corresponding text remains a significant challenge. This is particularly evident in knowledge-intensive and long-form content, where the relevance of an image is not just a matter of keyword matching but requires deep contextual

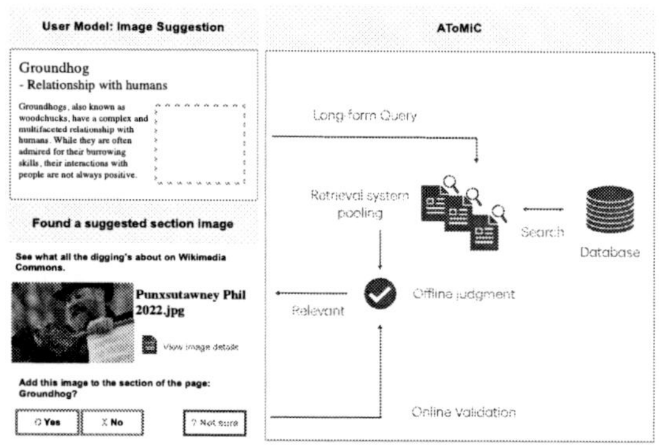

Figure 1: Conceptual plot illustrating the scope of AToMiC, featuring an image suggestion for the article *Groundhog - Relationship with humans*.

and semantic alignment with the text (Zhang et al., 2023; Dong et al., 2024; Zhang et al., 2024). Developing authoring tools to assist in multimedia content creation is therefore critical yet challenging for platforms such as Wikipedia.[1]

Recent advances in foundation models have significantly improved the ability to learn joint representations of images and text across diverse datasets (Radford et al., 2021; Li et al., 2022; Singh et al., 2022; Liu et al., 2024; Zhang et al., 2023; Beyer et al., 2024). These models leverage vast amounts of image–text data to align visual and textual inputs, achieving remarkable success in a variety of retrieval tasks. However, they are primarily designed to align structured, shorter texts, or alternative texts to perform effectively. More specifically, many models struggle to accurately recognize tailed entities represented in text (Hu et al., 2023; Chen et al., 2023). Taking the article in Figure1 as an example, recognizing entities like Punxsutawney Phil, a central figure in Groundhog Day celebration, can be challenging solely from an

[1]`https://www.mediawiki.org/wiki/Structured_Data_Across_Wikimedia/Image_Suggestions`

Proceedings of the First Workshop on Advancing Natural Language Processing for Wikipedia, pages 36–45
November 16, 2024

image or text description.[2] This reliance poses difficulties when models are applied to more complex tasks, such as retrieving images opted for long-form texts, e.g., a section, where queries are implicit, long-form, and require a deep understanding of context, semantics, and world knowledge.

To tackle the challenges, we initiated the AToMiC (Authoring Tools for Multimedia Content Creation) project, specifically designed for evaluating image–text retrieval within the context of multimedia content creation for Wikipedia articles. Unlike previous approaches, AToMiC focuses on the unique challenges posed by using entire, knowledge-intensive articles as implicit queries. This requires a sophisticated understanding of the article's content and its purpose, ensuring that the retrieved images not only match the text but also contribute meaningfully to the article's overall narrative and informational value to content creators.

We introduce two key retrieval tasks in assisting multimedia article composition:[3]

- Image Suggestion Task (T2M): This task focuses on text-to-image retrieval, where the goal is to retrieve images that best enhance specific sections of text.
- Image Promotion Task (M2T): This task involves image-to-text retrieval, where the objective is to identify the most suitable textual context for existing images.

To support these tasks, we worked with NIST to curate 24K and 14K graded relevance labels, respectively, using 16 different retrieval systems, ranging from widely used vision–language pretrained models (Radford et al., 2021; Li et al., 2022) to summarization-based systems (Long et al., 2024) and learned sparse retrieval systems (Nguyen et al., 2024). Our findings indicate that while many image–text retrieval models have been proposed in recent years, they still require strong signals from image captions to deliver relevant results. Additionally, we observed that integrating CLIP with a text-based learned sparse retrieval system (Formal et al., 2021, 2022) can enhance the overall effectiveness of a hybrid retrieval system, achieving approximately 0.4 in nDCG@10.

[2]`https://en.wikipedia.org/wiki/Groundhog_Day`

[3]In our context, "images" refer to both the pixel values and their associated captions, hence the task is aptly termed as Text-to-Media (T2M) and Media-to-Text (M2T), respectively.

We further validated the relevance labels in a real-world context by attaching relevant images to Wikipedia articles and obtaining feedback from experienced Wikipedia editors. Specifically, in June 2024, we selected 14 vital articles and attached 18 relevant images based on the relevance labels we curated. During the past three months, the survival rate of these images has been approximately 94%.[4] This result highlights the effectiveness of our proposed evaluation framework in real-world applications, extending beyond laboratory settings.

The remainder of this paper is structured as follows: Section 3 provides a detailed overview of the evaluation process; Section 4 presents the task outcomes; Section 5 offers an analysis of the resources and labels generated; Section 6 discuss our findings in applying AToMiC in the wild; and Section 7 concludes our discussion.

2 Related Work

Existing works such as WebQA (Chang et al., 2022), CIRR (Liu et al., 2021), FashionIQ (Wu et al., 2021), ReMuQ (Luo et al., 2023), OVEN (Hu et al., 2023), and INFOSEEK (Chen et al., 2023) have made substantial contributions to various multimodal retrieval tasks. For instance, WebQA excels in visual question answering tasks, using multimodal input to answer complex open-domain questions. CIRR and FashionIQ are tailored for composed image retrieval and attribute-based searches, particularly within the fashion industry, where image modifications based on textual input are common. ReMuQ focuses on retrieving content to answer multimodal questions, while OVEN emphasizes object-centric and zero-shot retrieval, respectively, often within knowledge-rich domains like Wikipedia. INFOSEEK enhances retrieval through semantic navigation and knowledge exploration, but it is better suited for explicit, well-defined queries.

3 Evaluation Overview

This section offers a thorough overview of AToMiC evaluation process in TREC 2023. We begin by introducing our foundational test collections, AToMiC, which serve as the cornerstone for our assessment. Following this, we explore the intricacies of our task design, providing a detailed examination of the challenges and objectives that shape the evaluation process. We then outline our evaluation protocols, focusing on critical aspects

[4]17 out of 18, as of August 2024

Task	Description	# Samples
T2M	Corpus (Images)	11,019,202
	Query (Train)	3,002,458
	Qrels (Train)	4,401,903
	Query (Eval)	74
	Qrels (Eval)	24,728
M2T	Corpus (Texts)	10,134,744
	Query (Train)	3,386,183
	Qrels (Train)	4,401,903
	Query (Eval)	61
	Qrels (Eval)	14,078

Table 1: Statistics of the AToMiC dataset. T2M: Image Suggestion; M2T: Image Promotion.

such as pooling depth and criteria for relevance judgments. To establish context and provide benchmarks, we introduce the baseline systems that serve as performance reference points. Additionally, we present participant reports, shedding light on the diverse approaches employed to address the tasks.

3.1 AToMiC Test Collection

AToMiC is an extension of the Wikipedia-based Image Text (WIT) dataset (Srinivasan et al., 2021), specifically designed to support two key retrieval tasks in multimedia content creation: image suggestion and image promotion (see subsection 3.2). Table 1 provides a summary of the key statistics. The corpus comprises approximately 10 million *documents*, integrating both text and image collections. To facilitate system development, we provide around 3 million *queries* and 4 million sparse *qrels* (relevance judgments) derived from image–text pairs extracted from Wikipedia.[5] Additionally, we offer 24K and 14K dense qrels for the 74 and 61 evaluation topics of the respective tasks.[6]

3.2 Task Design

In alignment with the AToMiC dataset's design principles, we have chosen evaluation topics that cater to the requirements of two distinct user models. Additionally, our selection of test topics takes into account the needs of both editors, who seek to enhance articles lacking images, and maintainers, who are responsible for monitoring the overall quality of all Wikipedia articles. Consequently, our emphasis lies on the selection of vital articles within Wikipedia to serve as evaluation topics for the tasks designed for these two user models: image suggestion (T2M) and image promotion (M2T).

[5]On average, there is only one image per section.

[6]Find more details in (Yang et al., 2023).

Image Suggestion (T2M). The Image Suggestion (T2M) task focuses on the scenario of identifying relevant images to enhance textual content. For this task, we selected 500 imageless sections from articles listed in Wikipedia's Level 3 Vital Articles.[7] The Vital Articles list is a carefully curated collection of articles considered essential for providing a comprehensive overview of human knowledge. These articles cover a wide range of topics and serve as a foundational reference point for readers seeking authoritative information.

Our focus on these specific sections stems from their critical importance within the Wikipedia ecosystem. By initially evaluating them in the English language, we aim to identify opportunities to improve the representation of vital content across other languages. Following the annotation process, we further refined the dataset by filtering out poorly performing and inappropriate sections, resulting in 74 test queries for this task, as shown in Table 1.

Image Promotion (M2T). The Image Promotion (M2T) task focuses on a search scenario where image providers aim to identify the most appropriate attachment points within an article's text sections. To simplify the image selection process, we employ a multi-stage filtering approach using images from the image suggestion task. Initially, we apply three fusion methods—top-K, RRF, and RBP—to combine the image ranking lists generated by our baseline systems for 200 T2M topics, with a pooling depth set at 20. We then merge the resulting image pools and remove duplicate images based on their IDs. Finally, we eliminate near-duplicate images using the `fastdup` library and randomly select 200 images as candidates for image topics.[8] After the annotation process, we further refine the dataset by filtering out poorly performing and inappropriate images, resulting in 61 test queries for this task, as detailed in Table 1.

Metrics. In assessing the effectiveness of retrieval systems, we anticipate dealing with ranked lists that prioritize the top positions as the most critical. Therefore, our primary metric of choice is the normalized Discounted Cumulative Gain (nDCG). This selection is particularly apt because we have access to graded annotation levels, which allows us to gauge the quality of our results with fine granularity. In addition to nDCG, we recognize the

[7]`https://en.wikipedia.org/wiki/Wikipedia:Vital_articles/Level/3`

[8]`https://github.com/visual-layer/fastdup`

importance of understanding the interplay between other widely used metrics prevalent in different research communities. Metrics such as mean Average Precision (mAP), Success, and Recall play vital roles in assessing retrieval effectiveness in various contexts. Investigating these metrics in conjunction with nDCG provides a more comprehensive view of system performance across different evaluation scenarios. By exploring these relationships, we aim to gain insights into the strengths and limitations of the retrieval systems involved in AToMiC.

3.3 Annotation Protocols

Our annotation process involves presenting annotators with candidates from participant runs, each with a specified pooling depth. Subsequently, after removing certain queries that do not meet the evaluation criteria, the final evaluation is performed for 80 queries for T2M and 70 queries for M2T. The objective of our annotation guidelines is to identify the most suitable image that complements the given section (or vice versa). However, it is important to note that we accept instances where the selected image provides value by illustrating the entire article, even if it does not correspond to the exact section under consideration.

Pooling. Pooling is a classical method adopted in early TREC evaluations and used to select documents for human assessment. This approach merges the top-ranking results from multiple runs into a single pool, with only the documents within this pool being evaluated. Collaborating with NIST, we adjust the depth of pooling based on the specific task at hand. For the Image Suggestion (T2M) task, we annotate the top 25 candidates during baseline assessments and expand this to 30 candidates for participant runs. Conversely, in the Image Promotion (M2T) task, we consistently annotate the top 30 candidates across all runs.

Relevance Judgments. Our annotation process involves categorizing candidate results into three graded relevance levels to capture the nuances of their suitability. NIST annotators make relevance judgments based on the following criteria:

- Non-Relevant (0): Candidates that are deemed not relevant to the task at hand fall into this category. They do not contribute meaningfully to the intended purpose.
- Relevant but Not Ideal (1): Candidates that possess some degree of relevance to the task but are not considered the best or most fitting options are categorized as relevant but not ideal. They provide value but may have room for improvement.
- Good Match (2): The highest level of relevance is assigned to candidates that are an excellent match for the task. These candidates align exceptionally well and serve the intended purpose effectively.

3.4 Baseline Systems

In our effort to enrich the diversity of annotations and submissions, we incorporate baseline runs based on three primary approaches for multimedia retrieval. These approaches utilize different techniques to represent multimedia information, thereby offering a comprehensive range of methods for evaluation. The baseline methods include:

Dense Retrieval Models. We employ representative dense retrieval models with pretrained vision–language models, specifically OpenCLIP (Ilharco et al., 2021), BLIP (Li et al., 2022), and FLAVA (Singh et al., 2022). We apply these models in a zero-shot fashion and only encode the pixel values of images without accessing their captions.

Traditional Sparse Retrieval. We employ traditional sparse retrieval using BM25, utilizing captions as the sole representation of images. This approach serves as a text-only baseline, providing a benchmark to evaluate the performance of more advanced techniques that integrate texts and images.

Learned Sparse Retrieval. We also utilize SPLADE (Formal et al., 2021, 2022), a learned sparse retrieval approach, to encode and index image captions. For this purpose, we specifically employ the SPLADE++ (ED) model (Formal et al., 2022).

Here is a breakdown of the individual baseline systems: (a) `b_bm25`: Traditional sparse retrieval using `Anserini` with default parameters $(k1, b) = (0.9, 0.4)$; (b) `b_splade_pp`: Learned sparse retrieval with the SPLADE++ (ED) model (Formal et al., 2022); (c) `b_clip_vit{g14,h14,l14,b32}`: Dense retrievers in various sizes provided by OpenCLIP (Ilharco et al., 2021); (d) `b_flava`: Dense retrieval using FLAVA (Singh et al., 2022); (e) `b_fsum_all`: An ensemble model that combines scores from all baseline systems by summing min-max normalized relevance scores.

3.5 Systems from Participants

UAmsterdam. UAmsterdam submitted T2M runs using Learned Sparse Retrieval techniques (Nguyen et al., 2024). Their approach consistently employed a DistilBERT query encoder, with multimedia representation varying between captions or images depending on the model. Training took around 18 hours on an A100 GPU, while indexing required approximately 80 hours. Their Anserini-based system processed fewer than 100 queries per second (QPS) using 60 CPUs. Notably, only images with English captions were included in the indexing process.

IRLab-Amsterdam. IRLab-Amsterdam submitted a single run that involved adapting a pre-existing multi-modal model (CLIP) into a Learned Sparse method. This adaptation was achieved by training a Multi-Layer Perceptron (MLP) and a Masked Language Modeling (MLM) head. The adaptation process took approximately 8 hours on an A6000 GPU, with indexing completed in just 30 minutes. Reported query latency was ≈ 3 seconds.

uogTr. The uogTr team submitted three runs using cascaded systems that combined a summarization model with CLIP (Long et al., 2024). Two runs utilized a pre-trained `base` model, while the third employed a fine-tuned `large` model. Pretraining took around 10 hours on four A6000 GPUs. Finetuning took 25 hours for the base and 75 hours for the large model.

4 Results

In this section, we present the results for two tasks: the Image Suggestion Task (T2M) and the Image Promotion Task (M2T) as shown in Table 2 and Table 3, respectively.

Image Suggestion Task (T2M). In our analysis of Recall@1K, the hybrid model achieved the best results. This outcome was anticipated, likely due to its ability to leverage different information. However, since the hybrid model includes multiple evaluated models, this could contribute to result variability.

Interestingly, there was no clear advantage between models using either image or caption representation. We suspect that this lack of distinction may stem from potential biases in the annotation process, which may have favored images with English captions due to the annotation's inherent difficulty (further analysis is provided in the subsequent section).

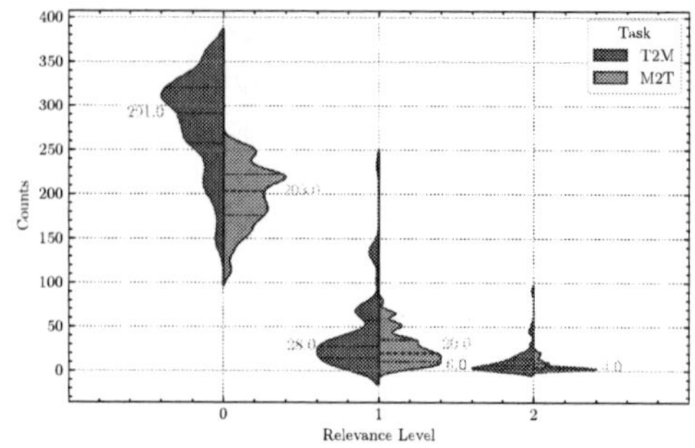

Figure 2: Violin plots of label counts for all topics, categorized by relevance level (0, 1, 2) and task types (T2M, M2T). The annotated values representing the median for each case.

We also observed that while the hybrid model faced challenges in terms of nDCG@10, it exhibited improvement in nDCG@1K. This positive development offers some optimism for the viability of the hybrid strategy, incorporating both captions and images to convey multimedia information effectively. In conclusion, it appears that there is substantial room for progress in this task. This assertion is supported by the notable difference in nDCG@10 scores observed here compared to the benchmarks commonly seen in TREC tasks.

Image Promotion Task (M2T). For M2T task, our first note is that this task exhibits less diversity in positive outcomes since teams from Amsterdam did not participate this task. The top two methods in terms of nDCG@10 also display notably high Recall@1K (up to 97%). This result was expected, considering that only one team participated in this task, supplemented by baseline methods.

Once again, akin to the T2M task, we observe limited advantages in employing the image alone for representation. The nDCG@10 scores in this task are comparatively low when compared to other tasks, signifying significant room for improvement. However, a notable distinction from the T2M task is that in the M2T task, the hybrid approach yielded the most successful results.

In summary, while the M2T task shows promise, it also highlights areas for improvement, particularly in enhancing the utilization of images for promoting content. Notably, the success of the hybrid approach in this task sets it apart from the T2M task.

Table 2: Image Suggestion (T2M) Results, ordered by nDCG@10.

Run ID	Team	Retrieval	Multimedia	mAP	nDCG@1K	nDCG@10	Recall@1K	Success@1	Success@10
UvA-IRLab	IRLab-Amsterdam	Learned-Sparse	Image	0.1526	0.4460	0.4060	0.6452	0.2973	0.6081
b_splade_pp	baselines	Learned-Sparse	Caption	0.1501	0.4461	0.4051	0.6452	0.2838	0.6081
b_fsum_all	baselines	Hybrid	Image+Caption	0.1183	0.5390	0.3109	0.8920	0.2297	0.5270
b_bm25	baselines	Sparse	Caption	0.0761	0.3257	0.3036	0.4820	0.1351	0.5541
UvA-IRLab-mlp-mlm-caption	UAmsterdam	Learned-Sparse	Caption	0.0757	0.2741	0.2317	0.4273	0.1486	0.4865
UvA-IRLab-mlp-mlm-img_cap	UAmsterdam	Learned-Sparse	Caption	0.0760	0.2751	0.2315	0.4286	0.1486	0.4865
finetune_large_t2i	uogTr	Dense	Image	0.0857	0.2949	0.2206	0.4475	0.1351	0.3514
b_clip_vith14_laion	baselines	Dense	Image	0.0674	0.3011	0.2139	0.4699	0.1486	0.3784
b_clip_vitg14_laion	baselines	Dense	Image	0.0626	0.3039	0.2075	0.4596	0.1081	0.3514
finetune_base	uogTr	Dense	Image	0.0427	0.2365	0.1841	0.3352	0.0676	0.3243
b_clip_vitl14_laion	baselines	Dense	Image	0.0538	0.2790	0.1817	0.4700	0.1622	0.3378
UvA-IRLab-mlp-mlm-cap1	UAmsterdam	Learned-Sparse	Caption	0.0234	0.1441	0.1426	0.2012	0.0811	0.2703
b_clip_vitb32_laion	baselines	Dense	Image	0.0248	0.1991	0.1396	0.2884	0.0135	0.2432
b_flava	baselines	Dense	Image	0.0031	0.0572	0.0752	0.0294	0.0000	0.0676
UvA-IRLab-mlp-mlm-images	UAmsterdam	Learned-Sparse	Image	0.0005	0.0179	0.0175	0.0286	0.0000	0.0405
pretrain_base	uogTr	Dense	Image	0.0000	0.0031	0.0050	0.0028	0.0000	0.0000

Table 3: Image Promotion (M2T) Results, ordered by nDCG@10

Run ID	Team	Retrieval	Multimedia	mAP	nDCG@1K	nDCG@10	Recall@1K	Success@1	Success@10
b_fsum_ all_i2t	baselines	Hybrid	Image+Caption	0.2100	0.6308	0.4029	0.9776	0.2131	0.6066
b_splade_pp_i2t	baselines	Learned-Sparse	Caption	0.2408	0.4687	0.3691	0.7821	0.1967	0.5574
b_clip_vitg14_laion_i2t	baselines	Dense	Image	0.0776	0.4243	0.2790	0.6849	0.0656	0.3279
b_bm25_i2t	baselines	Sparse	Caption	0.1992	0.3163	0.2784	0.4314	0.2295	0.4098
b_clip_vith14_laion_i2t	baselines	Dense	Image	0.0751	0.3996	0.2403	0.6634	0.0656	0.3934
b_clip_vitl14_laion_i2t	baselines	Dense	Image	0.0650	0.3703	0.2103	0.5996	0.0656	0.2623
finetune_base_i2t	uogTr	Dense	Image	0.0588	0.2695	0.1864	0.4828	0.1148	0.2295
b_clip_vitb32_laion_i2t	baselines	Dense	Image	0.0565	0.2755	0.1597	0.4761	0.0820	0.1967
finetune_large_i2t	uogTr	Dense	Image	0.0362	0.2516	0.1213	0.5403	0.0492	0.2131
b_flava_i2t	baselines	Dense	Image	0.0155	0.0916	0.0595	0.1644	0.0164	0.0492
pretrain_base_i2t	uogTr	Dense	Image	0.0018	0.0148	0.0110	0.0184	0.0000	0.0328

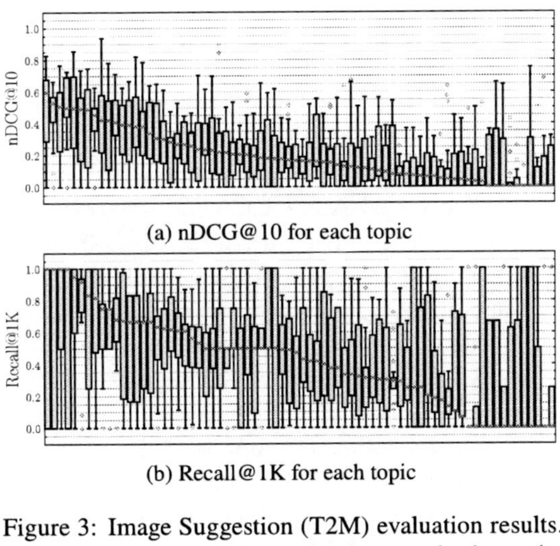

(a) nDCG@10 for each topic

(b) Recall@1K for each topic

Figure 3: Image Suggestion (T2M) evaluation results. The box plots present the evaluation metrics by topic, with (a) nDCG@10 and (b) Recall@1K.

5 Analysis

Label Distribution by Topic. Figure 2 presents the distribution of labels across different relevance levels for two tasks: Text-to-Media (T2M) and Media-to-Text (M2T). The plot depicts the label counts at each relevance level, with separate distributions for each task. Annotations indicate the median number of labels within each category, where blue represents T2M and orange represents M2T, across relevance levels 0, 1, and 2. Both tasks show a similar trend: the majority of labels fall into the lowest relevance level (`rel` = 0), with medians of 291.0 for T2M and 203.0 for M2T, while the number of highly relevant labels (`rel` = 2) is substantially lower, with medians of 6.0 for T2M and 4.0 for M2T. T2M generally has a higher median count at the lowest relevance level compared to M2T, whereas M2T displays a slightly higher median at the moderate relevance level (`rel` = 1), with medians of 28.0 for T2M and 20.0 for M2T. This distribution underscores the ongoing challenge of assigning higher relevance labels, especially for systems processing the nuanced content typical of English Wikipedia articles. The findings suggest a need for further algorithmic improvements to effectively identify highly relevant pairs.

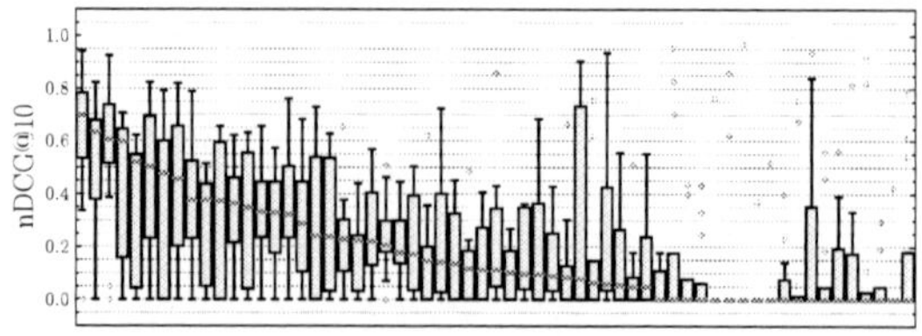

(a) nDCG@10 for each topic

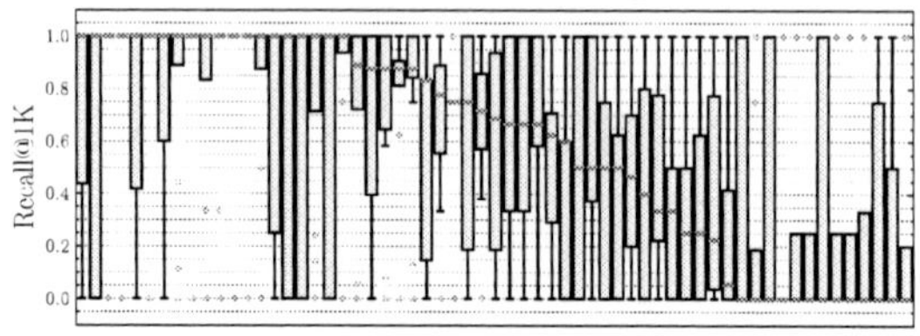

(b) Recall@1K for each topic

Figure 4: Image Promotion (M2T) evaluation results. The box plots present the evaluation metrics by topic, with (a) nDCG@10 and(b) Recall@1K.

Evaluation Metrics by Topic. This section analyzes the results of nDCG@10 and Recall@1K for the tasks T2M and M2T across all evaluated systems. To understand system effectivness across different test topics, we present results using box plots in Figure 3a, Figure 3b (for T2M), and Figure 4a, Figure 4b (for M2T). Upon closer examination of these figures, it becomes evident that both tasks exhibit similar trends. The systems tend to perform suboptimally in terms of nDCG@10 while maintaining relatively high Recall@1K scores. This suggests that there is substantial room for improvement in terms of early precision.

In particular, M2T demonstrates superior performance in terms of Recall@1K compared to T2M. This observation aligns with the insights gained from Figure 2: M2T has a higher proportion of relevant labels compared to T2M. We speculate that this observation may be attributed to annotators' tendencies to overlook images lacking English captions when performing the T2M task, resulting in more non-relevant labels. In contrast, for the M2T task, all candidates are well-structured English Wikipedia articles.

6 AToMiC in the Wild

To assess the model's performance in more challenging tasks and its applicability to real-world scenarios, we deployed the *offline* relevance labels generated by AToMiC onto *online* Wikipedia articles. By attaching relevant images to selected Wikipedia sections, we aimed to evaluate the longevity and impact of these images in an authentic editorial

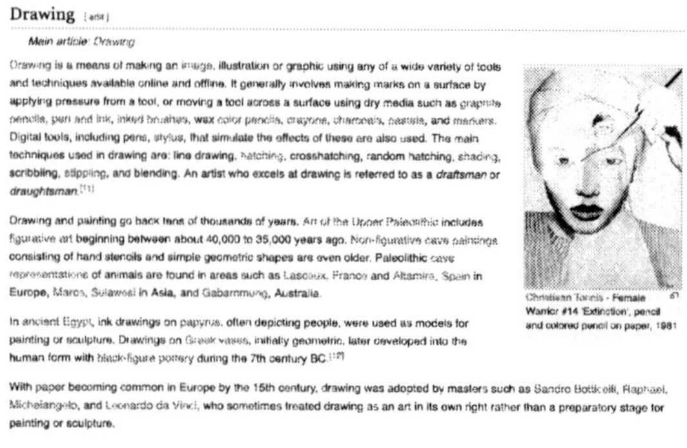

Figure 5: Example of an image attached to a Wikipedia article, Visual Arts - Drawing. The image was selected as a "Good match" (`rel` = 2) annotation from the AToMiC dataset.[11]

environment. Acknowledging Wikipedia's *not a lab* policy,[9] all uploaded images were vetted by humans as part of the standard Wikipedia editing process.

We selected 14 level-3 vital articles on Wikipedia and manually attached 18 images chosen from highly relevant (`rel` = 2) image–text pairs (see more details in Appendix B). This experiment was conducted in June 2024, and only one image was subsequently removed by Wikipedia editors. Several key insights emerged from this end-to-end experiment:

Real-World Applicability. We achieved a high retention rate of 94% (17 out of 18 images at the time of submission) for the selected relevant images. On one hand, Figure 5 illustrates a survival test sample from our experiment on the Wikipedia page for Visual Arts—Drawing. Originally, the *Drawing* section had no attached image. We selected this image from the highly relevant (`rel` = 2) annotations due to its strong relevance and comprehensive coverage of the content of the section. On the other hand, the only image was removed by Wikipedia editors because the article already contained a sufficient number of images.[10] This result highlights additional challenges, such as the need for page-level relevance optimization and the nuanced judgment required for precise annotation.

[9] `https://en.wikipedia.org/wiki/Wikipedia:What_Wikipedia_is_not`

[10] `https://en.wikipedia.org/w/index.php?title=Aircraft&diff=1227096926&oldid=1227092091`

[11] Source: `https://en.wikipedia.org/wiki/Visual_arts#Drawing`; screenshot captured on August 28, 2024.

Challenges. To ensure the feasibility of real-world experiments, we introduced an additional filtering process to identify the *golden* labels from the NIST annotations. This process involved manually refining the initial 832 (`rel = 2`) down to 18 images according to our judgment. After the filtering process, we found that the focus shifts towards selecting the most impactful image, the one that truly enhances the article's content, similar to optimizing for the NDCG@1 metric. This requires applying additional criteria to ensure that the chosen image not only meets relevance standards but also significantly elevates the *overall quality* of the article. The selected images should be visually compelling and convey *key ideas* or *added value* relevant to the *entire article*, rather than merely aligning with specific sentences or words, as demonstrated in Figure 5.

7 Conclusion

This research highlights significant advancements in multimedia content creation, particularly through the integration of diverse content modalities. The success of hybrid models in Image Suggestion and Image Promotion tasks underscores the value of combining multiple information sources to enhance content quality and address complex user queries. The strong performance in Recall@1K indicates a substantial leap forward in developing algorithms suited to a multimedia-rich online environment.

However, challenges remain in interpreting multimedia content, especially due to the complexity of visual and textual interrelations. Addressing these challenges requires careful consideration of context, cultural nuances, and potential biases. Expanding beyond English-language content is crucial to make the model more applicable to the multilingual and multicultural landscape.

Collaboration with platforms like Wikimedia underscores the importance of aligning AI research with real-world content needs. Practical, user-centered research is essential for the continued development of effective multimedia content creation systems. Looking ahead, key areas for future work include reducing English-centric bias through multilingual expansion, establishing a year-round evaluation event or continuous (Chiang et al., 2024), and enhancing collaboration with content platforms. Implementing preference-based evaluations will also offer better insights into user satisfaction and content relevance.

In sum, we curated and studied a new benchmark dataset for multimedia content creation and opens avenues for further refinement, particularly in expanding multilingual capabilities and ensuring alignment with diverse user expectations and ethical standards.

Acknowledgements

This research was supported in part by the Natural Sciences and Engineering Research Council (NSERC) of Canada.

References

Lucas Beyer, Andreas Steiner, André Susano Pinto, Alexander Kolesnikov, Xiao Wang, Daniel Salz, Maxim Neumann, Ibrahim Alabdulmohsin, Michael Tschannen, Emanuele Bugliarello, et al. 2024. PaliGemma: A versatile 3b VLM for transfer. *arXiv preprint arXiv:2407.07726.*

Yingshan Chang, Mridu Narang, Hisami Suzuki, Guihong Cao, Jianfeng Gao, and Yonatan Bisk. 2022. WebQA: Multihop and multimodal QA. In *Proc. of IEEE/CVF CVPR*, pages 16495–16504.

Yang Chen, Hexiang Hu, Yi Luan, Haitian Sun, Soravit Changpinyo, Alan Ritter, and Ming-Wei Chang. 2023. Can pre-trained vision and language models answer visual information-seeking questions? In *Proc. of EMNLP*, pages 14948–14968.

Wei-Lin Chiang, Lianmin Zheng, Ying Sheng, Anastasios Nikolas Angelopoulos, Tianle Li, Dacheng Li, Hao Zhang, Banghua Zhu, Michael Jordan, Joseph E Gonzalez, et al. 2024. Chatbot Arena: An open platform for evaluating llms by human preference. *arXiv preprint arXiv:2403.04132.*

Xiaoyi Dong, Pan Zhang, Yuhang Zang, Yuhang Cao, Bin Wang, Linke Ouyang, Xilin Wei, Songyang Zhang, Haodong Duan, Maosong Cao, et al. 2024. InternLM-XComposer-2: Mastering free-form text-image composition and comprehension in vision-language large model. *arXiv preprint arXiv:2401.16420.*

Thibault Formal, Carlos Lassance, Benjamin Piwowarski, and Stéphane Clinchant. 2022. From distillation to hard negative sampling: Making sparse neural ir models more effective. In *Proc. of SIGIR*, pages 2353–2359.

Thibault Formal, Benjamin Piwowarski, and Stéphane Clinchant. 2021. SPLADE: Sparse lexical and expansion model for first stage ranking. In *Proc. of SIGIR*, pages 2288–2292.

Hexiang Hu, Yi Luan, Yang Chen, Urvashi Khandelwal, Mandar Joshi, Kenton Lee, Kristina Toutanova, and Ming-Wei Chang. 2023. Open-domain visual entity recognition: Towards recognizing millions of wikipedia entities. In *Proc. of ICCV*, pages 12065–12075.

Gabriel Ilharco, Mitchell Wortsman, Ross Wightman, Cade Gordon, Nicholas Carlini, Rohan Taori, Achal Dave, Vaishaal Shankar, Hongseok Namkoong, John Miller, Hannaneh Hajishirzi, Ali Farhadi, and Ludwig Schmidt. 2021. OpenCLIP.

Junnan Li, Dongxu Li, Caiming Xiong, and Steven Hoi. 2022. BLIP: Bootstrapping language-image pre-training for unified vision-language understanding and generation. In *Proc. of ICML*.

Haotian Liu, Chunyuan Li, Qingyang Wu, and Yong Jae Lee. 2024. Visual instruction tuning. *Proc. of NeurIPS*, 36.

Zheyuan Liu, Cristian Rodriguez-Opazo, Damien Teney, and Stephen Gould. 2021. Image retrieval on real-life images with pre-trained vision-and-language models. In *Proc. of IEEE/CVF ICCV*, pages 2125–2134.

Zijun Long, Xuri Ge, Richard McCreadie, and Joemon M. Jose. 2024. CFIR: Fast and effective long-text to image retrieval for large corpora. In *Proc. of SIGIR*, page 2188–2198.

Man Luo, Zhiyuan Fang, Tejas Gokhale, Yezhou Yang, and Chitta Baral. 2023. End-to-end knowledge retrieval with multi-modal queries. In *Proc. of ACL*, pages 8573–8589.

Thong Nguyen, Mariya Hendriksen, Andrew Yates, and Maarten de Rijke. 2024. Multimodal learned sparse retrieval with probabilistic expansion control. In *Proc. of ECIR*, pages 448–464.

Alec Radford, Jong Wook Kim, Chris Hallacy, Aditya Ramesh, Gabriel Goh, Sandhini Agarwal, Girish Sastry, Amanda Askell, Pamela Mishkin, Jack Clark, et al. 2021. Learning transferable visual models from natural language supervision. In *Proc. of ICML*, pages 8748–8763.

Amanpreet Singh, Ronghang Hu, Vedanuj Goswami, Guillaume Couairon, Wojciech Galuba, Marcus Rohrbach, and Douwe Kiela. 2022. FLAVA: A foundational language and vision alignment model. In *Proc. of IEEE/CVF CVPR*, pages 15638–15650.

Krishna Srinivasan, Karthik Raman, Jiecao Chen, Michael Bendersky, and Marc Najork. 2021. WIT: Wikipedia-based image text dataset for multimodal multilingual machine learning. In *Proc. of SIGIR*, page 2443–2449.

Hui Wu, Yupeng Gao, Xiaoxiao Guo, Ziad Al-Halah, Steven Rennie, Kristen Grauman, and Rogerio Feris. 2021. FashionIQ: A new dataset towards retrieving images by natural language feedback. In *Proc. of IEEE/CVF CVPR*, pages 11307–11317.

Jheng-Hong Yang, Carlos Lassance, Rafael Sampaio De Rezende, Krishna Srinivasan, Miriam Redi, Stéphane Clinchant, and Jimmy Lin. 2023. AToMiC: An image/text retrieval test collection to support multimedia content creation. In *Proc. of SIGIR*, pages 2975–2984.

Pan Zhang, Xiaoyi Dong, Yuhang Zang, Yuhang Cao, Rui Qian, Lin Chen, Qipeng Guo, Haodong Duan, Bin Wang, Linke Ouyang, et al. 2024. InternLM-XComposer-2.5: A versatile large vision language model supporting long-contextual input and output. *arXiv preprint arXiv:2407.03320*.

Pan Zhang, Xiaoyi Dong Bin Wang, Yuhang Cao, Chao Xu, Linke Ouyang, Zhiyuan Zhao, Shuangrui Ding, Songyang Zhang, Haodong Duan, Hang Yan, et al. 2023. InternLM-XComposer: A vision-language large model for advanced text-image comprehension and composition. *arXiv preprint arXiv:2309.15112*.

A Case Study

T2M topic: Diabetes - Diagnosis. One example of topic on the T2M was the diagnosis section of the diabetes page. We depict 3 examples of good matches (rel=2) in Figure 6 note how even without an English caption there might be images that are relevant to it. We also noticed that some images without captions (or without English captions) got selected, which is a positive, but may have hindered teams that were not able to use images without English caption. Not surprisingly, this topic is also one with the worst median nDCG@10 and largest variation on Recall@1K (some models 100%, some 0% and an average of around 50%). Looking at the images the one without the caption looks like the perfect candidate for illustrating the section, while the other two are good matches.

M2T topic: Map of Kenya. In Figure 7, we present an image depicting a map of Kenya. We have chosen this particular image for analysis because it offers a distinct departure from traditional image caption datasets; it is not a typical "natural" image, but rather a map. Additionally, this image was assigned the highest number of positive sections. In total, we identified 90 sections related to this topic, out of which 24 were deemed to be particularly relevant. It is noteworthy that these relevant sections predominantly originate from the same set of pages, owing to the substantial volume of information available on English Wikipedia. For instance, we observed references to Geography, Demography, Politics, and the Outline of Kenya, which exist in English but may not have equivalents in other languages. This observation hints at the potential for discovering intriguing insights by exploring less densely populated languages on

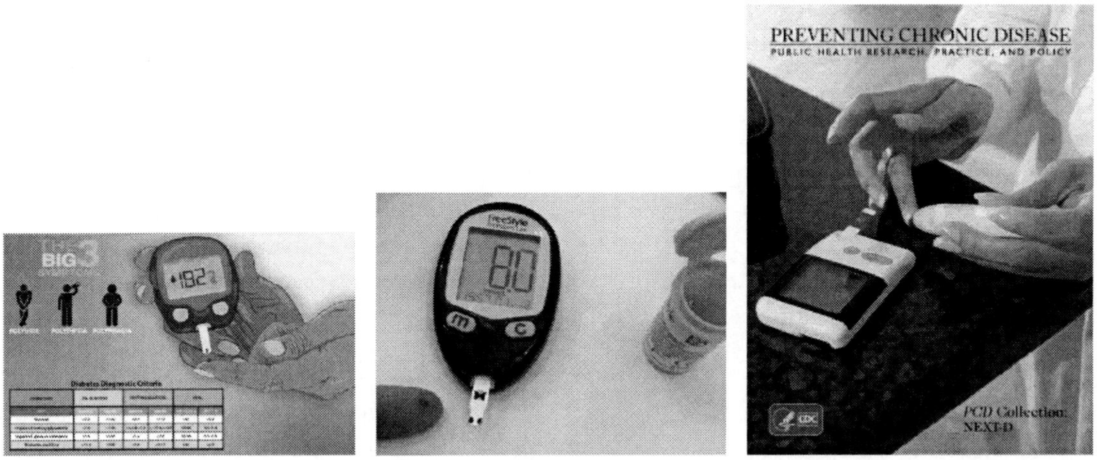

(a) Relevant image without caption

(b) Polish caption: Průběžné měření hladiny cukru v krvi

(c) English caption: CDC image showing the usage of a lancet and a blood glucose meter

Figure 6: Examples of relevant images for topic `projected-19572217-016`, Diabetes - Diagnosis.

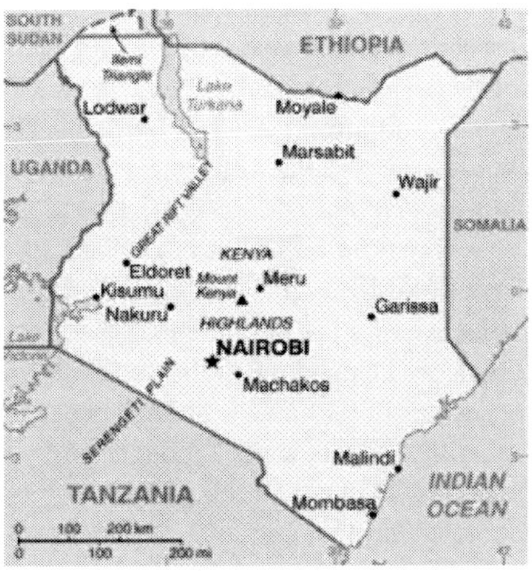

Figure 7: Example of M2T topic `1dd320ef-ad37-3c88-bcb5-aadd34f6deb2` - Map of Kenya

Wikipedia, as they may offer a more diverse range of multimedia content with fewer overlapping or redundant pages.

B In-the-Wild Evaluation

The following is the list of test topics (article - section) and the corresponding images that were uploaded to Wikipedia as part of the evaluation process:

- **Afterlife - Reincarnation**: (Uploaded 2 images)
- **Aircraft - History** (Uploaded 2 images)
- **Biotechnology - Definition** (Uploaded 1 image)
- **Grammar - Education** (Uploaded 2 images)
- **History of film - 1980S** (Uploaded 1 image)
- **Internal combustion engine - History** (Uploaded 1 image)
- **Iron age - History of the concept** (Uploaded 1 image)
- **Latin - Grammar** (Uploaded 1 image)
- **Mediterranean sea - Biogeochemistry** (Uploaded 1 image)
- **Orbit - History** (Uploaded 2 images)
- **Realism (arts) - Theatre** (Uploaded 1 image)
- **Roald Amundsen - Early life** (Uploaded 1 image)
- **Visual arts - Drawing** (Uploaded 1 image)
- **Wind - On other planets** (Uploaded 1 image)

WikiBias as an Extrapolation Corpus for Bias Detection

Karla Salas-Jimenez[1,2], Francisco López-Ponce,[1,2], Sergio-Luis Ojeda-Trueba[1], Gemma Bel-Enguix[1,3]
[1]Grupo de Ingeniería Lingüística - UNAM
[2]Posgrado en Ciencias e Ingeniería de la Computación - UNAM
[3]Departament de Filologia Catalana i Lingüística General - Universitat de Barcelona
{karla_dsj,francisco.lopez.ponce}@ciencias.unam.mx, {SOjedaT,gbele}@iingen.unam.mx

Abstract

This paper explores whether it is possible to train a machine learning model using Wikipedia data to detect subjectivity in sentences and generalize effectively to other domains. To achieve this, we performed experiments with the WikiBias corpus, the BABE corpus, and the CheckThat! Dataset. Various classical models for ML were tested, including Logistic Regression, SVC, and SVR, including characteristics such as Sentence Transformers similarity, probabilistic sentiment measures, and biased lexicons. Pre-trained models like DistilRoBERTa, as well as large language models like Gemma and GPT-4, were also tested for the same classification task.

1 Introduction

Subjectivity permeates all spheres and experiences of human life. Language, as a representation of reality, is not exempt from subjectivity. When an author's perspective is presented as absolute truth, the text is said to contain subjective bias. Technically, it is cognitively impossible to write a text or construct a corpus without some form of bias. Although showing the author's position is not always a wrong approach, and in some genres it is even considered advisable, this is not always the case. A multitude of textual content such as textbooks, scientific articles or news presentations need to maintain neutrality as much as possible by avoiding bias.

The creation of objective texts is a long standing concern for academia as well as for many areas of society. Science, law, information, politics and governmental communication, among others, require verifiable texts that leave aside the author's subjectivity. In journalism, for example, the objective, fact-based style has traditionally been encouraged.

In 2001 Wikipedia introduced its Neutral Point of View (NPOV) policy[1], which applies to all articles written in this collaborative encyclopedia. The NPOV encompasses the following principles: a) avoid stating opinions as facts, b) avoid stating seriously contested assertions as facts, c) avoid stating facts as opinions, d) prefer nonjudgmental language, and e) indicate the relative prominence of opposing views. To comply with this policy, published texts are periodically reviewed and neutralized.

In order to achieve neutral language, Wikipedia performs periodic reviews of articles, attempting to identify and eliminate bias elements. This has allowed the development of various resources by comparing original and de-biased versions of articles, such as the NPOV corpus (Recasens et al., 2013) and WikiBias (Pryzant et al., 2020).

Subjective bias is a problem that goes beyond the used lexicon. Depending on the domain in question various forms of bias appear. In this paper we ask if it is possible to train a ML model (using a bias detection dataset) that generalizes well enough to be extrapolated to other domains. The training corpus is the WikiBias corpus, explicitly elaborated on the neutralization processes of Wikipedia. We ask ourselves if the information learned from Wikipedia can correctly classify bias in different contexts.

The paper is structured as follows: Section 2 explains the state of the art corpora and algorithms for bias detection in English. The experiments performed with different corpora and the results are explained in section 3. Section 4 discusses the conclusions and future work. Finally, the paper closes with the limitations of this work in section 5.

2 Related Work

Bias detection systems are a recent development in NLP, which has grown in recent years in part due to research conducted with Wikipedia-based corpora. One of the first approaches corresponds

[1]Wikipedia: Neutral point of view

Proceedings of the First Workshop on Advancing Natural Language Processing for Wikipedia, pages 46–52
November 16, 2024

to (Recasens et al., 2013), who had the goal of identifying the word that introduces subjective bias. Their work was based on the study of Wikipedia reviews, considering the edition history of different articles (Max and Wisniewski, 2022; Zanzotto and Pennacchiotti, 2010). Recasens et al. (2013) proposed a classification of bias into two categories: framing bias (such as words of praise or specific perspectives) and epistemological bias (related to presupposed or implied propositions). They collected the NPOV Corpus for their study, which contains Wikipedia edits especially aimed at suppressing bias. To carry out the automatic identification of bias, the authors collect a 'bias lexicon' from the NPOV corpus. The presence or not of biased words serves a characteristic in a logistic regression system, obtaining 34% of accuracy. Pryzant et al. (2020) extended this corpus, and created the Wiki Neutrality Corpus (WNC), by adding a third type of bias: demographic bias, defined as text with presuppositions about particular genders, races, or other demographic categories (e.g. all engineers are male). In the work, the authors proposed two ways to neutralize the biased text: a modular approach, that divides the problem into two subtasks: detection and edition; and a concurrent system combining the two subtasks into a single step. In both cases, the detection was carried out using a BERT-based detector (Devlin et al., 2018), and a LSTM decoder.

More recently Zhong (2021), identified that the WNC corpus (Pryzant et al., 2020) has a series of issues: first, there's a lot of noise in the corpus, some sentence pairs are not related to bias mitigation, they're only style or grammar correction editions, but they're marked as biased. A second problem occurs in the mechanism of mitigation. Many times, it is necessary to make more than one correction in the sentence to neutralize it, a fact that was not initially contemplated. Therefore, the authors proposed a new corpus to provide a solution to these problems, the WikiBias corpus.

This resource has a fine labeling, indicating what type of bias is in each example: framing, epistemological or demographic. In addition to Wikipedia-based corpora, other resources have been created in recent years that focus on other domains, especially news. The MBIC (A Media Bias Annotation Dataset Including Annotator Characteristics) consists of 1700 sentences belonging to (Spinde et al., 2021) press news. The main feature of this corpus is the detailed information about the annotators of the corpus, so that this can help in bias detection. BABE (Bias Annotations By Experts) (Spinde et al., 2022) is a news corpus that consists of 3,700 sentences, 1,700 from MBIC (SG1) and an 2,000 additional texts (SG2). The texts, containing controversial topics, were extracted from 14 US news platforms from January 2017 to June 2020. For each sentence, the BABE corpus indicates the political posture, if the sentence is biased, and which words introduce this bias. In the last years, as part of a CLEF laboratory, the CheckThat! (Barrón-Cedeño et al., 2024) lab has been proposed. Task 2 of this lab aims to determine whether a sentence is subjective or not, and build their corpus, comprised of news sentences in English and Italian about politics, COVID-19, civil rights, and economy. It is worth noting that the annotators considered the quotations to be objective since they are not written by the author, as well as the emotions since they cannot be refuted (Ruggeri et al., 2023).

Regarding the methods of detection, in recent years, transformers have represented the state of the art in this field of study. Spinde et al. (2022) compares the performance of several models in the corpus BABE, reaching a highest result of F1=0.804 with BERT + distant. Raza et al. (2022) obtained an F1 of 0.75 with DistilBert. From the generative perspective, a lot of research has been carried out in order to detect and analyze LLM generated biased content (Fan et al., 2024; Hada et al., 2023). Lin proposes strategies to debias an LLM as well as to better understand biased answers (Lin et al., 2024).

3 Experiments and results

We test the performance of different models for bias detection. Our experiments include classic ML models trained with linguistic features, fine-tuned Transformers, and instruction-tuned LLMs. We used the DBias Python package (Raza et al., 2022), a Transformer based classifier, to generate a baseline.

3.1 Datasets to compare

Wikibias constitutes the primary corpus and is divided in three subsets: train, test, and validation sets. This corpus addresses general topics by drawing upon Wikipedia articles, as detailed in the section 2. With this training and validation sets, the models described below were developed, with the exception of section 3.4. The distribution of the classes of each of the sets used can be seen in the

Table 1.

To test the various models, three datasets were utilized: the Wikibias test set, the SG2 set from the BABE corpus and dev_test from CheckThat!.

The SG2 set from BABE was selected for use in this study due to the fact that the labels in this set were peer-reviewed, in contrast to the MBIC set, which was crowdsourced.

Furthermore, although both the SG2 set and the CheckThat! are news-based, they have been annotated under different agreements , which makes it appropriate to evaluate the models of the present study on both of them.

Corpus	Bias	No-Bias
WikiBias		
train	1975	3051
validation	403	663
test	784	1314
SG2	973	864
CheckThat!	532	298

Table 1: Distribution of classes in each corpus

3.2 ML models with features

For this approach, we used the following training characteristics: a) Sentence BERT (Reimers and Gurevych, 2019) similarity, b) sentiment analysis, based on the python package pysentimiento (Pérez et al., 2023), and c) the number of adjectives, adverbs and total words contained in the biased lexicons reported or collected by Recasens (Recasens et al., 2013).

Using these features, the following models were trained: Logistic Regression , Support Vector Classification (SVC), Support Vector Regression and Naive Bayes . Also we calculate the percentage of sentences in each class and incorporate the class-weight parameter into the models to address the issue of imbalance classes.

We took the best performing model (SVC, the rest of the models had an F1 value of 0.59 on average) and tested it with data from the other two mentioned corpora (SG2, CheckThat!). Results are shown in Table 5, in the SVC section.

The results show that the performance obtained in WikiBias is maintained in CheckThat!, and even improves when tested with SG2.

3.3 Transformers

We used DBias (Raza et al., 2022) to implement the first experiments with Transformers. DBias is a Python library that uses DistilBERT as a binary classifier for bias detection. The results serve as a baseline for our Transformer-based experiments.

In a second experiment. we implemented DistilRoberta as per standard Transformer usage. We passed all the sentences of the WikiBias corpus without any preprocessing through the pretrained model in order to fine-tune.

In a third experiment, we modified the input. Instead of one sentence, two sentences were given: the first one being the sentence obtained in the training corpus, the second one a masked version of it. We verified which words in the original sentence appear in Recasens' biased lexicon (Recasens et al., 2013). Those words were switched for the PBias word. Based on this new input, another set of fine-tuning and testing was carried out. Table 2 shows the results of these three experiments applied to the three corpora.

Model	Acc	Prec	Rec	F1
DBias				
WikiBias	0.54	0.65	0.54	0.57
SG2	0.667	0.67	0.66	0.66
CheckThat!	0.57	0.57	0.57	0.56
DestilRoberta				
WikiBias	0.72	0.63	0.61	0.62
SG2	0.69	0.75	0.59	0.66
CheckThat!	0.64	0.66	0.62	0.64
DestilRoberta sentence + mask				
WikiBias	0.61	0.59	0.61	**0.65**
SG2	0.70	0.66	0.85	**0.75**
CheckThat!	0.63	0.60	0.89	**0.71**

Table 2: Different experiments with Transformers applied to the corpora WikiBias, SG2, CheckThat!.

Notice that although the DBias package reports an F1 value of *0.75* on the MBIC (Raza et al., 2022), it does not perform equally well when tested on different corpus. The results are just slightly above a random classifier.

Moreover, the masked sentence approach proved to be the best methodology in this case. The use of carefully masked sentences that indicate word positions (and in a way word types) susceptible to bias, helped the model perform efficiently in all of the test scenarios. This can be seen in the increase of the F1 value by almost a decimal point in certain cases. Compared to the classic ML models the pretrained approach surpasses SVC.

Upon analyzing the previously reported performance, a follow up round of experiments was carried out. An examination of the instances in which the models exhibited errors revealed that these mainly corresponded to instances of epistemological bias. Thus, we ran an experiment in which these sentences were omitted. Additionally, the weight of the classes was incorporated into the loss function to address the imbalance of classes.

Inspired by this modification of training classes, we fine-tuned DistilRoberta 3 more times: first omitting epistemological bias during training, second using only epistemological bias, third using only framing bias. We decided to omit training only with demographic bias due to a lack of data for this final category. Table 3 describes the results of the second round of experiments.

	Acc	Prec	Rec	F1
Only framing and demographic				
WikiBias	0.70	0.67	0.69	0.68
SG2	0.63	0.64	0.63	0.63
CheckThat!	0.64	0.63	0.64	**0.64**
Only epistemological				
WikiBias	0.68	0.53	0.56	0.51
SG2	0.62	0.62	0.62	0.62
CheckThat!	0.53	0.54	0.54	0.53
Only framing				
WikiBias	0.70	0.68	0.70	**0.69**
SG2	0.65	0.66	0.65	**0.65**
CheckThat!	0.62	0.63	0.63	0.62

Table 3: Results of removal some biased sentences. The best results for each corpus are marked in bold.

It is worth noting that the performance in the WikiBias corpus improved following the elimination of sentences exhibiting epistemological biases. This suggests that this type of bias is harder to classify than the other two.

Other experiments were carried out, such as an ensemble of the SVM with DestilRoberta, in which the epistemological biases were also removed. Scores are not reported since this hybrid model did not improve previously shown results.

3.4 LLMs

Most of bias related research with LLMs focuses on detecting when an LLM produces a biased answer, nonetheless, for these experiments we focused on having LLMs classify sentences in order to detect bias on their own. State-of-the-art work shows that a structured Clue and Reasoning approach (Sun et al., 2023) has worked with widely used LLMs such as GPT3, for classification tasks. Due to token limits in newer models as well as a lack of computational resources this longer approach could not be replicated. Instead simpler zero-shot, one-shot, and few-shot learning variations were carried out for the classifying problem. Two models were evaluated using the WikiBias corpus. The selected models are Google's Gemma (Gemma Team, 2024) and OpenAI's GPT-4o (OpenAI, 2024).

For the zero-shot experiments a single instruction to determine if a sentence is biased was given, no information regarding the nature of bias was added. In the one-shot and few-shot cases the example sentences used were extracted solely from the WikiBias corpus. For the one-shot variation, the extracted sentence was initially chosen at random, but after a few experiments a framing bias sentence proved best, more info regarding prompts can be seen in Appendix A. For the few-shot variation one of each class was presented. Gemma's prompt had to be modified with start and end of turn tokens, where as for GPT the prompt was divided in three roles: system, user, and assistant.

<start_of_turn> user I want you to analyze this sentence {i}[2]*. Based on the following biased sentence I want you to determine if the previous sentence is biased. Example sentence: In 1995 he narrated the excellent TV miniseries Watergate. Think and reason before responding. Answer with a 0 or 1. 0 if there is no bias. 1 if there is.<end_of_turn>.*

For GPT we have the following:

System: *"You detect bias in sentences.",*

User: *f"Determine if the following sentence is biased or not. Answer only with 0 and 1. 0 if it isn't biased, 1 if it is. The sentence is {i}."*

Assistant: *"The following is an example of a biased sentence: in 1995 he narrated the excellent TV miniseries Watergate.".*

Table 4 shows each model's evaluation divided by the type learning variations on WikiBias corpus sentences, and Table 5 illustrates that the most optimal model is the DestilRoberta sentence + mask, which employs the three types of biases.

[2]It was implemented using f-strings, hence the {, }.

	Acc	Prec	Rec	F1
Gemma				
Zero-Shot	0.5	0.52	0.52	0.5
One-Shot	0.64	0.63	0.62	**0.62**
Few-Shot	0.46	0.22	0.22	0.22
GPT4o				
Zero-Shot	0.4	0.46	0.48	0.36
One-Shot	0.6	0.55	0.51	0.4
Few-Shot	0.38	0.4	0.41	0.34

Table 4: LLM for bias classification on WikiBias.

	Acc	Prec	Rec	F1
SVC				
WikiBias	0.66	0.61	0.60	0.60
SG2	0.63	0.64	0.64	0.63
CheckThat!	0.59	0.59	0.59	0.59
DestilRoberta sentence + mask				
WikiBias	0.61	0.59	0.61	**0.65**
SG2	0.70	0.66	0.85	**0.75**
CheckThat!	0.63	0.60	0.89	**0.71**
Gemma One-Shot				
WikiBias	0.64	0.63	0.62	0.62
SG2	0.51	0.34	0.34	0.32
CheckThat!	0.51	0.5	0.5	0.49

Table 5: The best results of each approach. The most favorable outcomes for each corpus are presented in bold.

4 Conclusion

Despite bias detection still being a challenging task in NLP, models trained on the WikiBias corpus are capable of detecting bias in news corpora such as SG2 and CheckThat!. These results indicate that the WikiBias corpus is a good resource for general bias detection, as it already contains more subtle biases. This is probably due to the fact that the goal of Wikipedia articles is to provide knowledge in an unaltered form. This presents inherent differences when compared to various media outlets that talk from a particular perspective and not only report hard facts. A fine grained analysis shows that epistemological bias is more challenging to identify, as it is often introduced through the use of frequent words such as "is," "many," and "so," which makes it dependent on the context of the discourse.

Analyzing results from the one-shot instance and the fine-tuned encoder models, we believe that framing bias represents a more recognizable form of bias for Transformer based methods. Both LLMs and Encoders perform at their best when their fine-tuning or instruction tuning is based on this type of bias. This could be due to the lexical nature of framing bias where adding one or two words instigate said bias.

Finally, we observed that simple instruction-tuned LLMs are not efficient for this task, barely reaching scores obtained by Encoders or classic ML models. Surprisingly few-shot learning was the worst performing instance of an LLM implementation. We theorize that having examples from various classes of bias, particularly without an explanation of each class, hinders the model since a lexical pattern of bias can't be generalized. Another factor might be the token related, adding two additional sentences might push the instruction prompt beyond an adequate amount of tokens.

5 Limitations

Detecting bias in sentences is a challenging task in Natural Language Processing (NLP). Biases can exist at various linguistic levels and often lack clear lexical representation. Among the three main types of bias—epistemological, framing, and demographic—epistemological biases are particularly difficult to detect and address, both for humans and computational algorithms. This difficulty is also evident in this study, as the different methods introduced in the paper fail to identify these biases effectively.

Because biased sentences can be hard for humans to distinguish, labeling also carries a degree of subjectivity. Some corpora include sociodemographic information about the annotators, providing additional information to the systems and algorithms so they can learn from the provided examples. However, this is not the case in our experiments, making the task even more challenging due to the inherent subjectivity.

Moreover, the task presents an additional layer of difficulty. The algorithms and techniques used in the experiments may already be biased. Transformers like DistilRoBERTa, for example, are trained on a large amount of biased data, which means that biases are inherently embedded in these models.

Acknowledgments

This research was funded by CONAHCYT (CF-2023-G-64) and PAPIIT project IT100822. G.B.E. is supported by a grant for the requalification of the Spanish university system from the Ministry of

Universities of the Government of Spain, financed by the European Union, NextGeneration EU (María Zambrano program, Universitat de Barcelona).

Karla Salas-Jimenez (CVU: 1291359), Francisco López-Ponce (CVU: 2045472), and Sergio-Luis Ojeda-Trueba (CVU: 2013549) thank the CONAHCYT graduate degree scholarship program.

References

Alberto Barrón-Cedeño, Firoj Alam, Tanmoy Chakraborty, Tamer Elsayed, Preslav Nakov, Piotr Przybyła, Julia Maria Struß, Fatima Haouari, Maram Hasanain, Federico Ruggeri, Xingyi Song, and Reem Suwaileh. 2024. The CLEF-2024 CheckThat! Lab: Check-Worthiness, Subjectivity, Persuasion, Roles, Authorities, and Adversarial Robustness. In *Advances in Information Retrieval*, pages 449–458, Cham. Springer Nature Switzerland.

Jacob Devlin, Ming-Wei Chang, Kenton Lee, and Kristina Toutanova. 2018. BERT: pre-training of deep bidirectional transformers for language understanding. *CoRR*, abs/1810.04805.

Zhiting Fan, Ruizhe Chen, Ruiling Xu, and Zuozhu Liu. 2024. Biasalert: A plug-and-play tool for social bias detection in llms. *Preprint*, arXiv:2407.10241.

Gemma Team. 2024. Gemma: Open models based on gemini research and technology. *Preprint*, arXiv:2403.08295.

Rishav Hada, Agrima Seth, Harshita Diddee, and Kalika Bali. 2023. "fifty shades of bias": Normative ratings of gender bias in GPT generated English text. In *Proceedings of the 2023 Conference on Empirical Methods in Natural Language Processing*, pages 1862–1876, Singapore. Association for Computational Linguistics.

Luyang Lin, Lingzhi Wang, Jinsong Guo, and Kam-Fai Wong. 2024. Investigating bias in llm-based bias detection: Disparities between llms and human perception. *Preprint*, arXiv:2403.14896.

Aurélien Max and Guillaume Wisniewski. 2022. Mining naturally-occurring corrections and paraphrases from wikipedia's revision history. *Preprint*, arXiv:2202.12575.

OpenAI. 2024. Gpt-4 technical report. *Preprint*, arXiv:2303.08774.

Reid Pryzant, Richard Diehl Martinez, Nathan Dass, Sadao Kurohashi, Dan Jurafsky, and Diyi Yang. 2020. Automatically neutralizing subjective bias in text. In *AAAI*.

Juan Manuel Pérez, Mariela Rajngewerc, Juan Carlos Giudici, Damián A. Furman, Franco Luque, Laura Alonso Alemany, and María Vanina Martínez. 2023. pysentimiento: A python toolkit for opinion mining and social nlp tasks. *Preprint*, arXiv:2106.09462.

Shaina Raza, Deepak John Reji, and Chen Ding. 2022. Dbias: detecting biases and ensuring fairness in news articles. *International Journal of Data Science and Analytics*, pages 1–21.

Marta Recasens, Cristian Danescu-Niculescu-Mizil, and Dan Jurafsky. 2013. Linguistic models for analyzing and detecting biased language. In *Proceedings of the 51st Annual Meeting of the Association for Computational Linguistics (Volume 1: Long Papers)*, pages 1650–1659.

Nils Reimers and Iryna Gurevych. 2019. Sentence-bert: Sentence embeddings using siamese bert-networks. In *Proceedings of the 2019 Conference on Empirical Methods in Natural Language Processing*. Association for Computational Linguistics.

Federico Ruggeri, Francesco Antici, Andrea Galassi, Katerina Korre, Arianna Muti, and Alberto Barrón-Cedeño. 2023. On the definition of prescriptive annotation guidelines for language-agnostic subjectivity detection. *Text2Story@ ECIR*, 3370:103–111.

T. Spinde, L. Rudnitckaia, K. Sinha, F. Hamborg, B. Gipp, and K. Donnay. 2021. Mbic – a media bias annotation dataset including annotator characteristics. *Preprint*, arXiv:2105.11910.

Timo Spinde, Manuel Plank, Jan-David Krieger, Terry Ruas, Bela Gipp, and Akiko Aizawa. 2022. Neural media bias detection using distant supervision with babe–bias annotations by experts. *arXiv preprint arXiv:2209.14557*.

Xiaofei Sun, Xiaoya Li, Jiwei Li, Fei Wu, Shangwei Guo, Tianwei Zhang, and Guoyin Wang. 2023. Text classification via large language models. In *Findings of the Association for Computational Linguistics: EMNLP 2023*, pages 8990–9005, Singapore. Association for Computational Linguistics.

Fabio Massimo Zanzotto and Marco Pennacchiotti. 2010. Expanding textual entailment corpora fromWikipedia using co-training. In *Proceedings of the 2nd Workshop on The People's Web Meets NLP: Collaboratively Constructed Semantic Resources*, pages 28–36, Beijing, China. Coling 2010 Organizing Committee.

Yang Zhong. 2021. *WIKIBIAS: Detecting multi-span subjective biases in language*. Ph.D. thesis, The Ohio State University.

A Prompts

The prompts seen in the article correspond to final prompts used for the reported experiments. Prompt engineering had to be carried out before actually obtaining said prompts, mainly working our way up from very simple instructions, sometimes even avoiding start of turn tokens. The following list includes the prompts previously used for Gemma. The brackets correspond to the f-string implementation.

1) Tell me if this is biased: {i}.
2) You detect bias in sentences. Is this sentence biased? {i}.
3) Determine if the following sentence is biased: {i}.

The following correspond to GPT prompts.

1) **System**: You detect bias. **User**: Determine if the following sentence is biased: {i}. **Assistant:** NONE.
2) **System**: You detect bias. **User**: The following sentence might contain bias, determine if so. **Assistant**: NONE.
3) **System**: You detect bias in sentences. **User**: Determine if the following sentence is biased or not. **Assistant**: A biased sentence contains a non objective point of view of said sentence.

As can be seen in both lists, initial prompts are very simple, sometimes even omitting that the model is analyzing sentences, as well as start and end of turn tokens or certain roles for GPT. The most interesting type of prompts are those like the second or third prompt for GPT. The second prompt doesn't tell the LLM that the sentence has bias, but it suggests that that is the case. This particularly triggered the LLM to produce mainly positive classifications. The third case contains an ambiguous definition of bias, leading to very inconclusive reasoning.

Similarly behaviour prompts, such as adding instructions to answer with 0 and 1s depending on each classification case, were added after various iterations of experiments. Said values were added in order to facilitate the classification reports.

HOAXPEDIA: A Unified Wikipedia Hoax Articles Dataset

Hsuvas Borkakoty[1], **Luis Espinosa-Anke**[1,2]
[1]Cardiff NLP, School of Computer Science and Informatics, Cardiff University, UK
[2]AMPLYFI, UK
{borkakotyh,espinosaankel}@cardiff.ac.uk

Abstract

Hoaxes are a recognised form of disinformation created deliberately, with potential serious implications in the credibility of reference knowledge resources such as Wikipedia. What makes detecting Wikipedia hoaxes hard is that they are often written according to the official style guidelines and would pass as legitimate articles from a written quality standard. In this work, we first confirm the above assumption with a systematic analysis of similarities and discrepancies between legitimate and hoax Wikipedia articles, and introduce HOAXPEDIA, a collection of 311 hoax articles (from existing literature and official Wikipedia lists), together with semantically similar legitimate articles, which together form a binary text classification dataset aimed at fostering research in automated hoax detection. We report results of several models, hoax-to-legit ratios, and the amount of text classifiers are exposed to (full article vs the article's definition alone). Our results suggest that detecting deceitful content in Wikipedia based on content alone is feasible but very hard. We complement our analysis with a study on the distributions in edit histories and find that looking at this feature alone yields better classification results. [1]

1 Introduction

Wikipedia is, as Hovy et al. (2013) define it, the "largest and most popular collaborative and multilingual resource of world and linguistic knowledge", and it is acknowledged that its accuracy is on par with or superior to, e.g., the Encyclopedia Britannica (Giles, 2005). However, as with any other online platform, Wikipedia is also the target of online vandalism, and *hoaxes*, a more obscure, less obvious form of vandalism[2], constitute a significant threat to Wikipedia's overall integrity (Kumar et al., 2016; Wong et al., 2021; Wang and McKeown, 2010), among others, because of its "publish first, ask questions later" policy (Asthana and Halfaker, 2018). Although Wikipedia employs community based New Page Patrol systems to check the credibility of a newly created article, the process is always in backlog[3], making it overwhelming (Schneider et al., 2014).

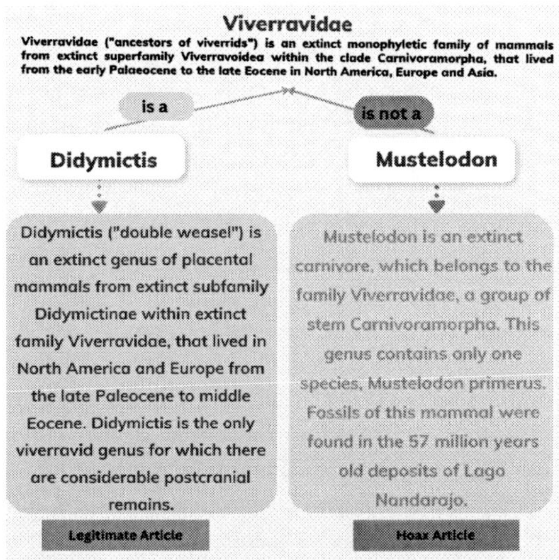

Figure 1: An example of the nature of the Hoaxpedia dataset. It contains hoax (red) articles as well as semantically similar legitimate articles (green), which pose a hard problem for a text-based classifier due to their textual similarities.

Hoax articles (as shown in Figure 1), are created to deliberately spread false information (Kumar et al., 2016), harm the credibility of Wikipedia as a knowledge resource and generate concerns

[1]The Dataset is available at: https://huggingface.co/datasets/hsuvaskakoty/hoaxpedia and associated codes are available at: https://github.com/hsuvas/hoaxpedia_dataset.git

[2]https://en.wikipedia.org/wiki/Wikipedia:Do_not_create_hoaxes.

[3]https://en.wikipedia.org/wiki/Wikipedia:New_pages_patrol.

Proceedings of the First Workshop on Advancing Natural Language Processing for Wikipedia, pages 53–66
November 16, 2024

among its users (Hu et al., 2007). Since manual inspection of quality is typically a lagging process (Dang and Ignat, 2016), the automatic detection of such articles is highly desirable. However, most works in the literature have centered their efforts on the metadata associated with hoax articles, e.g., user activity, appearance features or revision history (Zeng et al., 2006; Elebiary and Ciampaglia, 2023; Kumar et al., 2016; Wong et al., 2021; Hu et al., 2007; Susuri et al., 2017). For example, Adler et al. (2011) introduced a vandalism detection system using metadata, content and author reputation features, whereas Kumar et al. (2016) provide a comprehensive study of hoax articles and their timeline from discovery to deletion. In their work, the authors define the characteristics of a successful hoax, with a data-driven approach based on studying a dataset of 64 articles (both hoax and legitimate), on top of which they train statistical classifiers. Furthermore, other works have compared network traffic and features of hoax articles to those of other articles published the same day (Elebiary and Ciampaglia, 2023), and conclude that hoax articles attract more attention after creation than *cohort* (or legitimate) articles. Finally, Wong et al. (2021) study various Wikipedia vandalism types and introduce the Wiki-Reliability dataset, which comprises articles based on 41 author-compiled templates. This dataset contains 1,300 articles marked as hoax, which are legitimate articles with false information, a.k.a hoax facts (Kumar et al., 2016).

In this paper, we propose to study hoax detection only by looking at textual content. If successful, this would have obvious advantages in the transferrability of models to other platforms. To this end, we first construct a dataset (HOAXPEDIA) containing 311 hoax articles and around 30,000 *plausible negative examples*, i.e., legitimate Wikipedia articles that are semantically similar to hoax articles, so that the set of distractors *covers similar topics* (since similarity in style is assumed) to hoax articles (e.g., a newly discovered species). We also explore whether a Wikipedia definition (the first sentence of the article) can provide any kind of hints towards its veracity. Our results (reported at different ratios of hoax vs. legitimate articles) suggest that style and shallow features are certainly not the best predictors, but combining language models (LMs) with metadata features (e.g., an article's revision history) is a promising direction. Our contributions in this work can be summarised as follows.

- We systematically contrast a set of proven Wikipedia hoax articles with legitimate articles.
- We propose HOAXPEDIA, a novel Wikipedia Hoax article dataset with 311 hoax articles and 30,000 semantically similar legitimate articles collected from Wikipedia.
- We conduct binary classification experiments on HoaxPedia, using a range of language models (including LLMs), features, and hoax-to-legitimate ratio.

2 Related work

In what follows, we give a brief overview of disinformation detection, the datasets available for the community and the role of Wikipedia in disinformation detection, as our work falls in the intersection between disinformation detection and Wikipedia research.

Disinformation detection and datasets: Disinformation and misinformation are two types of false information, they differ in that misinformation is inaccurate information created or propagated unknowingly, whereas disinformation is inaccurate information deliberately created to mislead the intended consumer (Hernon, 1995; Fallis, 2014; Kumar et al., 2016; Ireton and Posetti, 2018). Nonetheless, both are harmful to information quality and reliability, thus posing risks toward different aspects of society (Su et al., 2020). Alam et al. (2021) survey disinformation detection from a multi-modal perspective (specifically, text, images, audio, and video), with text being the most common. Datasets used for disinformation detection can be divided based on the length of input or claim: short sentences (such as tweets or Reddit posts) vs articles (common type being news articles), where most of the datasets follow claim-evidence based format (Su et al., 2020). The short sentences or claim based datasets are mostly sourced from social media, such as X (formerly Twitter) (Castillo et al., 2011; Derczynski et al., 2017; Zubiaga et al., 2018; López and Madhyastha, 2021), Reddit (Gorrell et al., 2018; Qu et al., 2022), or fact checking websites like Politifact[4] (Wang, 2017), Snopes[5] (Vo and Lee, 2020), or a combination of different fact checking websites (Augenstein

[4]https://www.politifact.com/

[5]https://www.snopes.com/

et al., 2019). These datasets usually contain claims, verification labels and evidences to back the label. Article level datasets, on the other hand, are varied, and focus on state-backed propaganda (Heppell et al., 2023), German multi-label disinformation (the GerDISDETECT dataset) (Schütz et al., 2024), or narratives at conflict dataset containing news articles (Sinelnik and Hovy, 2024), which mostly focuses on news article or propaganda based disinformation spreading. The datasets mentioned above are specialized towards topic/trend based or news based disinformation, with no specialization on Wikipedia.

Wikipedia in disinformation detection: Wikipedia, as described by McDowell and Vetter (2020), serves as a source of information validation as backed by its large set of articles contributed by community. This is seen in action for fact verification task datasets such as FEVER (Thorne et al., 2018b), TabFactA (Chen et al., 2019), or the FNC-1 (Fake News Challenge-1) dataset (Pomerleau and Rao, 2017). Here, evidences for claims are collected from Wikipedia articles (eg. FEVER, FNC-1) and tables (eg. TabFactA). However, being a product of community effort, Wikipedia is also prone to vandalism and inaccurate contents (McDowell and Vetter, 2020), and the community outlines different policies to combat these issues[6]. We also find efforts to automatize the process of detecting vandalism contents from Natural Language Processing perspective. Previously, feature based approaches extracted from metadata and editor behaviour were used to detect vandalism (Wu et al., 2010; Javanmardi et al., 2011; Heindorf et al., 2016). Implementation of early warning systems based on metadata and editor behavior is found in the work of Kumar et al. (2015), where they propose a dataset of page metadata and a set of autoencoder-based classifiers. Yuan et al. (2017) propose an edit history based approach, where they use behaviour of users over time as feature to create the embedding space for multi-source LSTM networks (Hochreiter and Schmidhuber, 1997). Additionally, real-time machine learning based Wikipedia edit scoring system named ORES (Halfaker and Geiger, 2020), and multilingual vandalism detection system (Trokhymovych et al., 2023) contributes to a high-end edit based vandalism detection systems that are deployed in Wikipedia. However, these approaches do not consider article text as a marker to detect vandalism.

[6]https://en.wikipedia.org/wiki/Wikipedia:Vandalism

Data Source	Data points
Kumar et al. (2016)	64
Elebiary and Ciampaglia (2023)	95
Wikipedia List of Hoaxes	
Collected from Wikipedia	87
Collected from Internet archive	65
Total	311

Table 1: Data sources used to construct HOAXPEDIA and their corresponding number of data points from each source.

While Wikipedia marks hoax articles as form of vandalism (Thorne et al., 2018a), we argue that the vandalism and hoax detection fields have not yet met - although there are notable exceptions (Kumar et al., 2016; Wong et al., 2021), and thus our work aims to establish a stronger tie between them with a single dataset unifying existing work in addition to gathering any available proven hoax article from additional sources.

3 HOAXPEDIA Construction

HOAXPEDIA is constructed by unifying five different resources that contain known hoaxes, e.g., from Kumar et al. (2016); Elebiary and Ciampaglia (2023), as well as from the URLs available in the official Wikipedia hoaxes list[7] and the Internet Archive. Articles extracted from the Internet Archive are the ones that are deleted from Wikipedia but are redirected from the list of Hoaxes as 'Archived version' to the Internet Archive[8]. The statistics of the articles collected from different sources are given in Table 1. We manually verify each of the articles we collect from Wikipedia and Internet Archive as a hoax using their accompanied deletion discussion and reasons for citing them as a hoax.

In terms of negative examples, while we could have randomly sampled Wikipedia pages, this could have introduced a number of biases in the dataset, e.g., hoax articles contain historical events, personalities or artifacts, and thus we are interested in capturing a similar breadth of topics, entities and

[7]https://en.wikipedia.org/wiki/Wikipedia:List_of_hoaxes_on_Wikipedia

[8]Example archived article: https://web.archive.org/web/20230608103922/https://en.wikipedia.org/wiki/Rainbow_fish_%28mythology%29

sectors in the negative examples so that a classifier cannot use "shortcuts" for effective classification. These negative examples correspond to authentic content. This is achieved by verifying they do not carry the Db-hoax flag, which Wikipedia's New Page Patrol policy uses to mark potential hoaxes. Within this set, we extract negative examples as follows. Let H be the set of hoax articles, and W the set of candidate *legitimate* Wikipedia pages, with $T_H = \{t_{H^1}, \ldots, t_{H^p}\}$ and $T_W = \{t_{W^1}, \ldots, t_{W^q}\}$ their corresponding vector representations, and p and q the number of hoax and candidate Wikipedia articles, respectively. Then, for each SBERT (all-MiniLM-L6-v2) (Reimers and Gurevych, 2019) title embedding $t_{H^i} \in T_H$, we retrieve its top k nearest neighbors (NN) from T_W via cosine similarity $\cos$. We experiment with different values for k, specifically $k \in \{2, 10, 100\}$:

$$\text{NN}\,(t_{H^i}) = \{t_{W^j} : j \in J_k(t_{H^i})\}$$

where $J_k(t_{H^i})$ contains the top k cosine similarities in T_W for a given t_{H^i}, and

$$\cos\,(t_{H^i}, t_{W^j}) = \frac{t_{H^i} \cdot t_{W^j}}{||t_{H^i}||||t_{W^j}||}$$

The result of this process is a set of positive (hoax) articles and a set of negative examples, which we argue is similar in both style and topic, effectively removing topic bias from the dataset.

4 Text Based Analysis on HOAXPEDIA

For a better understanding of article structure, and leverage the text and its features to distinguish between hoax and legitimate articles, we run different analysis in surface level and designing classifiers to identify hoax articles. We do not consider metadata that comes along with the Wikipedia articles, as metadata are platform-specific, which we argue can have a negative impact on transferability.

4.1 Hoax vs. Legitimate, a Surface-Level Comparison

To maintain longevity and avoid detection, hoax articles follow Wikipedia guidelines and article structure. This raises the following question: *"how (dis)similar are hoaxes with respect to a hypothetical legitimate counterpart?"*. Upon inspection, we found comments in the deletion discussions such as *"I wouldn't have questioned it had I come across it organically"* (for the hoax article *The Heat is On* [9]), or *"The story may have a "credible feel" to it, but it lacks any sources"*, a comment on article *Chu Chi Zui*[10]. Comments like these highlight that hoaxes are generally well written (following Wikipedia's guidelines), and so we proceed to quantify their stylistic differences in a comparative analysis that looks at: (1) article text length; (2) sentence and word length; and (3) a readability metrics.

Article Text length distribution: Following the works of Kumar et al. (2016), we conduct a text length distribution analysis with hoax and legitimate articles, and verify they show a similar pattern (as shown in Figure 2), with similar medians for hoax and legitimate articles, specifically 1,057 and 1,777 words, respectively.

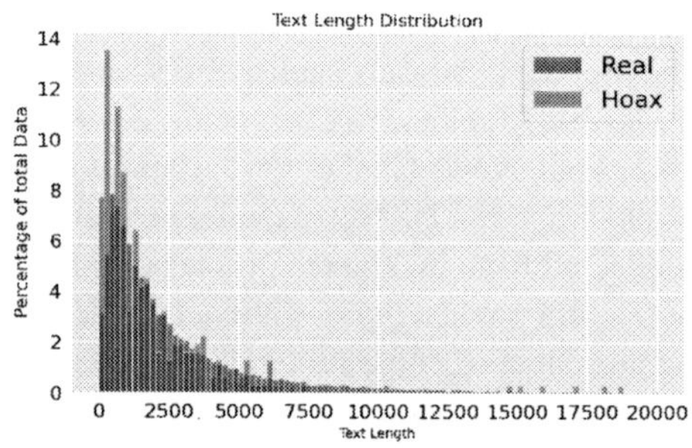

Figure 2: Text length distribution for hoax and legitimate articles (with percentage of data points shown in y-axis).

Average sentence and word length: Calculating average sentence and word length for hoaxes and legitimate articles separately can be a valuable proxy for identifying any obvious stylistic or linguistic (e.g., syntactic complexity) patterns. We visualize these in a series of box plots in Figure 3. They clearly show a similar style, with sentence and word length medians at 21.23 and 22.0, and 4.36 and 4.35 for legitimate and hoax articles respectively.

Readability Analysis: Readability analysis gives a quantifiable measure of the complexities in text, revealing distinguishable patterns for disguising disinformation through hoaxes or convey clear, factual content. For readability analysis, we use the Flesch-Kincaid (FK) Grading system (Flesch,

[9] https://en.wikipedia.org/wiki/Wikipedia:Articles_for_deletion/The_Heat_Is_On_(TV_series)
[10] https://en.wikipedia.org/wiki/Wikipedia:Articles_for_deletion/Chu_Chi_Zui

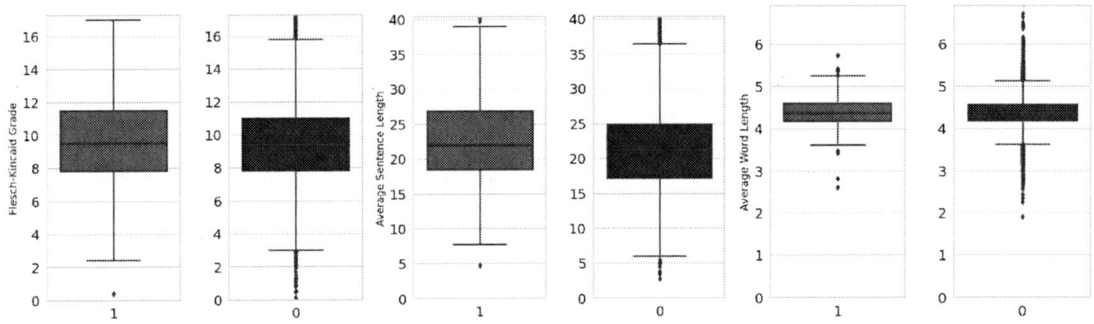

(a) Flesch-Kincaid Grade (b) Average Sentence Length (c) Average Word Length

Figure 3: Results of different stylistic analyses on Hoax (red) and legitimate (blue) articles.

2007), a metric that indicates comprehension difficulty when reading a passage in the context of contemporary academic English. After obtaining an average for both hoax and legitimate articles, we visualize these averages again in Figure 3, we find a median of 9.4 for legitimate articles and 9.5 for hoax articles, which again highlights the similarities between these articles.

4.2 Classification Experiments

We cast the problem of identifying hoax vs. legitimate articles as a binary classification problem. Our experiments are aimed to explore the impact of data imbalance and content length, and we evaluate a suite of pre-trained LMs as well as a set of open sourced LLMs. We split the dataset into non overlapping train and test (with 80:20 ratio for positive instances for definition and fulltext settings), due to the smaller number of positive instances (311), as well as for the fact that we want to test the models for their abilities on unseen test data. The experimental settings and results are discussed below.

4.2.1 Pre-trained Language Models

We evaluated the BERT family of models (BERT base and large (Devlin et al., 2019), RoBERTa-base and large (Liu et al., 2019), Albert-base and large (Lan et al., 2019)), as well as T5 (Base and Large) (Raffel et al., 2020) and Longformer (Base) (Beltagy et al., 2020) with the same training configuration (as mentioned in Appendix B) and generation objective as *Binary classification* for T5 models. In terms of data size, we consider the three different scenarios outlined in Section 3 (2x, 10x and 100x negative examples). This approach naturally increases the challenge for the classifiers. The details about the data used in different settings are given in Appendix A.

In addition to the three different settings for positive vs. negative ratios, we also explore *how much text is actually needed to catch a hoax*, or, in other words, *are definition sentences in hoax articles giving something away*? This is explored by running our experiments on the full Wikipedia articles, on one hand, and on the definition (first sentence alone), on the other. This latter setting is interesting from a lexicographic perspective because it helps us understand if the Wikipedia definitions show any pattern that a model could exploit. Moreover, from the practical point of view of building a classifier that could dynamically *"patrol"* Wikipedia and flag content automatically, a definition-only model would be more interpretable (with reduced ambiguity and focusing on core meaning/properties of the entity) and could have less parameters (handling smaller vocabularies, and compressed knowledge), which would have practical retraining/deployment implications in cost and turnaround.

We compare several classifiers and analyze whether model size (in number of parameters) is correlated with performance of data imbalance and content length scenarios, reporting the results in F1 on positive class (hoax). In definition only setting, we find that models evaluated on datasets that are relatively balanced (2 real articles for every hoax) show a stable performance, but they degrade drastically as the imbalance increases. RoBERTa proves to be most consistent, with an F1 of around 0.6 for all three settings, whereas Albert models perform poorly (with some interesting behavior discussed later). For the full text setting, we find that Longformer models performs well, with an F1 of 0.8. Surprisingly, the largest model we evaluated (T5-large) is not the best performing model, although this could point to underfitting (dataset being small for model this size). Another interesting behavior of T5-large is that in the 1H2R data split, performance on definition and full text setting are the same. On the other side, we find that Albert models are the ones showing the highest improvement when going from definition to full text. This is interesting, as it shows a small model may miss nuances in definitions but can still compete with, or even outperform, larger models.

A perhaps not too surprising observation is that all models improve after being exposed to more text, as seen in Table 2, increasing their F1 by about 20% on average and sometimes even up to 30%. This confirms that definitions alone are not a sufficiently strong signal for detecting hoax articles, although there are notable exceptions. Moreover, in terms of absolute performance, the RoBERTa models perform decently, although significantly below their full-text settings. It is interesting to note that the Longformer base yields much better results in the 1H100R split when exposed only to definitions. This is indeed a surprising and counterintuitive result that deserves future investigation.

Effect of Definitions on Classifying Hoaxes
We also test the importance of definition sentences in the full text setting though removing the definition sentence from each row and running classification on RoBERTa-Large, the most consistent model in our experiments. The results shown in Table 3, suggest that F1 decreases about 2% for the positive class when the definition sentence is missing. This shows that definitions show critical information about entities and events in Wikipedia, but often are not the place where hoax features would emerge, and therefore removing them from the full text does not change much of the story.

4.2.2 Large Language Models

We explore the capabilities of open-source Large Language Models (LLM) to detect hoax articles through our proposed dataset. We select Llama2-7B and 13B (Touvron et al., 2023), Llama3-8B (Dubey et al., 2024), and Mistral-7B models (Jiang et al., 2023) for the experiments, and the prompts used are given in the Appendix C. We consider prompt-based tuning and supervised fine-tuning (Touvron et al., 2023) as our experiment settings.

Prompting: For prompting, we consider zero-shot and few-shot prompts, as given in Appendix C, and the input setting are for both definition and fulltext. We report the results for F1-scores on positive class in Table 4. The results show that Llama2-13B models perform the best for both settings (definition and fulltext). Notably, performance difference between the definition and fulltext setting is marginal, as opposed to fine-tuned LMs in Table 2.

Fine-tuning: We fine-tune the LLMs with HOAXPEDIA in supervised fine-tuning (Touvron et al., 2023) paradigm. The results of fine-tuning as F1-scores for both definition and fulltext setting are shown in Table 5, with significant improvement across all the settings for all the models. Llama3 shows most consistency and is the best model across the scenarios, with a performance improvement of more than 25%.

4.2.3 Perplexity Experiments with LLMs

We consider perplexity as an indicator for LLMs to predict the distribution of Hoax and legitimate articles, with the hypothesis that LLMs will have difficulty predicting the contents of hoax articles, resulting in higher perplexity. We test the LLMs in both definition and fulltext settings. The average perplexity results for both settings are shown in Figure 4, revealing that there is a significant difference between the perplexity of hoax and legitimate articles in both settings. This suggests that LLMs struggle to predict the distribution of Hoax articles.

5 Comparing Revision Activities of Hoax and Legitimate Articles

Analysing the revision timelines of hoaxes and legitimate articles can reveal valuable insights into activity patterns on those articles from the Wikipedia community. We investigate the revision activity patterns by collecting timelines of hoax and legitimate articles (in all three hoax-to-legitimate ratios mentioned above) and add these timelines to HOAXPEDIA. However, since some of the hoax articles were deleted from Wikipedia at the time of this experiment, we were only able to obtain 164 hoax articles out of 311 in our dataset. We explore the revision history timelines of legitimate and hoax articles through changepoints and dense regions in timelines and experiment with the binary classification problem of identifying hoax articles through their timelines.

5.1 Exploratory Analysis

We analyze timeline patterns through the use of a dense region identification algorithm, namely Bayesian Online Changepoint Detection (BOCPD) (Adams and MacKay, 2007), followed by Kernel

Model	Model Size	Definition 1H2R	Definition 1H10R	Definition 1H100R	Fulltext 1H2R	Fulltext 1H10R	Fulltext 1H100R
Albert-base-v2	12M	0.23	0.17	0.06	0.67	0.47	0.11
Albert-large-v2	18M	0.28	0.30	0.15	0.72	0.63	0.30
BERT-base	110M	0.42	0.30	0.14	0.55	0.57	0.32
RoBERTa Base	123M	0.57	0.59	0.53	0.82	0.75	0.63
Longformer-base	149M	0.43	0.35	0.54	0.80	0.78	0.67
T5-Base	220M	0.48	0.25	0.14	0.51	0.27	0.23
BERT-large	340M	0.43	0.36	0.17	0.61	0.64	0.33
RoBERTa-large	354M	0.58	0.63	0.62	0.84	0.81	0.79
T5-large	770M	0.54	0.32	0.13	0.54	0.43	0.37

Table 2: F1 on the positive class - *hoax* at different degrees of data imbalance for definition-only and fulltext setup (H: Hoax, R: Real).

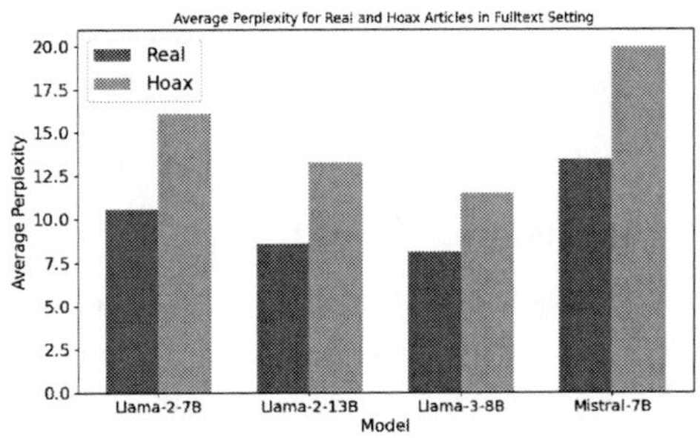

(a) Average perplexity scores for LLMs in the fulltext setup.

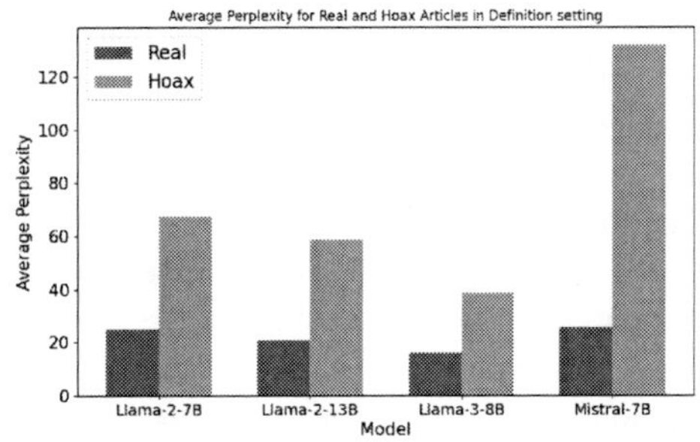

(b) Average perplexity scores for LLMs in the definition setup.

Figure 4: Average perplexity scores in fulltext and definition only setups for legitimate (real) and hoax articles.

Model	Setting	Precision	Recall	F1
RoBERTaL	1H2R	0.83	0.80	0.82
RoBERTaL	1H10R	0.82	0.71	0.76
RoBERTaL	1H100R	0.67	0.51	0.58

Table 3: Performance of RoBERTa-Large on binary classification without definition sentences in articles (with hoax to real ratio for fulltext setup in Settings column) on positive class - *hoax* (H: Hoax, R: Real).

Model Name	Zero-shot Definition	Zero-shot Fulltext	Few-shot Definition	Few-shot Fulltext
Llama2-7B	0.48	0.50	0.51	0.52
Llama2-13B	0.57	0.58	0.59	0.59
Llama3-8B	0.33	0.40	0.35	0.40
Mistral-7B	0.53	0.56	0.54	0.58

Table 4: F1 score on positive class - *hoax* for prompting experiment in zero and few shot setting for definition-only and fulltext setup.

Model	Definition 1H2R	Definition 1H10R	Definition 1H100R	Fulltext 1H2R	Fulltext 1H10R	Fulltext 1H100R
Llama2-7B	0.76	0.47	0.49	0.66	0.48	0.47
Llama2-13B	0.80	0.48	0.50	0.60	0.63	0.50
Llama3-8B	0.80	0.48	0.50	0.83	0.67	0.50
Mistral-7B	0.71	0.55	0.49	0.68	0.53	0.49

Table 5: F1 score for LLM fine-tuning in degrees of data imbalance for definition-only and fulltext setup (H: Hoax, R: Real).

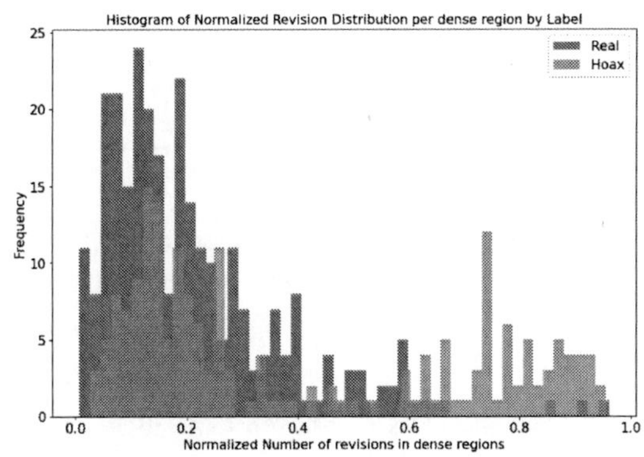

Figure 5: Histogram of normalized distribution for number of revisions in dense regions for hoax and legitimate (real) article.

Density Estimation (KDE) (Węglarczyk, 2018), with which we obtain dense regions, which are significantly active periods in a page's revision period in comparison with the overall distribution. Figure 6 shows a comparison of two timelines with highlighted dense regions. We can see that the number of revisions are generally low for hoax articles, and that their dense regions are mostly around the beginning and end of the article's timeline. This can be attributed to New Page Patrol (NPP) for spike in the beginning and detection with deletion discussion for the end. To quantify this evidence, we divide the revision timelines of hoax and legitimate articles into quartiles and compute a normalized count of dense regions. The result for each quartile is given in Table 6, and clearly shows that the proportion of dense regions happening at the beginning and at the end are higher (especially close to the end of the article's life) for hoax articles than for legitimate ones. We also show in a histogram the normalized distribution of hoax and legitimate (real) revisions in Figure 5, which provides a full-picture summary of these edits. The distribution shown here is the density of revisions for hoax and legitimate articles with respect to the frequency of articles in that density. Based on this analysis, we further find that legitimate articles have 5.40x more revisions on average (81.70 for legitimate vs. 15.11 for hoax), but if we look at the relative density of each revision, hoax articles undergo more activity per region (0.21 for legitimate articles vs. 0.39 of hoax articles), which suggests that for the hoax articles, there is a "disproportionate hyperfocus" of the community at very concrete points in the lifespan of the article.

Quartile	Hoax	Real
Q1	0.69	0.75
Q2	0.02	0.17
Q3	0.04	0.22
Q4	0.75	0.42

Table 6: Average distribution of dense regions per quartile (timeline divided into four parts) for hoax and legitimate (real) articles.

5.2 Revision History based Classification

We formulate the detection of hoaxes as a binary classification problem with features collected from article revision histories (each containing a series of timestamps) for hoax and legitimate articles. To create the feature vector, we group those timestamps by month and year (MM-YYYY) to create the vocabulary[11] for our model. We use this vocabulary to obtain the TF-IDF features (Sparck Jones, 1972). We train a Support Vector Machine (SVM) (Vapnik, 2013) classifier with the TF-IDF features. We report F1 scores for the positive class in Table 7, with good performance (0.88 for the 1H2R setting) of the SVM classifier, although the performance decreases due to the data imbalance. This further proves that the revision history can be an important feature in the detection of hoaxes. However, we also argue that timeline alone may not be enough, as it is a statistical feature prone to outliers. Moreover, hoaxes are defined based on it's contents, thus we encourage the importance of content as the important feature for hoax article detection.

Data Split	Precision	Recall	F1
1H2R	0.86	0.91	0.88
1H10R	0.89	0.78	0.83
1H100R	0.97	0.69	0.80

Table 7: Results of SVM timeline classifier for label 1 (Hoax) for all data splits.

6 Conclusion and Future Work

We have introduced HOAXPEDIA, a dataset containing hoax articles extracted from Wikipedia, from a number of sources, from official lists of hoaxes, existing datasets, and the Web Archive. We paired these hoax articles with similar legitimate articles, and after analyzing their main properties (concluding they are written with very similar style and content), we report the results of a number of binary classification experiments, where we explore the impact of (1) positive to negative ratio; and (2) going from the whole article to only the definition. This is different from previous work in that we have exclusively looked at the content of these hoax articles, rather than metadata such as traffic or longevity. For the future, we would like to explore the approaches (Arora et al., 2024; Field et al., 2022) to reduce spurious artifacts that might appear during the creation of the dataset to strengthen the dataset. Additionally, utilizing approaches for building Wikipedia corpus controlling for topic or readability (Johnson et al., 2021; Trokhymovych et al., 2024) can improve the overall quality of the dataset. We would also like to further refine what the criteria are used by Wikipedia editors to detect hoax articles, turn those insights into a ML model, and explore other types of non-obvious online vandalism.

7 Limitations

We present a new dataset named HOAXPEDIA and associated baselines from a wide variety of language models / large language models. Our study shows that these types of dataset can be helpful

[11]Appendix D explains the process of creating a vocabulary from the revision history

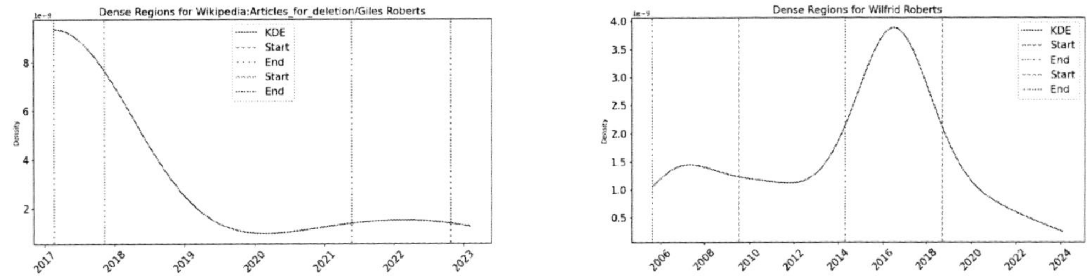

(a) Revision history Plot for an example Hoax article.

(b) Revision history plot for an example legitimate article.

Figure 6: Revision history based dense region plots for hoax and legitimate articles with dense regions marked with dotted lines.

in the area of free text disinformation detection. However, there are some limitations to our work that we aim to address here. The sets proposed here are small, with only 311 positive examples (hoaxes), which can be attributed to the fact that we only collect the examples that are explicitly labeled as hoaxes, rather than articles under discussion for hoaxes. Additionally, in our experiments, we do not conduct further investigation for model behaviors such as performance improvement of Longformer models in the hardest setting. We leave these analysis in future work, as the scope of this work is to introduce this dataset and establish the baseline results with pre-trained LMs and LLMs. Finally, we do not compare the results with existing work, mainly with (Kumar et al., 2016), since the approaches mentioned in existing work are metadata dependent with different sets of features/approaches in consideration, and our approach is based on article text, we argue that the results may not be comparable. We also acknowledge that Wikipedia is a multilingual effort, and our dataset only contains data from Wikipedia in the English language, which can be a major limitation in multilingual landscape. We keep the multilingual extension of the hoax dataset as one of the future work.

8 Ethics Statement

This paper is in the area of online vandalism and disinformation detection, hence a sensitive topic. All data and code will be made publicly available to contribute to the advancement of the field. However, we acknowledge that deceitful content can be also used with malicious intents, and we will make it clear in any associated documentation that any dataset or model released as a result of this paper should be used for ensuring a more transparent and trustworthy Internet.

References

Ryan Prescott Adams and David JC MacKay. 2007. Bayesian online changepoint detection. *arXiv preprint arXiv:0710.3742*.

B. Thomas Adler, Luca de Alfaro, Santiago M. Mola-Velasco, Paolo Rosso, and Andrew G. West. 2011. Wikipedia vandalism detection: Combining natural language, metadata, and reputation features. In *Computational Linguistics and Intelligent Text Processing*, pages 277–288, Berlin, Heidelberg. Springer Berlin Heidelberg.

Firoj Alam, Stefano Cresci, Tanmoy Chakraborty, Fabrizio Silvestri, Dimiter Dimitrov, Giovanni Da San Martino, Shaden Shaar, Hamed Firooz, and Preslav Nakov. 2021. A survey on multimodal disinformation detection. *arXiv preprint arXiv:2103.12541*.

Akhil Arora, Robert West, and Martin Gerlach. 2024. Orphan articles: The dark matter of wikipedia. In *Proceedings of the International AAAI Conference on Web and Social Media*, volume 18, pages 100–112.

Sumit Asthana and Aaron Halfaker. 2018. With few eyes, all hoaxes are deep. *Proc. ACM Hum.-Comput. Interact.*, 2(CSCW).

Isabelle Augenstein, Christina Lioma, Dongsheng Wang, Lucas Chaves Lima, Casper Hansen, Christian Hansen, and Jakob Grue Simonsen. 2019. Multifc: A real-world multi-domain dataset for evidence-based fact checking of claims. *arXiv preprint arXiv:1909.03242*.

Iz Beltagy, Matthew E Peters, and Arman Cohan. 2020. Longformer: The long-document transformer. *arXiv preprint arXiv:2004.05150*.

Carlos Castillo, Marcelo Mendoza, and Barbara Poblete. 2011. Information credibility on twitter. In *Proceedings of the 20th International Conference on World Wide Web*, WWW '11, page 675–684, New York, NY, USA. Association for Computing Machinery.

Wenhu Chen, Hongmin Wang, Jianshu Chen, Yunkai Zhang, Hong Wang, Shiyang Li, Xiyou Zhou, and William Yang Wang. 2019. Tabfact: A large-scale dataset for table-based fact verification. *arXiv preprint arXiv:1909.02164*.

Quang Vinh Dang and Claudia-Lavinia Ignat. 2016. Quality assessment of wikipedia articles without feature engineering. In *Proceedings of the 16th ACM/IEEE-CS on Joint Conference on Digital Libraries*, JCDL '16, page 27–30, New York, NY, USA. Association for Computing Machinery.

Leon Derczynski, Kalina Bontcheva, Maria Liakata, Rob Procter, Geraldine Wong Sak Hoi, and Arkaitz Zubiaga. 2017. Semeval-2017 task 8: Rumoureval: Determining rumour veracity and support for rumours. *arXiv preprint arXiv:1704.05972*.

Jacob Devlin, Ming-Wei Chang, Kenton Lee, and Kristina Toutanova. 2019. BERT: Pre-training of deep bidirectional transformers for language understanding. In *Proceedings of the 2019 Conference of the North American Chapter of the Association for Computational Linguistics: Human Language Technologies, Volume 1 (Long and Short Papers)*, pages 4171–4186, Minneapolis, Minnesota. Association for Computational Linguistics.

Abhimanyu Dubey, Abhinav Jauhri, Abhinav Pandey, Abhishek Kadian, Ahmad Al-Dahle, Aiesha Letman, Akhil Mathur, Alan Schelten, Amy Yang, Angela Fan, et al. 2024. The llama 3 herd of models. *arXiv preprint arXiv:2407.21783*.

Anis Elebiary and Giovanni Luca Ciampaglia. 2023. The role of online attention in the supply of disinformation in wikipedia. *arXiv preprint arXiv:2302.08576*.

Don Fallis. 2014. A functional analysis of disinformation. *IConference 2014 Proceedings*.

Anjalie Field, Chan Young Park, Kevin Z Lin, and Yulia Tsvetkov. 2022. Controlled analyses of social biases in wikipedia bios. In *Proceedings of the ACM Web Conference 2022*, pages 2624–2635.

Rudolf Flesch. 2007. Flesch-kincaid readability test. *Retrieved October*, 26(3):2007.

Jim Giles. 2005. Special report internet encyclopaedias go head to head. *nature*, 438(15):900–901.

Genevieve Gorrell, Kalina Bontcheva, Leon Derczynski, Elena Kochkina, Maria Liakata, and Arkaitz Zubiaga. 2018. Rumoureval 2019: Determining rumour veracity and support for rumours. *arXiv preprint arXiv:1809.06683*.

Aaron Halfaker and R Stuart Geiger. 2020. Ores: Lowering barriers with participatory machine learning in wikipedia. *Proceedings of the ACM on Human-Computer Interaction*, 4(CSCW2):1–37.

Stefan Heindorf, Martin Potthast, Benno Stein, and Gregor Engels. 2016. Vandalism detection in wikidata. In *Proceedings of the 25th ACM International on Conference on Information and Knowledge Management*, CIKM '16, page 327–336, New York, NY, USA. Association for Computing Machinery.

Freddy Heppell, Kalina Bontcheva, and Carolina Scarton. 2023. Analysing state-backed propaganda websites: a new dataset and linguistic study. *arXiv preprint arXiv:2310.14032*.

Peter Hernon. 1995. Disinformation and misinformation through the internet: Findings of an exploratory study. *Government Information Quarterly*, 12(2):133–139.

Sepp Hochreiter and Jürgen Schmidhuber. 1997. Long Short-Term Memory. *Neural Computation*, 9(8):1735–1780.

Eduard Hovy, Roberto Navigli, and Simone Paolo Ponzetto. 2013. Collaboratively built semi-structured content and artificial intelligence: The story so far. *Artificial Intelligence*, 194:2–27.

M. Hu, E. Lim, A. Sun, H. W. Lauw, and B. Vuong. 2007. Measuring article quality in wikipedia. *Proceedings of the Sixteenth ACM Conference on Conference on Information and Knowledge Management*.

Cherilyn Ireton and Julie Posetti. 2018. *Journalism, fake news & disinformation: handbook for journalism education and training*. Unesco Publishing.

Sara Javanmardi, David W. McDonald, and Cristina V. Lopes. 2011. Vandalism detection in wikipedia: a high-performing, feature-rich model and its reduction through lasso. In *Proceedings of the 7th International Symposium on Wikis and Open Collaboration*, WikiSym '11, page 82–90, New York, NY, USA. Association for Computing Machinery.

Albert Q Jiang, Alexandre Sablayrolles, Arthur Mensch, Chris Bamford, Devendra Singh Chaplot, Diego de las Casas, Florian Bressand, Gianna Lengyel, Guillaume Lample, Lucile Saulnier, et al. 2023. Mistral 7b. *arXiv preprint arXiv:2310.06825*.

Isaac Johnson, Martin Gerlach, and Diego Sáez-Trumper. 2021. Language-agnostic topic classification for wikipedia. In *Companion Proceedings of the Web Conference 2021*, pages 594–601.

Srijan Kumar, Francesca Spezzano, and VS Subrahmanian. 2015. Vews: A wikipedia vandal early warning system. In *Proceedings of the 21th ACM SIGKDD international conference on knowledge discovery and data mining*, pages 607–616.

Srijan Kumar, Robert West, and Jure Leskovec. 2016. Disinformation on the web: Impact, characteristics, and detection of wikipedia hoaxes. In *Proceedings of the 25th International World Wide Web Conference*.

Zhenzhong Lan, Mingda Chen, Sebastian Goodman, Kevin Gimpel, Piyush Sharma, and Radu Soricut. 2019. Albert: A lite bert for self-supervised learning of language representations. *arXiv preprint arXiv:1909.11942*.

Yinhan Liu, Myle Ott, Naman Goyal, Jingfei Du, Mandar Joshi, Danqi Chen, Omer Levy, Mike Lewis, Luke Zettlemoyer, and Veselin Stoyanov. 2019. Roberta: A robustly optimized bert pretraining approach. *arXiv preprint arXiv:1907.11692*.

Julio Amador Díaz López and Pranava Madhyastha. 2021. A focused analysis of twitter-based disinformation from foreign influence operations. In *Proceedings of the 1st International Workshop on Knowledge Graphs for Online Discourse Analysis (KnOD 2021) co-located with the 30th The Web Conference (WWW 2021)*, volume 2877. CEUR Workshop Proceedings.

Zachary J. McDowell and Matthew A. Vetter. 2020. It takes a village to combat a fake news army: Wikipedia's community and policies for information literacy. *Social Media + Society*, 6(3):2056305120937309.

Dean Pomerleau and Delip Rao. 2017. The fake news challenge: Exploring how artificial intelligence technologies could be leveraged to combat fake news. *Fake news challenge*.

Jingnong Qu, Liunian Harold Li, Jieyu Zhao, Sunipa Dev, and Kai-Wei Chang. 2022. Disinfomeme: A multimodal dataset for detecting meme intentionally spreading out disinformation. *arXiv preprint arXiv:2205.12617*.

Colin Raffel, Noam Shazeer, Adam Roberts, Katherine Lee, Sharan Narang, Michael Matena, Yanqi Zhou, Wei Li, and Peter J Liu. 2020. Exploring the limits of transfer learning with a unified text-to-text transformer. *The Journal of Machine Learning Research*, 21(1):5485–5551.

Nils Reimers and Iryna Gurevych. 2019. Sentence-bert: Sentence embeddings using siamese bert-networks. *arXiv preprint arXiv:1908.10084*.

Jodi Schneider, Bluma S. Gelley, and Aaron Halfaker. 2014. Accept, decline, postpone: How newcomer productivity is reduced in english wikipedia by prepublication review. In *Proceedings of The International Symposium on Open Collaboration*, OpenSym '14, page 1–10, New York, NY, USA. Association for Computing Machinery.

Mina Schütz, Daniela Pisoiu, Daria Liakhovets, Alexander Schindler, and Melanie Siegel. 2024. GerDISDETECT: A German multilabel dataset for disinformation detection. In *Proceedings of the 2024 Joint International Conference on Computational Linguistics, Language Resources and Evaluation (LREC-COLING 2024)*, pages 7683–7695, Torino, Italia. ELRA and ICCL.

Antonina Sinelnik and Dirk Hovy. 2024. Narratives at conflict: Computational analysis of news framing in multilingual disinformation campaigns. In *Proceedings of the 62nd Annual Meeting of the Association for Computational Linguistics (Volume 4: Student Research Workshop)*, pages 225–237, Bangkok, Thailand. Association for Computational Linguistics.

Karen Sparck Jones. 1972. A statistical interpretation of term specificity and its application in retrieval. *Journal of documentation*, 28(1):11–21.

Qi Su, Mingyu Wan, Xiaoqian Liu, Chu-Ren Huang, et al. 2020. Motivations, methods and metrics of misinformation detection: an nlp perspective. *Natural Language Processing Research*, 1(1-2):1–13.

Arsim Susuri, Mentor Hamiti, and Agni Dika. 2017. Detection of vandalism in wikipedia using metadata features – implementation in simple english and albanian sections. *Advances in Science, Technology and Engineering Systems Journal*, 2:1–7.

James Thorne, Andreas Vlachos, Christos Christodoulopoulos, and Arpit Mittal. 2018a. Fever: a large-scale dataset for fact extraction and verification. *arXiv preprint arXiv:1803.05355*.

James Thorne, Andreas Vlachos, Oana Cocarascu, Christos Christodoulopoulos, and Arpit Mittal. 2018b. The fact extraction and verification (fever) shared task. *arXiv preprint arXiv:1811.10971*.

Hugo Touvron, Louis Martin, Kevin Stone, Peter Albert, Amjad Almahairi, Yasmine Babaei, Nikolay Bashlykov, Soumya Batra, Prajjwal Bhargava, Shruti Bhosale, et al. 2023. Llama 2: Open foundation and fine-tuned chat models. *arXiv preprint arXiv:2307.09288*.

Mykola Trokhymovych, Muniza Aslam, Ai-Jou Chou, Ricardo Baeza-Yates, and Diego Saez-Trumper. 2023. Fair multilingual vandalism detection system for wikipedia. In *Proceedings of the 29th ACM SIGKDD Conference on Knowledge Discovery and Data Mining*, pages 4981–4990.

Mykola Trokhymovych, Indira Sen, and Martin Gerlach. 2024. An open multilingual system for scoring readability of wikipedia. *arXiv preprint arXiv:2406.01835*.

Vladimir Vapnik. 2013. *The nature of statistical learning theory*. Springer science & business media.

Nguyen Vo and Kyumin Lee. 2020. Where are the facts? searching for fact-checked information to alleviate the spread of fake news. *arXiv preprint arXiv:2010.03159*.

William Yang Wang. 2017. " liar, liar pants on fire": A new benchmark dataset for fake news detection. *arXiv preprint arXiv:1705.00648*.

William Yang Wang and Kathleen McKeown. 2010. "got you!": Automatic vandalism detection in Wikipedia with web-based shallow syntactic-semantic modeling. In *Proceedings of the 23rd International Conference on Computational Linguistics (Coling 2010)*, pages 1146–1154, Beijing, China. Coling 2010 Organizing Committee.

Stanisław Węglarczyk. 2018. Kernel density estimation and its application. In *ITM web of conferences*, volume 23, page 00037. EDP Sciences.

KayYen Wong, Miriam Redi, and Diego Saez-Trumper. 2021. Wiki-reliability: A large scale dataset for content reliability on wikipedia. In *Proceedings of the 44th International ACM SIGIR Conference on Research and Development in Information Retrieval*, SIGIR '21, page 2437–2442, New York, NY, USA. Association for Computing Machinery.

Qinyi Wu, Danesh Irani, Calton Pu, and Lakshmish Ramaswamy. 2010. Elusive vandalism detection in wikipedia: a text stability-based approach. In *Proceedings of the 19th ACM International Conference on Information and Knowledge Management*, CIKM '10, page 1797–1800, New York, NY, USA. Association for Computing Machinery.

Shuhan Yuan, Panpan Zheng, Xintao Wu, and Yang Xiang. 2017. Wikipedia vandal early detection: from user behavior to user embedding. In *Machine Learning and Knowledge Discovery in Databases: European Conference, ECML PKDD 2017, Skopje, Macedonia, September 18–22, 2017, Proceedings, Part I 17*, pages 832–846. Springer.

Honglei Zeng, Maher A. Alhossaini, Li Ding, Richard Fikes, and Deborah L. McGuinness. 2006. Computing trust from revision history. In *Proceedings of the 2006 International Conference on Privacy, Security and Trust: Bridge the Gap Between PST Technologies and Business Services*, PST '06, New York, NY, USA. Association for Computing Machinery.

Arkaitz Zubiaga, Ahmet Aker, Kalina Bontcheva, Maria Liakata, and Rob Procter. 2018. Detection and resolution of rumours in social media: A survey. *ACM Comput. Surv.*, 51(2).

A Dataset Details

We release our dataset in 3 settings as mentioned in Section 4.2. The settings with data splits and their corresponding sizes are mentioned in Table 8.

			Number of Instances		
Dataset Setting	Dataset Type	Split	Non-hoax	Hoax	Total
1Hoax2legitimate	Definition	Train	426	206	632
		Test	179	93	272
1Hoax2legitimate	Full Text	Train	456	232	688
		Test	200	96	296
1Hoax10legitimate	Definition	Train	2,225	203	2,428
		Test	940	104	1,044
1Hoax10legitimate	Full Text	Train	2,306	218	2,524
		Test	973	110	1,083
1Hoax100legitimate	Definition	Train	20,419	217	20,636
		Test	8,761	82	8,843
1Hoax100legitimate	Full Text	Train	22,274	222	22,496
		Test	9,534	106	9,640

Table 8: Dataset details in definition-only and fulltext settings with number of hoax and legitimate article splits.

B Language Model Training Details

We train our Language Models with the configuration given below. We use one NVIDIA RTX4090 to train the LMs, one NVIDIA V100 and one NVIDIA A100 GPU to train the LLMs.

- Learning rate: 2e-06
- Batch size: 4 (for Fulltext experiments) and 8 (For Definition experiments)
- Epochs: 30
- Loss Function: Weighted Cross Entropy Loss
- Gradient Accumulation Steps: 4
- Warm-up steps: 100

C Prompt for LLM in-context learning

The instruction prompt used for LLMs in their in-context learning with examples for few shot experiment are given below.

You are a helpful knowledge management expert and excel at identifying whether an input Wikipedia article is a hoax or not. Wikipedia defines a hoax as 'a deliberately fabricated falsehood made to masquerade as truth'. You take an Wikipedia article as input and return with the label citing hoax(Label 1) or real(Label 0) based only on the text of the article. Given an article from Wikipedia, your task is to analyze the article text to identify if the article is hoax or real. The Hoax and real articles are defined as follows:

- Hoax: An article that is deliberately fabricated falsehood made to masquerade as truth.
- Real: An article which contains information about an existing entity and are not fabricated.

Your output should be a JSON dictionary with label that you found. Here are the possible labels with what they mean:

- 0 : The article is real article.
- 1 : The article is a hoax article.

Your input will be in the following format:
INPUT: { Text: <Article text> }
OUTPUT: { Label: <One of the label from the possible labels: 0 and 1, where 0 is real article and 1 is hoax article.> }
Please respond with only the JSON dictionary containing label. You are instructed strictly to return output only in the format given above, nothing else. No yapping.

Here are the examples used in few-shot experiments.

Example 1:

INPUT:

```
{ Text:  Albion Dauti (born May
31, 1995 in Caracas, Venezuela) is
a Venezuelan telenovela actor and
presenter.  Albion Dauti was born
in Caracas, Venezuela. He studied
acting at the Faculty of Arts in
Caracas. In 2010 he started working
as a presenter in Venevision. }
```

OUTPUT:

```
{ Label: 1 }
```

Example 2:

INPUT:

```
{ Text: Michelle Madhok (born May
26, 1971) is the Founder and CEO of
White Cat Media Inc. - DBA SheFinds
Media, parent company of online
shopping publication SheFinds. com
and MomFinds.  com.  She writes
a weekly style column for New
York's Metro newspaper and appears
regularly on Fox News Channel, The
Today Show, and The Tyra Banks Show.
}
```

OUTPUT:

```
{ Label: 0 }
```

D Vocabulary creation for revision history classification

We generate the vocabulary for timeline via the following process.

1. We extract the revision history of each article and convert the all the timestamps to standardized date-time format.
2. Group the timestamps by month and year (MM-YYYY). We call this Binning.
3. Count the number of revisions for each bin.
4. Return a dictionary of month-year bins and their corresponding counts.

The Rise of AI-Generated Content in Wikipedia

Creston Brooks **Samuel Eggert** **Denis Peskoff**
Princeton University
{cabrooks, sameggert, dp2896}@princeton.edu

Abstract

The rise of AI-generated content in popular information sources raises significant concerns about accountability, accuracy, and bias amplification. Beyond directly impacting consumers, the widespread presence of this content poses questions for the long-term viability of training language models on vast internet sweeps. We use `GPTZero`, a proprietary AI detector, and `Binoculars`, an open-source alternative, to establish lower bounds on the presence of AI-generated content in recently created Wikipedia pages. Both detectors reveal a marked increase in AI-generated content in recent pages compared to those from before the release of GPT-3.5. With thresholds calibrated to achieve a 1% false positive rate on pre-GPT-3.5 articles, detectors flag over 5% of newly created English Wikipedia articles as AI-generated, with lower percentages for German, French, and Italian articles. Flagged Wikipedia articles are typically of lower quality and are often self-promotional or partial towards a specific viewpoint on controversial topics.

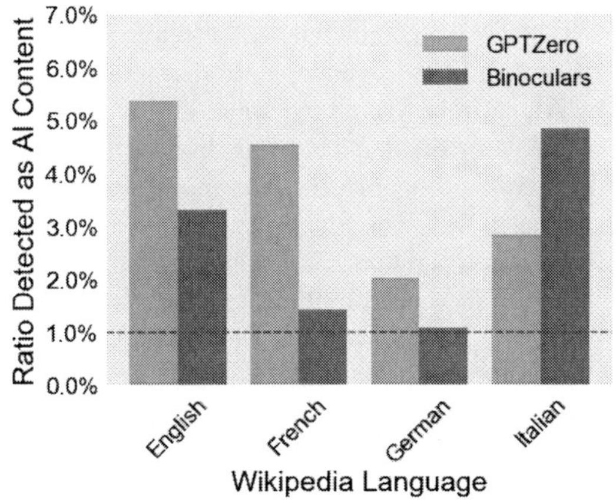

Figure 1: Using two tools, `GPTZero` and `Binoculars`, we detect that as many as 5% of 2,909 English Wikipedia articles created in August 2024 contain significant AI-generated content. The classification thresholds of both tools were calibrated to maintain a FPR of no more than 1% on a pre-GPT-3.5 Wikipedia baseline, as indicated by the red line.

1 AI-Generated Content

As Large Language Models (LLMs) have become increasingly advanced and more accessible, the risks of convincingly generated text grow in tandem with the benefits. While benefits include easier communication through machine translation, increased productivity, and new pedagogical opportunities, risks include the increased scale of disinformation and misinformation (Goldstein et al., 2023). Unchecked resampling of AI-generated data for training can even, in extreme cases, cripple model performance (Shumailov et al., 2024). Risks can be mitigated, however, to the extent that AI-generated data can be detected reliably at scale.

With the rapid release of generative LLMs, AI detection has been developing in parallel (Tang et al., 2024). Individuals (Ferrara, 2024), educators (Baidoo-Anu and Ansah, 2023; Khalil and Er, 2023), companies (Jabeur et al., 2023; Adelani et al., 2020), and governments (Androutsopoulou et al., 2019) seek reliable ways of validating that content has been generated by human authors rather than machines. Nonetheless, evaluating AI detectors across diverse contexts (e.g., length, domain, and level of integration with human writing) remains challenging (Bao et al., 2023; Sadasivan et al., 2023; Liang et al., 2023; Wang et al., 2024).

Wikipedia is a longstanding, publicly-curated reference source for an expansive and ever-growing set of topics. In the era of LLMs, it has become a standard source of training data due to its breadth of information, standards of curation, and flexible licensing. Therefore, it is an important testing ground for the proliferation of AI-generated content. We collect Wikipedia pages created in August 2024 and use a previously curated dataset of pages created prior to March 2022 as a pre-GPT-3.5 base-

Proceedings of the First Workshop on Advancing Natural Language Processing for Wikipedia, pages 67–79
November 16, 2024 ©2024 Association for Computational Linguistics

line for our experiments (Section 3).[1] We detect a noticeable increase in AI-generated content in the 2024 data and qualitatively assess flagged articles (Section 5). We compare these findings with preliminary experiments conducted on other contemporary sources (Section 6) and comment on the implications of AI-generated content (Section 7).

2 Detection Tools

We use two prominent detection tools which were suitably scalable for our study. `GPTZero` (Tian and Cui, 2023) is a commercial AI detector that reports the probabilities that an input text is entirely written by AI, entirely written by humans, or written by a combination of AI and humans. In our experiments we use the probability that an input text is entirely written by AI. The black-box nature of the tool limits any insight into its methodology.

An open-source method, `Binoculars` (Hans et al., 2024) uses two separate LLMs $\mathcal{M}_1$ $\mathcal{M}_2$ to score a text s for AI-likelihood by normalizing perplexity by a quantity termed cross-perplexity, which computes the average cross-entropy between the outputs of two models over a span of tokens:

$$B_{\mathcal{M}_1,\mathcal{M}_2}(s) = \frac{\log \text{PPL}_{\mathcal{M}_1}(s)}{\log \text{X-PPL}_{\mathcal{M}_1,\mathcal{M}_2}(s)}$$

The input text is classified as AI-generated if the score is lower than a determined threshold, calibrated according to a desired false positive rate (FPR). For our experiments, we use Falcon-7b and Falcon-7b-instruct (Almazrouei et al., 2023) to calculate cross-perplexity, following Hans et al. (2024) who report it as the best pair of LLMs for detection. Compared to competing open-source detectors, `Binoculars` reports superior performance across various domains including Wikipedia (Hans et al., 2024).

3 Wikipedia Data Sources

Wikipedia provides an accessible list of articles created within the past month for supported languages. We use the *New Pages* feature to collect articles created in August 2024 in English, French, German, and Italian (Table 2). These languages were also available in a set of Wikipedia pages collected before March 2022.[2]

[1] Our data collection and evaluation code is available at `github.com/brooksca3/wiki_collection`.

[2] `https://huggingface.co/datasets/legacy-datasets/wikipedia`

Although GPT-3 was released in June 2020, the significant public uptake in generating text with LLMs occurred in March 2022 with the release of GPT-3.5 and exploded with ChatGPT in November 2022 (Wu et al., 2023). Thus, the dataset of articles created prior to March 2022 allows us to establish a FPR for the tools in detecting AI-generated content post-GPT-3.5.

Language	**Pre-March 2022**	**August 2024**
English	2965	2909
German	4399	3907
Italian	2306	3003
French	4351	3138

Table 1: Number of Wikipedia pages collected for each language before March 2022 and in August 2024 after removing articles containing fewer than 100 words. We take random subsets of our data pools to stay within budget constraints.

4 Detection as a Lower Bound

Following Latona et al.'s (2024) approach for measuring AI content in conference reviews, we estimate a lower bound for AI-generated articles by subtracting the percentage of pre-March 2022 articles classified as AI by a given tool from the percentage of August 2024 articles classified as AI. As we do not have ground-truth examples of AI-generated articles, we do not attempt to estimate the false negative rate (FNR). Doing so would require creating artificial positive examples by simulating the various ways Wikipedia authors might use LLMs to assist in writing—taking into account different models, prompts, and the extent of human integration, among other factors.

Although we cannot speculate on how `GPTZero` scores text, Falcon models are trained on Wikipedia data (Almazrouei et al., 2023), and `Binoculars` is known to assign false positives to text in its models' training data (Hans et al., 2024). Additionally, the tools we use are primarily for detecting AI-generated content in English. While `GPTZero` supports Spanish and French, it is not designed for other languages (GPTZero, 2024), and using it out-of-domain may increase FNRs. For non-English texts, `Binoculars` reports similar FPRs but higher FNRs (Hans et al., 2024). The higher the FNRs, the more AI-generated articles slip past the detectors. Therefore, while the numbers we report represent a lower bound, the actual amount of AI-generated content could be substantially higher.

Language	Footnotes per Sentence		Outgoing Links per Word	
	AI-Detected Articles	All New Articles	AI-Detected Articles	All New Articles
English	0.667	**0.972**	0.383	**1.77**
French	0.370	**0.441**	0.474	**1.58**
German	0.180	**0.211**	0.382	**0.754**
Italian	**0.549**	0.501	1.16	**1.64**

Table 2: Mean values for footnotes per sentence and outgoing links per word in all articles created in August 2024, as well as those detected as AI-generated by either `GPTZero` or `Binoculars`, with thresholds set to induce a 1% FPR for each tool. The number of AI articles are 207, 174, 249, and 206 for English, French, German, and Italian.

Our methodology assumes that the pre-March 2022 and August 2024 data distributions are comparable, with increased AI use being the primary factor affecting detection. One concern is that pre-March 2022 pages may be more polished due to years of editing. However, we observe that a higher number of edits weakly correlates with a higher AI-detection score for pre-March 2022 articles (Appendix D), suggesting that the FPRs for those articles may even be inflated. While the base assumption cannot be watertight, we observe a relatively consistent distribution of page categories between the two data pools, and we rely on the consistency of our chosen tools' reported FPRs.

5 Trends in Pages Flagged for AI

As seen in Figure 1, we estimate that 4.36% of 2,909 English Wikipedia articles created in August 2024 contain significant AI-generated content.[3] We set the classification thresholds of both tools to induce a detection rate of no more than 1% on pre-March 2022 articles. With these thresholds, `GPTZero` classifies 156 English articles as AI-generated, and `Binoculars` classifies 96. Among these, there is an overlap of 45 articles classified as AI independently by the two tools. Notably, there is no overlap between the 39 and 31 pre-March 2022 English articles flagged as AI-generated by the tools. Hence, there is a strong shared signal in assumed true positives but tool-specific noise in false positives.

The quality of articles detected as AI-generated is generally lower on at least two axes. Table 2 shows how, compared to all articles created in August 2024, AI-generated ones use fewer references and are less integrated into the Wikipedia nexus.[4]

[3] 5.36% detection rate with 1% FPR.

[4] We normalize by sentence and word count to remove length as a confounding factor, since longer articles may have more footnotes and links without being higher quality.

5.1 Manual Inspection

We inspect each of the 45 English articles flagged as AI-generated by both `GPTZero` and `Binoculars` by examining their edit histories and the activity logs of their creators to better understand the motivations for using LLMs to create Wikipedia pages. We observe that several of the 45 pages are authored by the same individuals, which is unsurprising, as users who use AI in one article are likely to use it in others. Most of the 45 pages are flagged by moderators and bots with some warning, e.g., "*This article does not cite any sources. Please help improve this article by adding citations to reliable sources*" or even "*This article may incorporate text from a large language model.*" We observe distinct trends after inspecting the user and page histories.

5.2 Advertisement

One prominent motive is self-promotion. Of the 45 flagged pages, we identify eight that were created to promote organizations such as small businesses, restaurants, or websites. These pages are often the first to be created by their respective users and typically lack any citations beyond links to the entity being promoted. One page links to a personal YouTube video promoting a winery with fewer than 100 views. Another describes an estate in the United Kingdom, claiming it has formerly had notable residents. This is subsequently deleted by a moderator who notes:

> "*Reference links are all dead apart from one for the town council, which makes no mention of the estate. One link is actually labelled 'fictional'... Article reads like an advert for the house, which is coincidentally up for sale at the moment.*"

Other self-promoting pages are deleted by moderators who remark: "*unambiguous advertising which only promotes a company, group, product, service, person, or point of view.*"

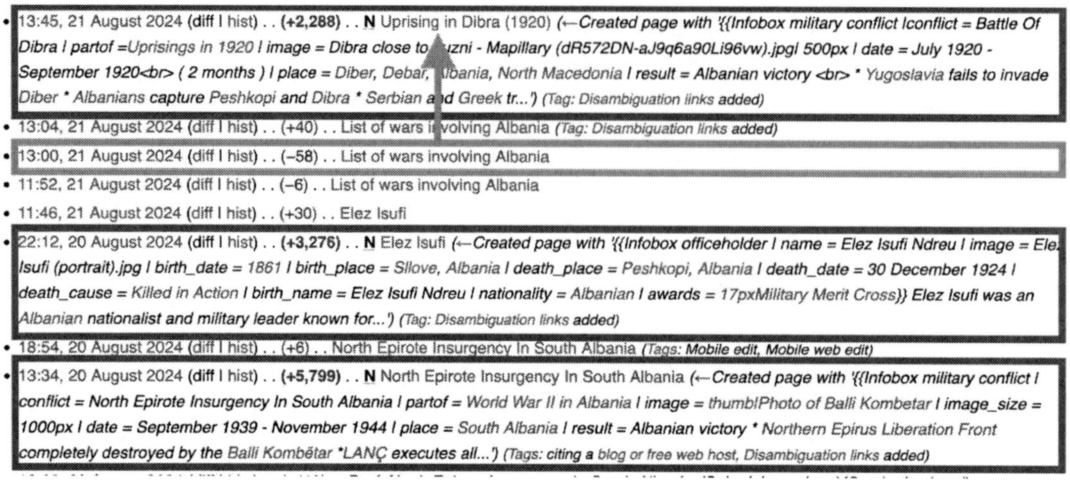

Figure 2: The activity of this user, who was flagged for instigating an 'Edit War,' reveals that within a single day, they created three articles (red border), all identified as AI-generated. Notably, at 13:00 (green border), the user edited the outcome of 'War in Dibra' from *'Mixed Results'* to *'Victory'* and removed key text, just an hour before creating a new page titled 'Uprising in Dibra.' That page (see Figure 3) has since been deleted by moderators.

5.3 Pages Pushing Polarization

While the immediate beneficiaries of advertisement are obvious, we also identify pages that advocate a particular viewpoint on often polarizing political topics. We identify eight such pages out of the flagged 45. One user created five articles on English Wikipedia, detected by both tools as AI-generated, on contentious moments in Albanian history. The same user's profile garnered a warning from Wikipedia for engaging in an 'Edit War' with other users (Figure 2). The user changed outcomes of an Albanian conflict from *'Mixed Results'* to *'Victory'* and deleted supporting text, before using AI to generate an entirely new page on said conflict. The Wikimedia community has since removed the flagged pages and banned the user in question for sockpuppetry.[5] In other cases, users created articles ostensibly on one topic, such as types of weapons or political movements, but dedicated the majority of the pages' content to discussing specific political figures. We find two such articles that espouse non-neutral views on JD Vance and Volodymyr Zelensky.

5.4 Machine Translation

AI detection tools can flag instances of machine translation. We find three cases where users explicitly documented their work as translations, including pages on Portuguese history and legal cases in Ghana. Outside of the 45 articles flagged by both tools, we identify a top contributor of Italian Wikipedia who created 57 articles flagged as AI-generated by `Binoculars`, but not by `GPTZero`.[6] This user notes in their sandbox that they translated these articles from French Wikipedia, a common practice in the Wikimedia editor community (Zhu and Walker, 2024).

Despite producing fluent and accurate translations, state-of-the-art LLMs still introduce observable biases (Hendy et al., 2023). Even beyond these biases, machine translation complicates the process of vetting pages flagged for AI content: an AI-generated article in one language can be translated and propagated into other languages. For example, Wikipedia communities like Cebuano and Swedish contain millions of pages made through automatic methods (Alshahrani et al., 2023).

5.5 Writing Tool

Other pages, which are often well-structured with high-quality citations, seem to have been written by users who are knowledgeable in certain niches and are employing an LLM as a writing tool. Several of the flagged pages are created by users who churn out dozens of articles within specific categories, including snake breeds, types of fungi, Indian cuisine, and American football players. One flagged page points us to a user who seemingly uses AI to cre-

[5] Sockpuppetry is the practice of using multiple accounts to mislead other editors (Solorio et al., 2013).

[6] These 57 translated pages are the reason `Binoculars` has a higher detection rate than `GPTZero` for Italian in Figure 1.

ate chapter-by-chapter books summaries. Another page details an ongoing criminal case in India and is flagged by moderators with a warning reminding editors to treat subjects as innocent until proven guilty.

6 Detection Beyond Wikipedia

Wikipedia has a distinct genre and brand of contributor. To contextualize our findings and motivate further research, we conduct a preliminary investigation into two other genres—comment-section debates and press releases—on platforms where contributors may have different motivations for using generative AI compared to those on Wikipedia. We hope this encourages closer examination of AI-generated content across different domains with varying contributor incentives.[7]

6.1 Reddit

Comments on contentious subreddits—Israel-Palestine, public opinion on Democrats, public opinion on Republicans—are updated daily on Kaggle, a popular data science platform. We randomly sample 3,000 user comments from 2024 containing at least 100 words.

Less than 1% of the collected comments receive a `GPTZero` score above 0.5, which may mean (1) few are AI-generated, (2) such content is censored or (3) AI presence is difficult for detectors to discern in this domain. Despite being rare, some comments flagged as AI-generated are potentially worrisome: one urges others how to vote in an upcoming election (Appendix B).

6.2 Press Releases

The United Nations "remains the one place on Earth where all the world's nations can gather together, discuss common problems, and find shared solutions that benefit all of humanity".[8] Country teams of the United Nations provide frequent updates about developments in that country. We collect 8,326 press releases across 60 country teams from the United Nations from 2013 to 2024; country teams have websites in the format of https://{country}.un.org.[9]

As many as 20% of press releases published in 2024 received a `GPTZero` AI-generation score of at least 0.5, compared to 12.5% in 2023, 1.6% in 2022, and less than 1% in all years prior.[10] The marked increase in UN press releases flagged as AI may stem from translations into English, although the individuals named as authors of the articles often hold degrees from institutions in English-speaking countries. We include three examples of flagged press releases in Appendix C.

7 Implications and Conclusion

Not all AI-generated text is nefarious. If a human authors the primary content and approves an AI-generated summary or translation, AI may be considered a writing aide. Shao et al. (2024) have even designed a retrieval-based LLM workflow for writing Wikipedia-like articles and gathered perspectives from experienced Wikipedia editors on using it—the editors unanimously agreed that it would be helpful in their pre-writing stage. Moreover, LLM-enabled translation can reduce language barriers in domains of information sharing (Katsnelson, 2022; Berdejo-Espinola and Amano, 2023).

However, the increasing ease with which it is possible to generate content at scale to overrepresent a particular perspective has predictable and dangerous consequences. People are more likely to believe statements that are frequently repeated, since familiarity is easily confused with validity (Hasher et al., 1977; Unkelbach et al., 2019). Consumer confidence is a key determiner of economic strength, and confidence in the economy is based in part on how strong individuals perceive others' confidence to be. To the extent that AI-generated outputs show less variability than human-generated texts, we can expect peaks of polarization to continue to increase (Bail et al., 2018; Heltzel and Laurin, 2020), undermining the useful wisdom of crowds (Surowiecki, 2005; Bender et al., 2021).

Continued work is needed to understand differences in LLMs and human speech and the implications of widespread AI-generated data (Guo et al., 2023; Sadasivan et al., 2023; Liang et al., 2024). The motives to discreetly propagate AI-generated text online vary across platforms, and measuring the prevalence of AI-generated content is a necessary step in understanding these motives.

[7] Full details about the sources we evaluated and instructions for replicating the evaluation are available at our repository: `github.com/brooksca3/wiki_collection`.

[8] `https://www.un.org/`

[9] Due to licensing uncertainties, we do not release the press releases; however, we release the scripts used to collect them.

[10] 90/447 press releases from 2024 are flagged, 170/1360 from 2023, and 20/1268 from 2022.

Limitations

The proprietary nature of `GPTZero` makes experiments costly to run ($1000 for our study). `Binoculars` requires non-trivial RAM and compute to run at scale. These factors bound the scale of the study we are able to conduct and limit our ability to draw generalizable conclusions. We hope that future efforts can replicate this work at a larger scale and across more domains.

Future work should also consider a broader suite of AI detectors. We considered two other open-source AI detection tools but did not use them. `Ghostbuster` (Verma et al., 2024) requires training on specific LLM features and `Fast-DetectGPT` (Bao et al., 2023) reports lower true positive rates than `Binoculars` across all domains considered.

Moreover, we focus on English and other high resource languages given their availability in the sources we consider. In the multilingual setting, Liang et al. (2023) detect bias in AI detectors against non-native speakers, Wang et al. (2024) create a multilingual dataset to study detection, and Ignat et al. (2024) study multilingual detection in the context of hotel reviews.

Ethical Considerations

Detecting AI may have unexpected negative consequences for people implicated as having generated that text. We have therefore been encouraged to omit any identifying information in the specific pages we discuss; however, we will provide more specific data to researchers upon request provided that it not be disseminated further.

We are relying on public internet content. All sources that we investigate are public-facing in nature. The Wikipedia data we collect is under a Creative Commons CC0 License. The Reddit data is distributed through Kaggle under a Open Data Commons Attribution License (ODC-By) v1.0. There is no clear license for United Nations country teams. Individual use *and* download of the data is explicitly permitted by the parent organization.

Acknowledgements

We thank Adele Goldberg for funding support along with Brandon Stewart, Preeti Chemiti, and Rob Voigt for valuable feedback and advice. We are grateful to the Princeton Language and Intelligence (PLI) for providing computational resources. Peskoff is supported by the National Science Foundation under Grant #2127309 to the Computing Research Association for the CIFellows 2021 Project.

References

David Ifeoluwa Adelani, Haotian Mai, Fuming Fang, Huy H Nguyen, Junichi Yamagishi, and Isao Echizen. 2020. Generating sentiment-preserving fake online reviews using neural language models and their human-and machine-based detection. In *Advanced information networking and applications: Proceedings of the 34th international conference on advanced information networking and applications (AINA-2020)*, pages 1341–1354. Springer.

Ebtesam Almazrouei, Hamza Alobeidli, Abdulaziz Alshamsi, Alessandro Cappelli, Ruxandra Cojocaru, Merouane Debbah, Etienne Goffinet, Daniel Heslow, Julien Launay, Quentin Malartic, et al. 2023. Falcon-40b: an open large language model with state-of-the-art performance. 2023. *URL https://falconllm. tii. ae.*

Saied Alshahrani, Norah Alshahrani, and Jeanna Matthews. 2023. Depth+: An enhanced depth metric for wikipedia corpora quality. In *Proceedings of the 3rd Workshop on Trustworthy Natural Language Processing (TrustNLP 2023)*, pages 175–189.

Aggeliki Androutsopoulou, Nikos Karacapilidis, Euripidis Loukis, and Yannis Charalabidis. 2019. Transforming the communication between citizens and government through ai-guided chatbots. *Government information quarterly*, 36(2):358–367.

David Baidoo-Anu and Leticia Owusu Ansah. 2023. Education in the era of generative artificial intelligence (ai): Understanding the potential benefits of chatgpt in promoting teaching and learning. *Journal of AI*, 7(1):52–62.

Christopher A Bail, Lisa P Argyle, Taylor W Brown, John P Bumpus, Haohan Chen, MB Fallin Hunzaker, Jaemin Lee, Marcus Mann, Friedolin Merhout, and Alexander Volfovsky. 2018. Exposure to opposing views on social media can increase political polarization. *Proceedings of the National Academy of Sciences*, 115(37):9216–9221.

Guangsheng Bao, Yanbin Zhao, Zhiyang Teng, Linyi Yang, and Yue Zhang. 2023. Fast-detectgpt: Efficient zero-shot detection of machine-generated text via conditional probability curvature. *arXiv preprint arXiv:2310.05130*.

Emily M Bender, Timnit Gebru, Angelina McMillan-Major, and Shmargaret Shmitchell. 2021. On the dangers of stochastic parrots: Can language models be too big? In *Proceedings of the 2021 ACM conference on fairness, accountability, and transparency*, pages 610–623.

Violeta Berdejo-Espinola and Tatsuya Amano. 2023. Ai tools can improve equity in science. *Science*, 379(6636):991–991.

Emilio Ferrara. 2024. Genai against humanity: Nefarious applications of generative artificial intelligence and large language models. *Journal of Computational Social Science*, pages 1–21.

Josh A Goldstein, Girish Sastry, Micah Musser, Renee DiResta, Matthew Gentzel, and Katerina Sedova. 2023. Generative language models and automated influence operations: Emerging threats and potential mitigations. *arXiv preprint arXiv:2301.04246*.

GPTZero. 2024. Introducing gptzero's multilingual ai detection. `https://gptzero.me/news/multilingualdetection/`.

Biyang Guo, Xin Zhang, Ziyuan Wang, Minqi Jiang, Jinran Nie, Yuxuan Ding, Jianwei Yue, and Yupeng Wu. 2023. How close is chatgpt to human experts? comparison corpus, evaluation, and detection. *arXiv preprint arxiv:2301.07597*.

Abhimanyu Hans, Avi Schwarzschild, Valeriia Cherepanova, Hamid Kazemi, Aniruddha Saha, Micah Goldblum, Jonas Geiping, and Tom Goldstein. 2024. Spotting llms with binoculars: Zero-shot detection of machine-generated text. *Preprint*, arXiv:2401.12070.

L. Hasher, D. Goldstein, and T. Toppino. 1977. Frequency and the conference of referential validity. *Journal of Verbal Learning and Verbal Behavior*, 16:107–112.

Greg Heltzel and Kristin Laurin. 2020. Polarization in america: Two possible futures. *Current Opinion in Behavioral Sciences*, 34:179–184.

Amr Hendy, Mohamed Abdelrehim, Amr Sharaf, Vikas Raunak, Mohamed Gabr, Hitokazu Matsushita, Young Jin Kim, Mohamed Afify, and Hany Hassan Awadalla. 2023. How good are gpt models at machine translation? a comprehensive evaluation. *arXiv preprint arXiv:2302.09210*.

Oana Ignat, Xiaomeng Xu, and Rada Mihalcea. 2024. Maide-up: Multilingual deception detection of gpt-generated hotel reviews. *arXiv preprint arXiv:2404.12938*.

Sami Ben Jabeur, Hossein Ballouk, Wissal Ben Arfi, and Jean-Michel Sahut. 2023. Artificial intelligence applications in fake review detection: Bibliometric analysis and future avenues for research. *Journal of Business Research*, 158:113631.

Alla Katsnelson. 2022. Poor english skills? new ais help researchers to write better. *Nature*, 609(7925):208–209.

Mohammad Khalil and Erkan Er. 2023. Will chatgpt g et you caught? rethinking of plagiarism detection. In *International Conference on Human-Computer Interaction*, pages 475–487. Springer.

Giuseppe Russo Latona, Manoel Horta Ribeiro, Tim R. Davidson, Veniamin Veselovsky, and Robert West. 2024. The ai review lottery: Widespread ai-assisted peer reviews boost paper scores and acceptance rates. *ArXiv*, abs/2405.02150.

Weixin Liang, Mert Yuksekgonul, Yining Mao, Eric Wu, and James Zou. 2023. Gpt detectors are biased against non-native english writers. *Patterns*, 4(7):100779.

Weixin Liang, Yaohui Zhang, Zhengxuan Wu, Haley Lepp, Wenlong Ji, Xuandong Zhao, Hancheng Cao, Sheng Liu, Siyu He, Zhi Huang, et al. 2024. Mapping the increasing use of llms in scientific papers. *arXiv preprint arXiv:2404.01268*.

Vinu Sankar Sadasivan, Aounon Kumar, Sriram Balasubramanian, Wenxiao Wang, and Soheil Feizi. 2023. Can ai-generated text be reliably detected? *arXiv preprint arXiv:2303.11156*.

Yijia Shao, Yucheng Jiang, Theodore A Kanell, Peter Xu, Omar Khattab, and Monica S Lam. 2024. Assisting in writing wikipedia-like articles from scratch with large language models. *arXiv preprint arXiv:2402.14207*.

Ilia Shumailov, Zakhar Shumaylov, Yiren Zhao, Nicolas Papernot, Ross Anderson, and Yarin Gal. 2024. Ai models collapse when trained on recursively generated data. *Nature*, 631(8022):755–759.

Thamar Solorio, Ragib Hasan, and Mainul Mizan. 2013. A case study of sockpuppet detection in wikipedia. In *Proceedings of the Workshop on Language Analysis in Social Media*, pages 59–68.

James Surowiecki. 2005. *The Wisdom of Crowds*. Anchor.

Ruixiang Tang, Yu-Neng Chuang, and Xia Hu. 2024. The science of detecting llm-generated text. *Communications of the ACM*, 67(4):50–59.

Edward Tian and Alexander Cui. 2023. Gptzero: Towards detection of ai-generated text using zero-shot and supervised methods".

C. Unkelbach, A. Koch, R. R. Silva, and T. Garcia-Marques. 2019. Truth by repetition: Explanations and implications. *Current Directions in Psychological Science*, 28(3):247–253.

Vivek Verma, Eve Fleisig, Nicholas Tomlin, and Dan Klein. 2024. Ghostbuster: Detecting text ghostwritten by large language models. In *Proceedings of the 2024 Conference of the North American Chapter of the Association for Computational Linguistics: Human Language Technologies*.

Yuxia Wang, Jonibek Mansurov, Petar Ivanov, Jinyan Su, Artem Shelmanov, Akim Tsvigun, Chenxi Whitehouse, Osama Mohammed Afzal, Tarek Mahmoud, Toru Sasaki, Thomas Arnold, Alham Aji, Nizar Habash, Iryna Gurevych, and Preslav Nakov. 2024.

M4: Multi-generator, multi-domain, and multi-lingual black-box machine-generated text detection. In *Proceedings of the 18th Conference of the European Chapter of the Association for Computational Linguistics (Volume 1: Long Papers)*, pages 1369–1407, St. Julian's, Malta. Association for Computational Linguistics.

Tianyu Wu, Shizhu He, Jingping Liu, Siqi Sun, Kang Liu, Qing-Long Han, and Yang Tang. 2023. A brief overview of chatgpt: The history, status quo and potential future development. *IEEE/CAA Journal of Automatica Sinica*, 10(5):1122–1136.

Kai Zhu and Dylan Walker. 2024. The promise and pitfalls of ai technology in bridging digital language divide: Insights from machine translation on wikipedia. *SSRN*.

Appendix

A (Deleted) Wikipedia Page Classified as AI-Generated

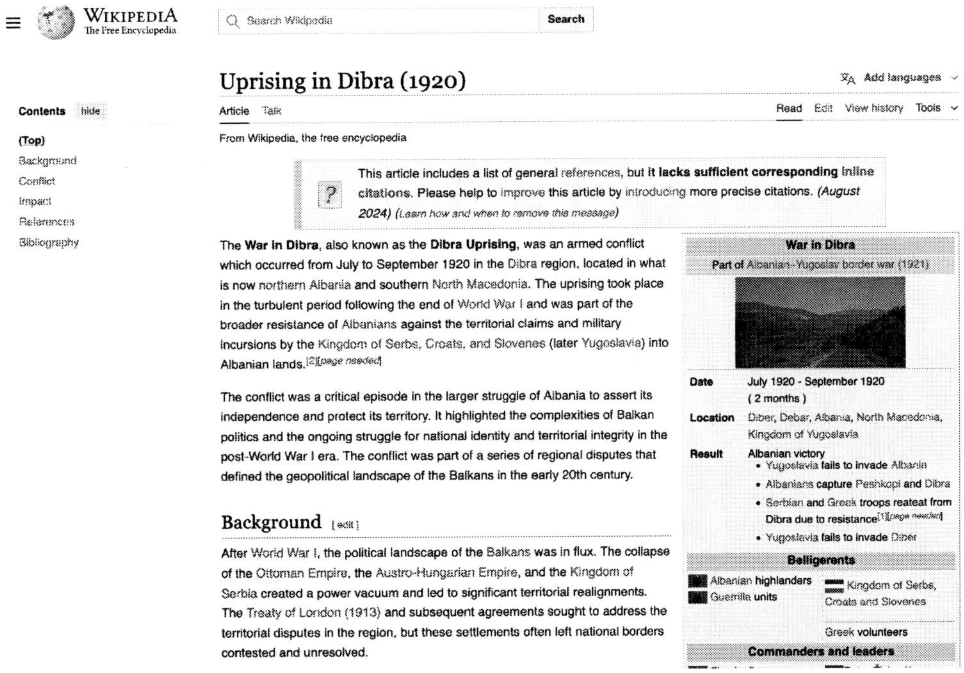

Figure 3: Wikipedia page flagged as AI-generated and deleted by moderators.

B Reddit Post Classified as AI-Generated

The following comment encouraging Americans to vote for a third-party candidate was flagged as AI.

> *While the acknowledgment of the symbolic rejection of the two-party system is understood, the contention here lies in the practical consequences of a third-party vote. It's crucial to recognize that the call for voting third party isn't solely symbolic but a strategic push for a more diverse political landscape over time. The argument asserts that voting for anyone other than Biden increases Trump's chance of victory. However, this perspective assumes a binary outcome, overlooking the potential long-term impact of promoting alternative voices. A shift toward a multi-party system is a gradual process, and fostering this change requires voters to make choices aligned with their principles. Moreover, characterizing the choice between a "bland moderate Democrat" and an "extremely corrupt, authoritarian Republican" as high stakes underscores the need for broader political options. Supporting third parties now can pave the way for a more representative democracy in the future, where voters aren't limited to perceived lesser evils. While the current election might seem high-stakes, it's crucial to consider the long-term goal of breaking the duopoly for a healthier democracy. Third-party votes, rather than being mere protests, can be strategic steps toward that transformative change.*

C Examples of UN Press Releases Classified as AI-Generated

In this section, we present three examples of UN press releases flagged by our tools as likely AI-generated. We re-emphasize that AI detection can produce false positives, and no individual classification should be considered definitive.

C.1 UN Belize Press Release

The United Nations in Belize expresses its deep concern over the recent tragic incidents that have claimed the lives of women and children both in their homes and public spaces

```
https://belize.un.org/en/263463-united-nations-belize-expresses-its-deep-concern
-over-recent-tragic-incidents-have-claimed
```

```
The United Nations in Belize expresses its deep concern over the recent tragic
incidents that have claimed the lives of women and children both in their homes
and public spaces. The right to life is fundamental and should be expected and
respected by all in Belize. We offer our condolences to families affected by these
recent tragic cases of domestic and gender-based violence and commit to continue
supporting the Government and people of Belize in the pursuit of freedom from
violence. We all collectively have a role to play in ensuring that Belize remains
a safe, secure, and inclusive society for everyone. The United Nations works to
support Belize's commitment to eliminate all forms of violence especially against
women and girls making the recent events even more distressing. The United Nations
is fully committed to support the Government of Belize and civil society in concrete
actions to realize the rights of all women and children, allowing them to live
lives free of violence including preventive support and the attention of mental
health aspects and consequences of those affected.
```

Table 3: Press Release by the United Nations in Belize, 15 March 2024

C.2 (Abridged) UN Bangladesh Press

UNOPS' Roundtable Discussion on the 'Invest in Women: Accelerate Progress'

https://bangladesh.un.org/en/264789-unops-roundtable-discussion-%C2%A0%E2%80%98invest-%C2%A0women-accelerate-progress%E2%80%99

Dhaka, Bangladesh - UNOPS Bangladesh hosted the 9th episode of "SDG Café," a monthly roundtable discussion series dedicated to addressing pressing development challenges and co-creating innovative solutions.

As part of UNOPS's commitment to getting Agenda 2030 back on track, this episode places the spotlight on the Sustainable Development Goals (SDG 5), dedicated to advancing gender equality and empowering women in Bangladesh and beyond. This roundtable took place on March 21, 2024 with the theme, 'Invest in Women: Accelerate Progress'.

The session focused on highlighting the importance of investing in women to foster inclusive and sustainable economic growth, in line with SDG 5. Addressing the enduring gender disparities in investment, especially in developing nations, the talks revolved around discussing obstacles, prospects, and inventive approaches to boost investment in businesses owned by women, elevate women into leadership positions, and advance initiatives supporting gender parity.

The highlight of the event was the keynote speeches delivered by esteemed personalities Rubana Huq, Vice-chancellor of Asian University for Women and Chairperson of Mohammadi Group, and Azmeri Haque Badhon, renowned Bangladeshi actress. Huq's address emphasized the urgency of accelerating investment in women, drawing from her extensive experience in academia and business leadership.

...

Table 4: Press Release by the United Nations in Bangladesh, 2 May 2024

C.3 (Abridged) UN Turkmenistan Press Release

Consultative meeting with national stakeholders on Advancing Cross-Border Paperless Trade in Turkmenistan

`https://turkmenistan.un.org/en/269295-consultative-meeting-national-stakeholders-advancing-cross-border-paperless-trade`

Turkmenistan, Ashgabat - The United Nations Resident Coordinator's Office (UN RCO) in Turkmenistan and the United Nations Economic and Social Commission for Asia and the Pacific (ESCAP) jointly organized a two-day workshop titled "Towards a National Strategy in Advancing Cross-Border Paperless Trade in Turkmenistan." The event, held on 20-21 May 2024 at the UN House in Ashgabat, brought together national stakeholders and development partners to discuss and strategize the implementation of cross-border paperless trade initiatives in Turkmenistan. The opening day of the workshop featured esteemed speakers including Ms. Rupa Chanda, Director of Trade, Investment and Innovation Division at ESCAP, Mr. Dmitry Shlapachenko, UN Resident Coordinator in Turkmenistan, and Mr. Myrat Myradov, Head of Legal Regulations and Coordination at the Foreign Economic Relations Department, Ministry of Trade and Foreign Economic Relations of Turkmenistan.

The first day's sessions included a comprehensive review of key initiatives by various ministries and agencies, aimed at enhancing trade facilitation in Turkmenistan. Development partners, Asian Development Bank, USAID, GIZ, International Trade Center, also presented their contributions in this domain, fostering a better understanding of the current trade facilitation landscape in the country...

The workshop concluded with a practical group exercise, followed by group presentations, and summarizing the outcomes and proposed strategies for advancing cross-border paperless trade in Turkmenistan. The event underscored Turkmenistan's commitment to embracing innovative solutions for trade facilitation and integration into the global digital economy. Turkmenistan joined the CPTA in May 2022 and has actively participated in its implementation. A readiness assessment was conducted, resulting in a study report published in December 2022.

Table 5: Press Release by the United Nations in Turkmenistan, 22 May 2024

D AI Detection Scores vs. Page Edits Across Languages

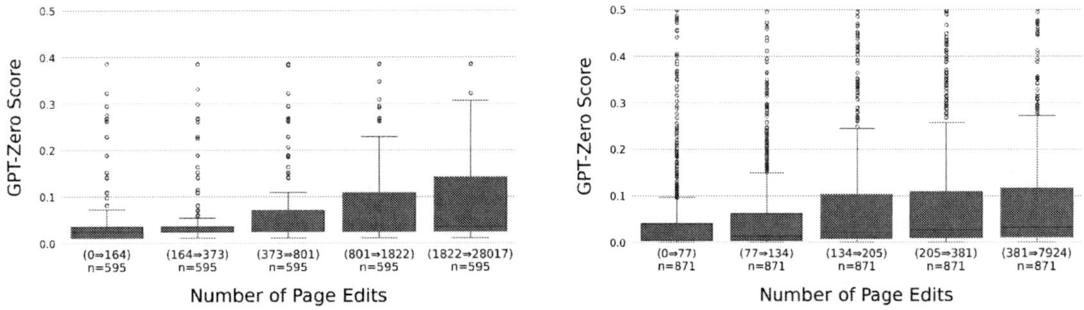

Figure 4: GPTZero scores compared to the number of page edits for English (left) and French (right) articles created before March 2022. Pages with more edits in English receive higher GPTZero scores.

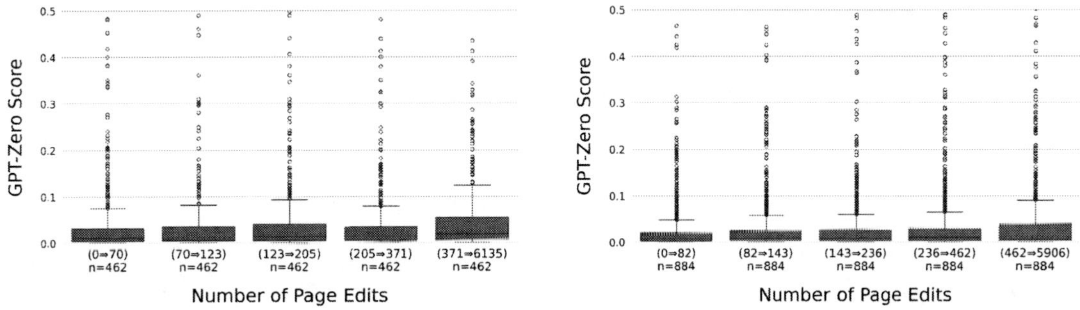

Figure 5: GPTZero scores compared to the number of page edits for Italian (left) and German (right) articles created before March 2022.

Embedded Topic Models Enhanced by Wikification

Takashi Shibuya **Takehito Utsuro**
Degree Programs in Systems and Information Engineering,
Graduate School of Science and Technology, University of Tsukuba
s2430171@_u.tsukuba.ac.jp utsuro@_iit.tsukuba.ac.jp

Abstract

Topic modeling analyzes a collection of documents to learn meaningful patterns of words. However, previous topic models consider only the spelling of words and do not take into consideration the homography of words. In this study, we incorporate the Wikipedia knowledge into a neural topic model to make it aware of named entities. We evaluate our method on two datasets, 1) news articles of *New York Times* and 2) the AIDA-CoNLL dataset. Our experiments show that our method improves the performance of neural topic models in generalizability. Moreover, we analyze frequent terms in each topic and the temporal dependencies between topics to demonstrate that our entity-aware topic models can capture the time-series development of topics well.

1 Introduction

Probabilistic topic models such as latent Dirichlet allocation (LDA) (Blei et al., 2003) and embedded topic model (ETM) (Dieng et al., 2020) have been utilized for analyzing a collection of documents and discovering the underlying semantic structure. Such topic models have also been extended to dynamic topic models (Blei and Lafferty, 2006; Hida et al., 2018; Dieng et al., 2019; Cvejoski et al., 2023), which can capture the chronological transition of topics, motivated by the fact that documents (such as magazines, academic journals, news articles, and social media content) feature trends and themes that change with time.

However, previous (dynamic) topic models consider only the spelling of words and do not take into consideration the homography of words such as "*apple*" and "*amazon*". We hypothesize that this unawareness of the word homography harms the performance of topic models because one meaning of a word will tend to be used in some specific topics but another meaning of the same spelled word will appear in other topics more frequently. For instance, the entity "Amazon.com" will tend to appear in business news or technology articles, whereas documents about the environment will discuss the entity "Amazon rainforest" more often than "Amazon.com". Although the word "*Amazon*" can thus refer to a different entity depending on a context, existing topic models are not aware of such homography of the word "*Amazon*" and regard the word as unique.

To address the above issue, we propose a method of analyzing a collection of documents based on entity knowledge on Wikipedia. Our proposed method relies on two technologies: 1) entity linking (wikification) and 2) entity embedding (Wikipedia2Vec (Yamada et al., 2020)). Entity linking (wikification) is a natural language processing technique that assigns an entity mention in a document to a specific entity in a target knowledge base (Wikipedia). For example, an entity linker can recognize which a word "apple" in a document means, "Apple Inc.", "Big Apple", or another. We adopt entity linking as a preprocessing of topic modeling. Next, we incorporate entity embeddings (vector representations of entities in a knowledge base) into a neural topic model according to the result of the entity linking. Previous neural topic models utilize only conventional word embeddings, which are unaware of the homography of words. On the other hand, our proposed method uses not only word embeddings but also entity embeddings, which enables neural topic models to distinguish between multiple entities that share their spelling. We hypothesize that our entity-aware method improves the performance of neural topic models. We empirically show the effectiveness of our method on two datasets: 1) a collection of news articles of *New York Times* published between 1996 and 2020 and 2) the AIDA-CoNLL dataset (Hoffart et al., 2011). We adopt two topic models, ETM and dynamic ETM (Dieng et al., 2019), as baselines and quantitatively show that entity linking

Proceedings of the First Workshop on Advancing Natural Language Processing for Wikipedia, pages 80–90
November 16, 2024

improves the performance of neural topic models. Furthermore, we demonstrate that topics and their temporal change extracted by trained dynamic topic models are reasonable by manually analyzing frequent terms of each topic. We summarize our contributions as follows:

- We propose a method to make neural topic models aware of named entities. Our method utilizes entity linking (wikification) as preprocessing and incorporates entity embeddings (Wikipedia2Vec) into neural topic models.
- We quantitatively demonstrate that our proposed method improves the performance of neural topic models on a dataset containing many homographic words such as "apple".
- We manually analyze topics extracted by trained topic models and verify that our proposed method brings high interpretability because frequent terms in each topic are expressed with Wikipedia entries.
- We also show that our method does not harm the performance even on a dataset that does not include many homographic words (if entity linking is accurate enough).

2 Related Work

2.1 Neural Topic Models

Our method builds on a combination of topic models and word embeddings, following a surge of previous methods that leverage word embeddings to improve the performance of probabilistic topic models. Some methods incorporate word similarity into the topic model (Petterson et al., 2010; Xie et al., 2015; Zhao et al., 2017). Other methods combine LDA with word embeddings by first converting the discrete text into continuous observations of embeddings (Das et al., 2015; Batmanghelich et al., 2016; Xun et al., 2016, 2017). Another line of research improves topic modeling inference utilizing deep neural networks (Cong et al., 2017; Zhang et al., 2018; Card et al., 2018). These methods reduce the dimension of the text data through amortized inference and the variational auto-encoder (Kingma and Welling, 2014). Finally, Dieng et al. (2020) proposed the embedded topic model (ETM) that makes use of word embeddings and uses amortization in its inference procedure.

2.2 Dynamic Topic Models

The seminal work of Blei and Lafferty (2006) introduced dynamic latent Dirichlet allocation (D-LDA), which uses a state space model on the parameters of a topic distribution, thus allowing the distribution parameters to change with time. Dieng et al. (2019) proposed an extension of D-LDA, dynamic embedded topic model (D-ETM), that better fits the distribution of words via the use of distributed representations for both the words and the topics. Furthermore, Miyamoto et al. (2023) introduced the self-attention mechanism into the neural network used in amortized variational inference.

2.3 Entity Embeddings

Entity embeddings have been studied mainly in the context of named entity disambiguation (NED). Bordes et al. (2011); Socher et al. (2013); Lin et al. (2015) focus on knowledge graph embeddings and propose vector representations of entities to primarily address the knowledge base (KB) link prediction task. Wang et al. (2014) proposed the joint modeling of the embedding of words and entities and revealed that such joint modeling improves performance in several entity-related tasks including the link prediction task. Yaghoobzadeh and Schütze (2015) built embeddings of words and entities on a corpus with annotated entities using the skip-gram model to address the entity typing task. Finally, Yamada et al. (2016) proposed an embedding method that consists of three models: 1) the conventional skip-gram model that learns to predict neighboring words given the target word in text corpora, 2) the anchor context model that learns to predict neighboring words given the target entity using anchors and their context words in the KB, and 3) the KB graph model that learns to estimate neighboring entities given the target entity in the link graph of the KB. To the best of our knowledge, our study is the first attempt to incorporate entity embeddings into embedded topic models.

2.4 Topic Models with Wikipedia

There have been several works where topic models are applied to Wikipedia. Most such studies worked on cross-lingual topic modeling by harnessing Wikipedia's cross-linguality (Ni et al., 2009; Boyd-Graber and Blei, 2009; Zhang et al., 2013; Hao and Paul, 2018; Piccardi and West, 2021). In Wikipedia, each article describes a concept, and each concept is usually described in multiple languages. They proposed formulations of cross-lingual topic models and verified the efficacy of their proposed topic models trained on Wikipedia articles and links. Aside from the above studies, Miz et al. (2020) applied topic models to Wikipedia for analyzing popular topics in different language editions. In contrast to these works, our method utilizes Wikipedia entities identified by entity linking to make embedded topic models capable of dealing with the homography of words in arbitrary documents.

3 Topic Models

Here, we review topic models on which our method is based: LDA, ETM, D-ETM. In the following, we consider a collection of D documents, where the vocabulary contains V distinct terms. Let $w_{dn} \in \{1, \ldots, V\}$ denote the n-th word in the d-th document.

3.1 Latent Dirichlet Allocation (LDA)

LDA is a probabilistic generative model of documents (Blei et al., 2003). It posits K topics, and the distribution over the vocabulary for each topic k is represented $\boldsymbol{\beta}_k \in \mathbb{R}^V$. It assumes each document comes from a mixture of topics, where the topics are shared across the given documents and the mixture proportions are unique for each document. Specifically, LDA considers a vector of topic proportions $\boldsymbol{\theta}_d \in \mathbb{R}^K$ for each document d; each element θ_{dk} expresses how prevalent the k-th topic is in the document d. In the generative process of LDA, each word is assigned to topic k with the probability θ_{dk}, and the word is then drawn from the distribution $\boldsymbol{\beta}_k$. The generative process for each document is as follows:

1. Draw topic proportion: $\boldsymbol{\theta}_d \sim \text{Dirichlet}(\boldsymbol{\eta}_\theta)$
2. For each word n in d:
    (a) Draw topic assignment: $z_{dn} \sim \text{Cat}(\boldsymbol{\theta}_d)$
    (b) Draw word: $w_{dn} \sim \text{Cat}(\boldsymbol{\beta}_{z_{dn}})$.

Here, $\text{Cat}(\cdot)$ denotes a categorical distribution. LDA places a Dirichlet prior on the topics, $\boldsymbol{\beta}_k \sim \text{Dirichlet}(\boldsymbol{\alpha}_\beta)$. The two concentration parameters of the Dirichlet distributions, $\boldsymbol{\alpha}_\beta$ and $\boldsymbol{\eta}_\theta$, are fixed model hyperparameters.

3.2 Embedded Topic Model (ETM)

ETM (Dieng et al., 2020) is a neural topic model powered by word embeddings (Mikolov et al., 2013) and a neural network. Here, let $\boldsymbol{\rho}$ be an $L \times V$ matrix, which contains L-dimensional embeddings of the words in the vocabulary. Each column $\boldsymbol{\rho}_v \in \mathbb{R}^L$ corresponds to the embedding of the v-th term. ETM uses this embedding matrix $\boldsymbol{\rho}$ to define the word distribution of each topic, $\boldsymbol{\beta}_k = \text{softmax}(\boldsymbol{\rho}^\top \boldsymbol{\alpha}_k)$. $\boldsymbol{\alpha}_k$ is an embedding representation of the k-th topic in the semantic space of words, called topic embedding. The generative process of ETM is analogous to LDA as follows:

1. Draw topic proportion: $\boldsymbol{\theta}_d \sim \mathcal{LN}(\mathbf{0}, \boldsymbol{I})$
2. For each word n in d:
    (a) Draw topic assignment: $z_{dn} \sim \text{Cat}(\boldsymbol{\theta}_d)$
    (b) Draw word: $w_{dn} \sim \text{Cat}(\boldsymbol{\beta}_{z_{dn}})$.

Here, $\mathcal{LN}(\cdot, \cdot)$ denotes a logistic-normal distribution (Atchison and Shen, 1980). The intuition behind ETM is that the embedding representations of semantically related words are similar to each other, they will interact with the topic embeddings $\boldsymbol{\alpha}_k$ similarly, and then they will be assigned to similar topics.

3.3 Dynamic Embedded Topic Model (D-ETM)

D-ETM (Dieng et al., 2019) analyzes time-series documents by introducing Markov chains to the topic embeddings $\boldsymbol{\alpha}_k$ and the topic proportion mean. As in ETM, D-ETM considers an embedding matrix $\boldsymbol{\rho} \in \mathbb{R}^{L \times V}$, such that each column $\boldsymbol{\rho}_v \in \mathbb{R}^L$ corresponds to the embedding of the v-th term. D-ETM posits an topic embedding $\boldsymbol{\alpha}_k^{(t)} \in \mathbb{R}^L$ for each topic k at a time stamp $t \in \{1, \ldots, T\}$. This means D-ETM represents each topic with a time-varying vector. Then, the word distribution for the k-th topic in the time step t is defined by $\boldsymbol{\beta}_k^{(t)} = \text{softmax}(\boldsymbol{\rho}^\top \boldsymbol{\alpha}_k^{(t)})$. Here, the generative process of D-ETM for documents is described as follows:

1. For time step $t = 0$:
    (a) Draw initial topic embedding: $\boldsymbol{\alpha}_k^{(0)} \sim \mathcal{N}(\mathbf{0}, I)$ for $k \in \{1, \ldots, K\}$
    (b) Draw initial topic proportion mean: $\boldsymbol{\eta}_0 \sim \mathcal{N}(\mathbf{0}, I)$
2. For each time step $t \in \{1, \ldots, T\}$:
    (a) Draw topic embedding: $\boldsymbol{\alpha}_k^{(t)} \sim \mathcal{N}(\boldsymbol{\alpha}_k^{(t-1)}, \sigma^2 I)$ for $k \in \{1, \ldots, K\}$

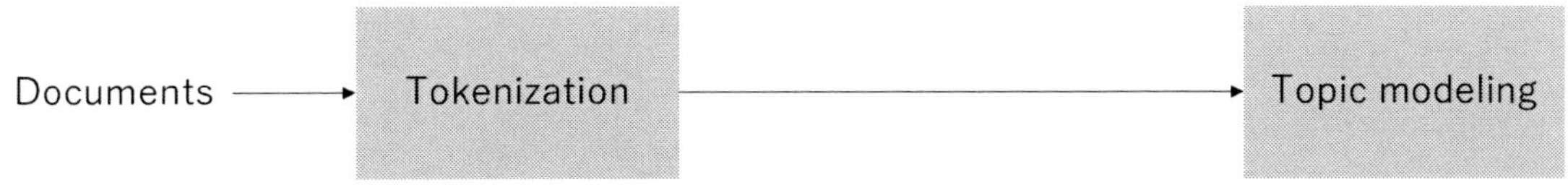

(b) Conventional topic models

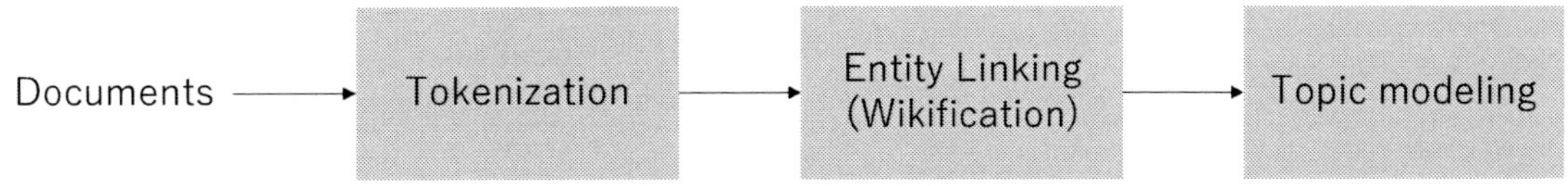

(b) Our proposed topic model

Figure 1: Processing flows of conventional topic models and our proposed topic model.

(b) Draw topic proportion mean:
$\boldsymbol{\eta}_t \sim \mathcal{N}(\boldsymbol{\eta}_{t-1}, \delta^2 I)$

3. For each document $d \in \{1, \ldots, D\}$:
   (a) Draw topic proportion:
   $\boldsymbol{\theta}_d \sim \mathcal{LN}(\boldsymbol{\eta}_{t_d}, \gamma^2 I)$
   (b) For each word n in d:
      i. Draw topic assignment:
      $\boldsymbol{z}_{dn} \sim \text{Cat}(\boldsymbol{\theta}_d)$
      ii. Draw word:
      $w_{dn} \sim \text{Cat}(\boldsymbol{\beta}^{(t_d)}_{\boldsymbol{z}_{dn}})$,

where $\mathcal{N}(\cdot, \cdot)$ denotes a normal distribution distribution. σ, δ, and γ are model hyperparameters, each of which controls the variance of the corresponding normal distribution. t_d denotes the time stamp of the document d. Step 2(a) encourages smooth variations of the topic embeddings, and Step 2(b) describes time-varying priors over the topic proportions $\boldsymbol{\theta}_d$.

In this study, we incorporate entity knowledge into ETM or D-ETM by utilizing not only word embeddings but also entity embeddings, which enables topic models to be aware of named entities. To the best of our knowledge, our study is the first attempt to apply entity embeddings to embedded topic models. In the next section, we will explain how we introduce entity embeddings into embedded topic models.

4 Proposed Method

In this study, we propose a method of incorporating word disambiguation results into a neural topic model. We depict the processing flows of conventional topic models and our proposed method in Figure 1. In previous embedded topic models such as ETM and D-ETM, given documents are first tokenized, and then the word embedding matrix $\boldsymbol{\rho}$ is built by tiling the pretrained word embeddings such as skip-gram (Mikolov et al., 2013) corresponding to tokenized words. On the other hand, we incorporate entity information extracted by entity linking (EL) into the word embedding matrix $\boldsymbol{\rho}$ of an ETM/D-ETM. We explain the details of our method below.

4.1 Incorporation of Entity Linking

Here, we explain a way of building the embedding matrix $\boldsymbol{\rho}$ based on EL results. EL is a task that assigns a unique identity to an entity mention in text. In this study, we use an entity embedding instead of a word embedding if an entity linker identifies a phrase in a document as an entry in a knowledge base (KB) as depicted in Figure 2. Specifically, we utilize entity embedding trained with the Wikipedia2Vec toolkit (Yamada et al., 2020). The Wikipedia2Vec toolkit can learn the embeddings of both words and entities by using Wikipedia's text and hyperlinks. We can incorporate distributed representations of not only words but also entities into neural models with them. For example, if a word "amazon" is identified as a KB entry "Amazon (company)" in a document, we adopt the entity embedding corresponding to "Amazon (company)". If "*amazon*" is identified as a KB entry "Amazon rainforest" in another document (or another place of the same document), we use the entity embedding for "Amazon rainforest". If "*amazon*" is not identified to any KB entry, we adopt the word embedding corresponding to "*amazon*". Thus we deal with the entity "Amazon (company)", the entity "Amazon rainforest", and the word "*amazon*" as distinct items. Through the above procedure, we

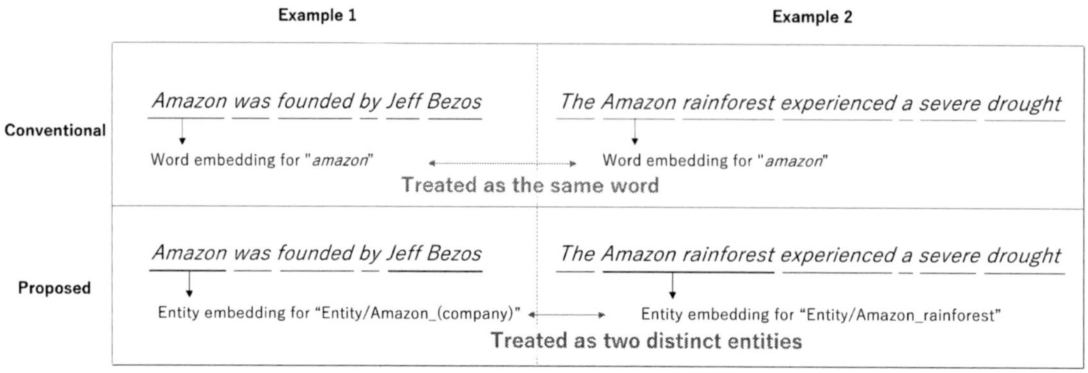

Figure 2: Difference between conventional embedded topic models and our proposed topic model.

can incorporate EL results into a neural topic model and make it aware of named entities. In the next section, we will evaluate the performance of our proposed method.

5 Experiments

In this section, we conduct two experiments. First, we evaluate our method on our original dataset, which requires a topic model to be aware of named entities. Our first experiment aims to verify that our method is effective in a case where word disambiguation is important. Next, we evaluate our method on the AIDA-CoNLL dataset (Hoffart et al., 2011). The AIDA-CoNLL dataset provides manual entity annotations. In this second experiment, we aim to assess 1) whether our method of incorporating entity information does not harm the performance of topic models even in a case where word disambiguation is not necessarily required and 2) how largely the off-the-shelve entity linker used in our pipeline deteriorates the performance in comparison with the use of the gold entity annotations.

5.1 Fine-Grained Topic Modeling

5.1.1 Experimental Setup

Dataset. In this experiment, we use archive news articles of *New York Times*[1]. We extract two subsets of articles published between the years 1996 and 2020: 1) a collection of 6,651 documents that include the word "*apple*" and 2) a collection of 3,070 documents that include "*amazon*". We regard each of the two collections as a single dataset and assess if our proposed method can train a more generalizable topic model by disambiguating homographic words, "*apple*" and "*amazon*". We randomly split each collection into 3:1:1 for training, validation, and test sets. Following Miyamoto et al. (2023), we filter out words that appear in 70% or more of documents and words included in a predefined stop-word list before building an embedding matrix $\boldsymbol{\rho}$. We group documents published within five consecutive years into a single time step. For example, news articles published between 1996 and 2000 are grouped.

Compared Models. We use **ETM** (Dieng et al., 2020) and **DSNTM** (Miyamoto et al., 2023) (one implementation of D-ETM (Dieng et al., 2019)) as baseline models, where only tokenization is applied to documents. ETM is not a dynamic topic model and does not consider time stamp information, whereas DSNTM is a dynamic topic model and can capture the chronological transition of topics. We assess if our method is effective in each model. We compare **ETM+EL** and **DSNTM+EL** (where we use entity embeddings for entities identified by an entity linker) with their corresponding baselines to see if our proposed method is effective.

Implementation Details. We set the number of topics $K = 10$ for all models. The variances of the prior distributions are set $\delta^2 = \sigma^2 = 0.005$ and $\gamma^2 = 1$. We use 500-dimensional word/entity embeddings (window size: 10)[2] pretrained with the Wikipedia2Vec toolkit (Yamada et al., 2020)[3]. Regarding other hyperparameters, we follow the official implementation of DSNTM[4]. For the preprocessing of documents, we utilize the tokenizer and entity linker implemented in the Stanford CoreNLP

[1] https://developer.nytimes.com

[2] http://wikipedia2vec.s3.amazonaws.com/models/en/2018-04-20/enwiki_20180420_win10_500d.txt.bz2

[3] https://wikipedia2vec.github.io/wikipedia2vec/

[4] https://github.com/miyamotononno/DSNTM

Method	*"apple"*	*"amazon"*
ETM	5753.3 ± 227.2	5086.7 ± 304.8
ETM+EL	5228.9 ± 730.9	6412.4 ± 731.3
DSNTM (Miyamoto et al., 2023)	4597.9 ± 270.0	4587.6 ± 349.0
DSNTM+EL	**3578.6** ± 141.4	4038.7 ± 65.9

Table 1: Results for perplexity with 95% confidence interval (CI) on our *New York Times* dataset. The lower, the better. EL means entity linking.

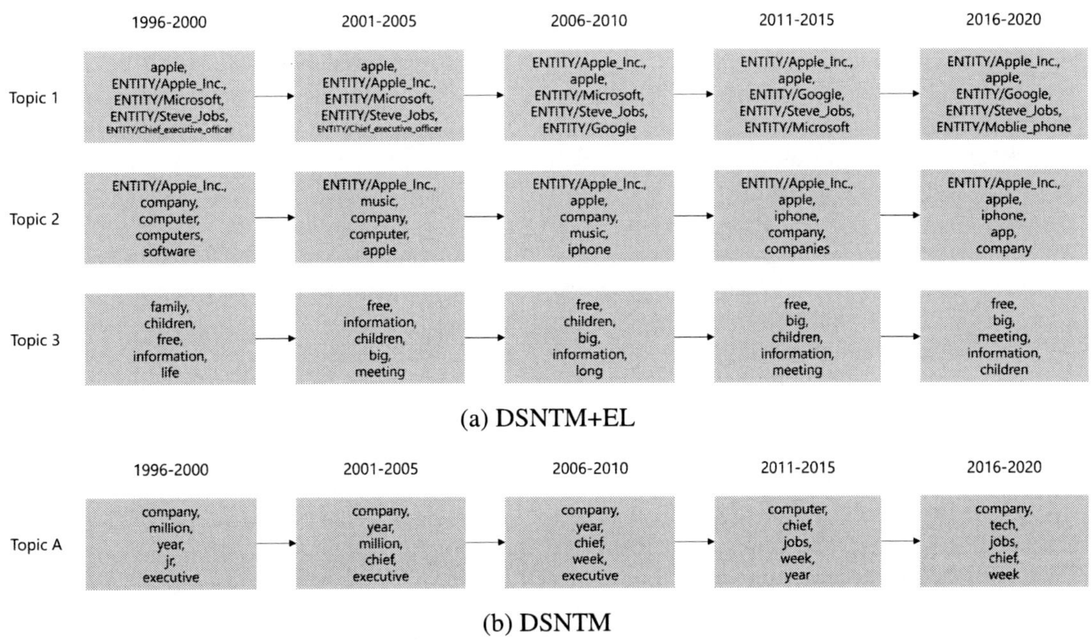

Figure 3: Examples of topic transition. We present the top five most frequent terms in each topic.

toolkit (Manning et al., 2014).[5] We call these CoreNLP analyzers through the Stanza library (Qi et al., 2020)[6].

5.1.2 Quantitative Evaluation

We use perplexity (Rosen-Zvi et al., 2004) to evaluate the generalizability of a topic model. Although there is a discussion on how to properly evaluate topic models (Chang et al., 2009; Hoyle et al., 2021), perplexity is still a widely-used objective metric (Hida et al., 2018; Miyamoto et al., 2023). It measures the ability to predict words in unseen documents. In training, we apply early stopping based on the performance of a validation set. We train each model eight times with different random seeds and report the average performance and its 95% confidence interval on a test set.

The results are shown in Table 1. We can find two tendencies in the results. The first one is that EL tends to improve the performance except for ETM on the *"amazon"* dataset. In particular, DSNTM+EL achieves lower perplexity than DSNTM. This demonstrates that word disambiguation by EL is effective in analyzing a collection of documents with a topic model. We will discuss the reason why our method does not work well with ETM on the *"amazon"* dataset in a later section. The second tendency is that DSNTM+EL performs better than ETM+EL. This means that modeling a temporal change of topics is effective even when EL is combined.

5.1.3 Qualitative Analysis

Visualization of Topic Transition. We present an overview of the topic transition process extracted by a trained DSNTM+EL model on the *"apple"* dataset in Figure 3(a). The topics in the first, second, and third rows (Topics 1, 2, and 3)

[5] Although more accurate entity linkers (Shavarani and Sarkar, 2023; Wang et al., 2024) are publicly available, we choose the one implemented in the Stanford CoreNLP due to the limitation of computing resources.

[6] https://github.com/stanfordnlp/stanza

Word/Entity 1	Word/Entity 2	Cosine similarity
ENTITY/Apple_Inc.	*apple*	0.67
ENTITY/Apple_Inc.	ENTITY/Steve_Jobs	0.59
ENTITY/Apple_Inc.	*steve*	0.27
ENTITY/Apple_Inc.	*jobs*	0.28
apple	ENTITY/Steve_Jobs	0.52
apple	*steve*	0.30
apple	*jobs*	0.30

Table 2: Word similarities of two words/entities on Wikipedia2Vec (Yamada et al., 2020).

represent business/management, products/services, and *New York City*, respectively. When we look into Topic 1, the word "*apple*", the entity "ENTITY/Apple_Inc.", and the entity "ENTITY/Steve_Jobs" are frequently used constantly between 1996 and 2020, whereas the entity "ENTITY/Google" emerges after 2006. This is reasonable because Google was founded in 1998 and went public via an initial public offering (IPO) in 2004. Google was never mentioned before 1998 and not often before 2004. This demonstrates that DSNTM+EL successfully finds the transition of frequent terms in each topic and that we can easily understand the trends of topics by visualization. This is true for "*iphone*" (released in 2007) in Topic 2 as well. Regarding Topic 3, one might think this topic has nothing to do with the word "*apple*" at a glance, but this topic is related to *New York City*. *New York City* sometimes is called its nickname, "*Big Apple*". This topic consists of articles about *New York City*, especially entertainment such as *Big Apple Circus* and *Big Apple Chorus*. Then, the word "*big*" is listed as a frequent term.[7]

We also show the transition of a topic (Topic A) extracted by a trained DSNTM model in Figure 3(b). According to the frequent terms, Topic A is similar to Topic 1 in Figure 3(a). This means that a conventional topic model can analyze documents in a similar way. However, our method involving entity linking into its preprocessing comes with higher interpretability as frequent terms are expressed with not only words but also entities. The word "*jobs*" in Topic A means *Steve Jobs* in almost all cases, but DSNTM+EL shows that Topic 1 is related to *Steve Jobs* in a much easier-to-understand manner. This high interpretability is another advantage of our proposed method in addition to lower perplexities.

Influence of Entity Embedding. We investigate why entity linking (EL) boosts the performance of neural topic models. Some words have multiple meanings, whereas previous topic models deal with such words without being aware of meanings, considering only their spelling. In such an approach, a topic model can take into consideration neither who "*steve*" is nor whether "*jobs*" is a person's name or a common noun. In our proposed method, we try to disambiguate words, and use entity embedding trained with the Wikipedia2Vec toolkit (Yamada et al., 2020) instead of conventional word embedding if a word is linked to a KB entry.

Here, let us show some properties of the entity embedding used. We show the cosine similarities between some words/entities in Table 2. As shown, "ENTITY/Steve_Jobs" is much closer to "ENTITY/Apple_Inc." than the words "*steve*" and "*jobs*". This is because the word "*jobs*" can be a noun word (the plural form of "*job*"), and even "*steve*" can be the name of another person. Then, their embedding vectors are trained in various contexts. On the other hand, "ENTITY/Steve_Jobs" tends to appear in articles relevant to *Apple Inc.*, and then its entity embedding is trained in a narrow range of contexts. As a result, the entity embedding of "ENTITY/Steve_Jobs" has a large similarity to the entity embedding of "ENTITY/Apple_Inc.", while the word embeddings of "*steve*" and "*jobs*" go far from the entity embedding of "ENTITY/Apple_Inc.".

In ETM and DSNTM, a topic embedding $\boldsymbol{\alpha}_k^{(t)}$ is multiplied with a static word/entity embedding matrix $\boldsymbol{\rho}$ to estimate a distribution of terms, $w_{dn} \sim \mathrm{Cat}(\mathrm{softmax}(\boldsymbol{\rho}^\top \boldsymbol{\alpha}_{z_{dn}}^{(t_d)}))$ (See Section 3). This means that, if word/entity embedding vectors cluster based on their used context, topic embedding can be easily trained. Actually, entity embedding has such a property as we explained in the previous paragraph. Thus, entity embedding can help neural topic models extract topics from documents.

Dependency on Entity Linking. In contrast to our aim, entity linking (EL) does not boost the

[7]Ideally, entity linkers should recognize those entities correctly, but the entity linker used in our pipeline is not so accurate. As a result, the word "*big*" is listed.

Method	Tokenization & entity linking	Perplexity
ETM	Gold annotation	5380.5 ± 246.2
ETM+EL (ours)	Gold annotation	**5010.1** ± 448.8
ETM	Stanford CoreNLP	5404.9 ± 225.0
ETM+EL (ours)	Stanford CoreNLP	6558.1 ± 979.4

Table 3: Results for perplexity with 95% confidence interval (CI) on the AIDA-CoNLL dataset (Hoffart et al., 2011). The lower, the better. EL means entity linking.

performance of ETM on the "*amazon*" dataset, different from the "*apple*" dataset. We find that the accuracy of entity linking is not so good on the "*amazon*" dataset and that the entity linker fails to assign entity mentions to correct KB entries. Our proposed method is a pipeline of 1) preprocessing with an entity linker and 2) neural topic modeling. If the preprocessing is not accurate, the successive topic modeling will naturally be affected. We hypothesize that the latest, more accurate entity linkers (Shavarani and Sarkar, 2023; Wang et al., 2024) can boost the performance of neural topic models more. To verify our hypothesis, we will conduct an experiment on a dataset that contains manual entity annotations in the next section.

5.2 Coarse-Grained Topic Modeling

In this section, we evaluate our method on a dataset accompanied with gold entity annotations, to assess 1) whether our method of incorporating entity information does not harm the performance of topic models even in a case where word disambiguation is not necessarily required and 2) how largely the off-the-shelf entity linker used in our pipeline deteriorates the performance in comparison with the use of the gold entity annotations.

5.2.1 Experimental Setup

Dataset. In this experiment, we use the AIDA-CoNLL dataset (Hoffart et al., 2011)[8]. This dataset contains manual Wikipedia annotations for the 1,393 Reuters news stories originally published for the CoNLL-2003 Named Entity Recognition Shared Task (Tjong Kim Sang and De Meulder, 2003). The number of Wikipedia annotations is 27,817. The dataset consists of `train`, `testa`, and `testb` splits, which contain 946, 216, and 231 documents, respectively. We utilize the three splits as training, validation, and test sets. As in our previous experiment, we filter out words that appear in 70% or more of documents and words included in the predefined stop-word list before building an embedding matrix ρ. In contrast to the *New York Times* dataset used in the previous experiment, which is created by collecting news articles that include a specific word such as "*apple*", the AIDA-CoNLL dataset was made without such an intention. It should include much less ambiguous words.

Compared Models. We use **ETM** (Dieng et al., 2020) as a baseline model. As the AIDA-CoNLL dataset provides gold annotations of entity linking (including tokenization), we can assess the influence of the off-the-shelf tokenizer and entity linker on the performance of our entire pipeline by comparing results from using gold annotations and results from using annotations by the tokenizer and entity linker. Therefore, we evaluate the following four models. 1) **ETM** that utilizes the gold annotations, 2) **ETM+EL** that uses the gold annotations, 3) **ETM** that utilizes annotations provided by Stanford CoreNLP, and 4) **ETM+EL** that uses annotations given by Stanford CoreNLP. Since the AIDA-CoNLL dataset does not include time stamp information, we do not adopt a dynamic topic model in this experiment.

Implementation Details. In this experiment, we use 300-dimensional word/entity embeddings (window size: 10)[9] because we encountered training instability with 500-dimensional word/entity embeddings. Regarding all other hyperparameters and implementations, we follow the previous experiment.

5.2.2 Results

The results are shown in Table 3. First, we can see that when the gold annotations are provided, entity linking improves the performance of ETM, even though the used AIDA-CoNLL dataset does not include as many homographic words as our *New York Times* dataset used in the previous experiment. This demonstrates that our method is potentially generalizable and can perform well on various data. Second, we observe that using information anno-

[8] `https://www.mpi-inf.mpg.de/departments/databases-and-information-systems/research/ambiverse-nlu/aida`

[9] `http://wikipedia2vec.s3.amazonaws.com/models/en/2018-04-20/enwiki_20180420_win10_300d.txt.bz2`

tated by the Stanford CoreNLP entity linker deteriorates the performance. As the knowledge base supported by the entity linker is not identical to that used for the annotations in the AIDA-CoNLL dataset, the accuracy of the entity linker can not be calculated so easily. However, we can attribute the performance gap between the two cases, 1) gold annotations and 2) the CoreNLP entity linker, to the accuracy of the entity linker. We believe that the latest, more accurate entity linkers (Shavarani and Sarkar, 2023; Wang et al., 2024) can boost the performance of neural topic models.

6 Conclusion

In this study, we proposed a method of analyzing a collection of documents after disambiguating homographic words. We incorporated entity information extracted by entity linking into neural topic models. Our experimental results demonstrated that entity linking improves the generalizability of topic models by disambiguating words such as "*apple*" and "*amazon*". In addition, our method offers higher interpretability as frequent terms in each topic are represented with not only words but also entities.

Limitations

Our models heavily rely on word/entity embedding as with other neural topic models. If the word/entity embedding contains some bias, our models will be affected by the bias.

Besides, topic models, including our models, sometimes infer incorrect information about topics, such as the frequent terms appearing in topics, the topic proportion in each document, and the dependencies among topics. There would be the potential risk of inducing misunderstandings among users.

Ethics Statement

Our study complies with the ACL Ethics Policy. We used *PyTorch* (BSD-style license), *New York Times* articles[10], the AIDA-CoNLL dataset (Creative Commons Attribution 3.0 license). Our study was conducted under their licenses and terms.

Acknowledgments

We thank anonymous reviewers for helpful feedback on our draft.

[10]`https://developer.nytimes.com/terms`

References

J. Atchison and S.M. Shen. 1980. Logistic-normal distributions:Some properties and uses. *Biometrika*, 67(2):261–272.

Kayhan Batmanghelich, Ardavan Saeedi, Karthik Narasimhan, and Sam Gershman. 2016. Nonparametric spherical topic modeling with word embeddings. In *Proceedings of the 54th Annual Meeting of the Association for Computational Linguistics (Volume 2: Short Papers)*, pages 537–542, Berlin, Germany. Association for Computational Linguistics.

David M. Blei and John D. Lafferty. 2006. Dynamic topic models. In *Proceedings of the 23rd International Conference on Machine Learning*, ICML '06, page 113–120, New York, NY, USA. Association for Computing Machinery.

David M. Blei, Andrew Y. Ng, and Michael I. Jordan. 2003. Latent Dirichlet allocation. *J. Mach. Learn. Res.*, 3(null):993–1022.

Antoine Bordes, Jason Weston, Ronan Collobert, and Yoshua Bengio. 2011. Learning structured embeddings of knowledge bases. *Proceedings of the AAAI Conference on Artificial Intelligence*, 25(1):301–306.

Jordan Boyd-Graber and David M. Blei. 2009. Multilingual topic models for unaligned text. In *Proceedings of the Twenty-Fifth Conference on Uncertainty in Artificial Intelligence*, UAI '09, page 75–82, Arlington, Virginia, USA. AUAI Press.

Dallas Card, Chenhao Tan, and Noah A. Smith. 2018. Neural models for documents with metadata. In *Proceedings of the 56th Annual Meeting of the Association for Computational Linguistics (Volume 1: Long Papers)*, pages 2031–2040, Melbourne, Australia. Association for Computational Linguistics.

Jonathan Chang, Sean Gerrish, Chong Wang, Jordan Boyd-graber, and David Blei. 2009. Reading tea leaves: How humans interpret topic models. In *Advances in Neural Information Processing Systems*, volume 22. Curran Associates, Inc.

Yulai Cong, Bo Chen, Hongwei Liu, and Mingyuan Zhou. 2017. Deep latent Dirichlet allocation with topic-layer-adaptive stochastic gradient Riemannian MCMC. In *Proceedings of the 34th International Conference on Machine Learning*, volume 70 of *Proceedings of Machine Learning Research*, pages 864–873. PMLR.

Kostadin Cvejoski, Ramsés J. Sánchez, and César Ojeda. 2023. Neural dynamic focused topic model. *Proceedings of the AAAI Conference on Artificial Intelligence*, 37(11):12719–12727.

Rajarshi Das, Manzil Zaheer, and Chris Dyer. 2015. Gaussian LDA for topic models with word embeddings. In *Proceedings of the 53rd Annual Meeting of the Association for Computational Linguistics and the 7th International Joint Conference on*

Natural Language Processing (Volume 1: Long Papers), pages 795–804, Beijing, China. Association for Computational Linguistics.

Adji B. Dieng, Francisco J. R. Ruiz, and David M. Blei. 2019. The dynamic embedded topic model. *Preprint*, arXiv:1907.05545.

Adji B. Dieng, Francisco J. R. Ruiz, and David M. Blei. 2020. Topic modeling in embedding spaces. *Transactions of the Association for Computational Linguistics*, 8:439–453.

Shudong Hao and Michael J. Paul. 2018. Learning multilingual topics from incomparable corpora. In *Proceedings of the 27th International Conference on Computational Linguistics*, pages 2595–2609, Santa Fe, New Mexico, USA. Association for Computational Linguistics.

Rem Hida, Naoya Takeishi, Takehisa Yairi, and Koichi Hori. 2018. Dynamic and static topic model for analyzing time-series document collections. In *Proceedings of the 56th Annual Meeting of the Association for Computational Linguistics (Volume 2: Short Papers)*, pages 516–520, Melbourne, Australia. Association for Computational Linguistics.

Johannes Hoffart, Mohamed Amir Yosef, Ilaria Bordino, Hagen Fürstenau, Manfred Pinkal, Marc Spaniol, Bilyana Taneva, Stefan Thater, and Gerhard Weikum. 2011. Robust disambiguation of named entities in text. In *Proceedings of the 2011 Conference on Empirical Methods in Natural Language Processing*, pages 782–792, Edinburgh, Scotland, UK. Association for Computational Linguistics.

Alexander Hoyle, Pranav Goel, Andrew Hian-Cheong, Denis Peskov, Jordan Boyd-Graber, and Philip Resnik. 2021. Is automated topic model evaluation broken? the incoherence of coherence. In *Advances in Neural Information Processing Systems*, volume 34, pages 2018–2033. Curran Associates, Inc.

Diederik Kingma and Max Welling. 2014. Efficient gradient-based inference through transformations between Bayes nets and neural nets. In *Proceedings of the 31st International Conference on Machine Learning*, volume 32 of *Proceedings of Machine Learning Research*, pages 1782–1790, Bejing, China. PMLR.

Yankai Lin, Zhiyuan Liu, Maosong Sun, Yang Liu, and Xuan Zhu. 2015. Learning entity and relation embeddings for knowledge graph completion. *Proceedings of the AAAI Conference on Artificial Intelligence*, 29(1).

Christopher Manning, Mihai Surdeanu, John Bauer, Jenny Finkel, Steven Bethard, and David McClosky. 2014. The Stanford CoreNLP natural language processing toolkit. In *Proceedings of 52nd Annual Meeting of the Association for Computational Linguistics: System Demonstrations*, pages 55–60, Baltimore, Maryland. Association for Computational Linguistics.

Tomas Mikolov, Ilya Sutskever, Kai Chen, Greg S Corrado, and Jeff Dean. 2013. Distributed representations of words and phrases and their compositionality. In *Advances in Neural Information Processing Systems*, volume 26. Curran Associates, Inc.

Nozomu Miyamoto, Masaru Isonuma, Sho Takase, Junichiro Mori, and Ichiro Sakata. 2023. Dynamic structured neural topic model with self-attention mechanism. In *Findings of the Association for Computational Linguistics: ACL 2023*, pages 5916–5930, Toronto, Canada. Association for Computational Linguistics.

Volodymyr Miz, Joëlle Hanna, Nicolas Aspert, Benjamin Ricaud, and Pierre Vandergheynst. 2020. What is trending on Wikipedia? capturing trends and language biases across Wikipedia editions. In *Companion Proceedings of the Web Conference 2020*, WWW '20, page 794–801, New York, NY, USA. Association for Computing Machinery.

Xiaochuan Ni, Jian-Tao Sun, Jian Hu, and Zheng Chen. 2009. Mining multilingual topics from Wikipedia. In *Proceedings of the 18th International Conference on World Wide Web*, WWW '09, page 1155–1156, New York, NY, USA. Association for Computing Machinery.

James Petterson, Wray Buntine, Shravan Narayanamurthy, Tibério Caetano, and Alex Smola. 2010. Word features for latent Dirichlet allocation. In *Advances in Neural Information Processing Systems*, volume 23. Curran Associates, Inc.

Tiziano Piccardi and Robert West. 2021. Crosslingual topic modeling with WikiPDA. In *Proceedings of the Web Conference 2021*, WWW '21, page 3032–3041, New York, NY, USA. Association for Computing Machinery.

Peng Qi, Yuhao Zhang, Yuhui Zhang, Jason Bolton, and Christopher D. Manning. 2020. Stanza: A python natural language processing toolkit for many human languages. In *Proceedings of the 58th Annual Meeting of the Association for Computational Linguistics: System Demonstrations*, pages 101–108, Online. Association for Computational Linguistics.

Michal Rosen-Zvi, Thomas Griffiths, Mark Steyvers, and Padhraic Smyth. 2004. The author-topic model for authors and documents. In *Proceedings of the 20th Conference on Uncertainty in Artificial Intelligence*, UAI '04, page 487–494, Arlington, Virginia, USA. AUAI Press.

Hassan Shavarani and Anoop Sarkar. 2023. SpEL: Structured prediction for entity linking. In *Proceedings of the 2023 Conference on Empirical Methods in Natural Language Processing*, pages 11123–11137, Singapore. Association for Computational Linguistics.

Richard Socher, Danqi Chen, Christopher D Manning, and Andrew Ng. 2013. Reasoning with neural tensor networks for knowledge base completion. In *Advances in Neural Information Processing Systems*, volume 26. Curran Associates, Inc.

Erik F. Tjong Kim Sang and Fien De Meulder. 2003. Introduction to the CoNLL-2003 shared task: Language-independent named entity recognition. In *Proceedings of the Seventh Conference on Natural Language Learning at HLT-NAACL 2003*, pages 142–147.

Junxiong Wang, Ali Mousavi, Omar Attia, Ronak Pradeep, Saloni Potdar, Alexander Rush, Umar Farooq Minhas, and Yunyao Li. 2024. Entity disambiguation via fusion entity decoding. In *Proceedings of the 2024 Conference of the North American Chapter of the Association for Computational Linguistics: Human Language Technologies (Volume 1: Long Papers)*, pages 6524–6536, Mexico City, Mexico. Association for Computational Linguistics.

Zhen Wang, Jianwen Zhang, Jianlin Feng, and Zheng Chen. 2014. Knowledge graph and text jointly embedding. In *Proceedings of the 2014 Conference on Empirical Methods in Natural Language Processing (EMNLP)*, pages 1591–1601, Doha, Qatar. Association for Computational Linguistics.

Pengtao Xie, Diyi Yang, and Eric Xing. 2015. Incorporating word correlation knowledge into topic modeling. In *Proceedings of the 2015 Conference of the North American Chapter of the Association for Computational Linguistics: Human Language Technologies*, pages 725–734, Denver, Colorado. Association for Computational Linguistics.

Guangxu Xun, Vishrawas Gopalakrishnan, Fenglong Ma, Yaliang Li, Jing Gao, and Aidong Zhang. 2016. Topic discovery for short texts using word embeddings. In *2016 IEEE 16th International Conference on Data Mining (ICDM)*, pages 1299–1304.

Guangxu Xun, Yaliang Li, Wayne Xin Zhao, Jing Gao, and Aidong Zhang. 2017. A correlated topic model using word embeddings. In *Proceedings of the Twenty-Sixth International Joint Conference on Artificial Intelligence, IJCAI-17*, pages 4207–4213.

Yadollah Yaghoobzadeh and Hinrich Schütze. 2015. Corpus-level fine-grained entity typing using contextual information. In *Proceedings of the 2015 Conference on Empirical Methods in Natural Language Processing*, pages 715–725, Lisbon, Portugal. Association for Computational Linguistics.

Ikuya Yamada, Akari Asai, Jin Sakuma, Hiroyuki Shindo, Hideaki Takeda, Yoshiyasu Takefuji, and Yuji Matsumoto. 2020. Wikipedia2Vec: An efficient toolkit for learning and visualizing the embeddings of words and entities from Wikipedia. In *Proceedings of the 2020 Conference on Empirical Methods in Natural Language Processing: System Demonstrations*, pages 23–30, Online. Association for Computational Linguistics.

Ikuya Yamada, Hiroyuki Shindo, Hideaki Takeda, and Yoshiyasu Takefuji. 2016. Joint learning of the embedding of words and entities for named entity disambiguation. In *Proceedings of the 20th SIGNLL Conference on Computational Natural Language Learning*, pages 250–259, Berlin, Germany. Association for Computational Linguistics.

Hao Zhang, Bo Chen, Dandan Guo, and Mingyuan Zhou. 2018. WHAI: Weibull hybrid autoencoding inference for deep topic modeling. In *International Conference on Learning Representations*.

Tao Zhang, Kang Liu, and Jun Zhao. 2013. Cross lingual entity linking with bilingual topic model. In *Proceedings of the Twenty-Third International Joint Conference on Artificial Intelligence*, IJCAI '13, page 2218–2224. AAAI Press.

He Zhao, Lan Du, Wray Buntine, and Gang Liu. 2017. MetaLDA: A topic model that efficiently incorporates meta information. In *2017 IEEE International Conference on Data Mining (ICDM)*, pages 635–644.

Wikimedia data for AI: a review of Wikimedia datasets for NLP tasks and AI-assisted editing

Isaac Johnson
Wikimedia Foundation
United States
isaac@wikimedia.org

Lucie-Aimée Kaffee
Hugging Face
Germany
lucie.kaffee@huggingface.co

Miriam Redi
Wikimedia Foundation
United Kingdom
mredi@wikimedia.org

Abstract

Wikimedia content is used extensively by the AI community and within the language modeling community in particular. In this paper, we provide a review of the different ways in which Wikimedia data is curated to use in NLP tasks across pre-training, post-training, and model evaluations. We point to opportunities for greater use of Wikimedia content but also identify ways in which the language modeling community could better center the needs of Wikimedia editors. In particular, we call for incorporating additional sources of Wikimedia data, a greater focus on benchmarks for LLMs that encode Wikimedia principles, and greater multilingualism in Wikimedia-derived datasets.

1 Introduction

Wikimedia data—especially Wikipedia—has been essential to the progression of AI over the past several years. In particular, Wikipedia text is key to natural language processing (NLP): it is generally long-form (meaning lots of context to learn from), "well-written",[1] and high-quality (Gao et al., 2020). The BERT language model (Devlin, 2018) that was introduced in 2018 and is often considered the first modern LLM uses English Wikipedia as a majority of its data. Even today, with much larger language models, English Wikipedia is often weighted heavily when trained—e.g., (Brown, 2020; Longpre et al., 2024).

The usage of Wikimedia data for AI has both been beneficial as a source of high-quality data for NLP researchers and for directing attention to the Wikimedia projects. This relationship, however, has largely been incidental to Wikimedia's mission and openness, and many of the advances of NLP have not made it back to the Wikimedia projects. For example, the Wikimedia Foundation regularly publishes snapshots of the content on the Wikimedia projects. These "dumps" have been made available since at least 2005.[2] While researchers have long been considered an expected end-user, this data was not pre-processed in any way to support the NLP community. As a result, researchers used many different approaches for pre-processing this raw text to produce natural-language text for use in training models.[3] More recently, there have been explicit efforts to bring the Wikimedia and the ML communities closer together such as the Wiki-M3L[4] and NLP for Wikipedia[5] workshops, and standardized datasets such as Hugging Face's Wikipedia text,[6] There have also been concerns that the AI ecosystem might be depleting the very projects upon which it is built and stronger calls for developers of AI tools to view the knowledge commons not just a repository from which to extract data, but as a community to give back to—e.g., Commons (2023) and Foundation (2024).

In this paper, we make an effort to catalog the many AI and NLP-related datasets that draw on the Wikimedia projects to identify what gaps and opportunities exist. We frame this review following the calls for AI developers to contribute more to the knowledge commons. Specifically, we select the datasets in this paper with a focus on how NLP might be made more beneficial for the Wikimedia editor communities. Editors not only do the difficult work of synthesizing sources into the encyclopedic text consumed by readers and AI alike, they also engage in rich discussion and sensemaking around source reliability, fairly portraying content, and evaluating complex questions of nota-

[1] https://en.wikipedia.org/wiki/Wikipedia:Manual_of_Style

[2] https://meta.wikimedia.org/w/index.php?title=Data_dumps&oldid=216530

[3] See Johnson and Lescak (2022) for examples.

[4] https://meta.wikimedia.org/wiki/Wiki-M3L

[5] https://meta.wikimedia.org/wiki/NLP_for_Wikipedia_(EMNLP_2024)

[6] https://huggingface.co/datasets/wikimedia/wikipedia

Proceedings of the First Workshop on Advancing Natural Language Processing for Wikipedia, pages 91–101
November 16, 2024 ©2024 Association for Computational Linguistics

bility. Their work is guided by core content policies, which AI models must also be able to adhere to in order to be useful to the editing community. In the course of the analysis, we identify three major opportunities:

- Extend and diversify the subset of Wikimedia data used in AI research. This could include regular datasets of images along with associated captions for multimodal modeling, more attention paid to talk pages or other collaboration spaces on Wikipedia, and greater usage of the high-quality transcribed documents produced by Wikisource communities.

- Consider the needs of Wikimedia editors in evaluation of LLMs. While Wikipedia data is well-represented within common benchmark datasets, these tasks are almost exclusively oriented towards reader goals. Work is needed to extend benchmarks to better encode the needs of Wikimedia editors.

- Continue to extend models to be more multilingual, open-source, and compact to meet the needs of the Wikimedia projects.

2 Approach

To guide the knowledge of Wikimedia datasets and tasks that are relevant to this work, we searched for individual Wikimedia projects on Hugging Face's dataset search[7] and relied heavily on the authors' long experience working with Wikimedia data, developing natural language technologies, and collaborating with the Wikimedia communities. We list characteristic (not all) datasets for each stage of training, focusing on datasets and tasks that are oriented back towards the Wikimedia projects and that are at most a decade old. While we made an effort to build an exhaustive list, given the highly distributed nature of the Wikimedia movement and its research community, this overview might present some gaps. However, we believe that such potential gaps should not affect our conclusions in major ways, and we treat this as the start of a catalog that we will work to update as we learn more and more datasets are created.

The current training paradigms of LLMs depend on datasets at three major stages: pre-training, post-training, and evaluation.[8] Across these three stages, we detail how raw data is converted into datasets, tasks, and benchmarks to support the objectives of each stage. We see data, like the Wikimedia dumps, as relatively raw versions of what appears on the Wikimedia projects but in a form that is not directly useful for language models. We define datasets as data that has undergone pre-processing to anticipate a specific need, such as cleaning text to bring it closer to natural language. This pre-processing is important for turning Wikimedia content into high-quality datasets for language models to learn basic patterns of language (pre-training). We define tasks as datasets with explicit inputs and outputs that can be used to fine-tune models to complete a given action (post-training). In the final stage, benchmarks are curated tasks that allow for easy comparison of models to determine their usefulness to the Wikimedia projects (evaluation). While Wikimedia data has long been available and researchers have developed many datasets and tasks from this data, Wikimedia benchmarks have received less attention but are also an important mechanism for enabling members of the Wikimedia NLP community to encode our expectations for language models that are using Wikimedia content.

2.1 What makes a dataset helpful to Wikimedia?

There are many many datasets that use Wikimedia data but not all of them relate to tasks that are clearly of value to the Wikimedia editor community.[9] For example, SQuAD (Rajpurkar et al., 2016) is a Q&A dataset that is derived from Wikipedia that has played important role within the NLP community, but Q&A does not necessarily map to a task where AI could directly help Wikimedia editors. While different editors and communities will have different needs, we highlight a few core principles that guide these needs and would ideally be expressed in datasets and the resulting models trained on Wikimedia data:

- **Multilinguality**: Wikipedia alone exists in over 300 languages and providing equitable support to these different communities means

[7] https://huggingface.co/datasets

[8] See (Dubey et al., 2024) for a good rundown of pre-training/post-training and Bowman and Dahl (2021) for a good overview of evaluation of LLMs.

[9] We focus here on editors, but there are many other contributors to the Wikimedia projects that are also valuable stakeholders for future consideration such as campaign organizers or tool developers.

building NLP tools that can handle their diversity.

- **Core content policies**: editors follow three core content policies[10] that guide content on Wikipedia and useful models would need to do the same: Neutral Point-of-View (NPOV; fair representation of significant viewpoints), Verifiability (citations), and No Original Research (do not reach conclusions beyond the reliable sources).
- **Openness**: "free" and "open" are important to Wikimedia in many ways.[11] In this context, language models are most useful when they are open-source and small enough to be reasonably hosted by the community, e.g., through the non-profit Wikimedia Foundation.

2.2 From data to benchmarks: a case study

Wikipedia articles offer an illustrative example of how data can be curated to support the three stages of training while adhering to the principles listed above. Starting with raw data, regular snapshots of the content of the Wikimedia projects have long been available as freely-downloadable dumps of article wikitext (the markup language used to write Wikipedia articles). For these dumps to be useful for most natural language applications—i.e. converted from raw data into a dataset—researchers both need to apply some basic filtering at the page level to remove non-content pages such as redirects and strip out the wikitext syntax from the pages to leave something closer to natural language.[12] These resulting natural language datasets are useful for pre-training but still require the identification of specific inputs and outputs to be converted into a task that can be used for post-training. As an example of post-training, Qian et al. (2023) explore the task of writing short articles using an extensive dataset of Wikipedia article titles as inputs and the cleaned article text as expected outputs. Their metrics for automatic evaluation of the generated articles focus on language fluency and factualness. While this work is valuable for NLP fields like knowledge-intensive Q&A, it only briefly explores metrics that capture Wikimedia principles such as Verifiability (appropriate citations). This makes the work less useful to the Wikimedia community as a benchmark that could allow for direct comparison of LLMs at assisting Wikimedians in producing high-quality content.

In contrast, FreshWiki (Shao et al., 2024) more directly aims to be this benchmark: it is a curated dataset of English Wikipedia articles that have been assessed to be of high quality (more likely to adhere to Wikimedia content policies) and that have been written largely after a specific cut-off date (to avoid data leakage due to memorization of Wikipedia content by LLMs). FreshWiki further incorporates citations in the expected output and adds metrics to measure how faithful the content is to its citations (see Table 2). While FreshWiki currently only exists in English, this same process could be extended to other language editions as there is nothing English-specific about it. Shao et al. (2024) evaluate GPT-4's performance, which is neither compact nor open-source, on FreshWiki because (Gao et al., 2023) had previously shown that more open models (LLaMA-2 70B) performed well at generating text but still lagged behind GPT-4 in terms of correctly citing sources. Altogether, FreshWiki was able to better model Wikipedia's core content policies but exposed gaps in open models in this domain and is a framework that can be easily extended to be more multilingual.

3 A review of curated Wikimedia data

3.1 Pre-training: from data to datasets

Pre-training datasets for language models are collections of unsupervised text—i.e. no explicit task associated with them – that can be used to train language models to understand the basic relationships between words (tokens).[13] These datasets are maximally useful when they are large, high-quality, and diverse. Datasets of Wikipedia articles are the prime example of this but they are not the only source of pre-training datasets available from the Wikimedia projects. Here, the needs of the Wikimedia projects are generally well-aligned with the needs of NLP researchers: better pre-training data means better models which can then be used to support the Wikimedia projects.

We distinguish here between whether data (raw content) is available and if there are standard datasets (pre-processed text). Table 1 shows two clear gaps: 1) raw data about image pixels and their associated text for pre-training of multimodal mod-

[10] https://en.wikipedia.org/wiki/Wikipedia:Core_content_policies

[11] https://w.wiki/B5zh

[12] See Guo et al. (2020) for an illustrative example.

[13] While we focus on language models, we also include some image-text data here.

Major source of text	Data available?	Pre-processed dataset?
Wikipedia articles	Various dumps[14]	Hugging Face[15]
Wikimedia Talk pages	Various dumps	One-offs such as WikiConv (Hua et al., 2018)
Commons Images + captions / alt-text	None	One-offs such as WIT (Srinivasan et al., 2021) or Concadia (Kreiss et al., 2022)
Wikisource transcriptions	Various dumps	Hugging Face[16]
Wikisource image-transcription pairs	None	None
Other Wikimedia projects (Wikibooks, Wikivoyage, Wikiversity, Wiktionary)	Various dumps	None

Table 1: Major data(sets) of Wikimedia content.

els is lacking, and, 2) even when the raw data is available, it is rare that standardized, pre-processed datasets are available that lower the barrier to access for researchers.[17]

We encourage continued work to identify good practices for converting the other data sources listed in Table 1 into datasets. Each content source will bring its own challenges but the popularity of the Hugging Face Wikipedia dataset proves its value.[18] For example, Wikisource offers an exciting opportunity to diversify the knowledge on which language models are being trained given the contributions by the Wikisource communities in digitizing knowledge from languages that have historically been underrepresented online.[19] Generating image datasets[20] will take much more work and resources given the massive size of the imagery hosted on Wikimedia Commons but would be a worthy addition to the outsized role that Wikimedia content plays in pre-training datasets.

One very positive aspect of the state of Wikimedia content for pre-training is that all of the data and almost all of the datasets are massively multilingual. While each of Wikipedia's over 300 language editions has varying norms and content, tools for converting this data into datasets generally are language-agnostic—i.e. they are stripping out syntax or making other choices that do not rely on tokenization or language-specific semantics. This helps to fuel a positive feedback loop of more multilingual content leading to more multilingual AI and thus more support for growing these language editions (Costa-jussà et al., 2022). As will be seen below, this wealth of language data unfortunately does not always hold for post-training datasets.

3.2 Post-training: from datasets to tasks

Post-training datasets for language models are collections of supervised tasks that can be used to fine-tune models to be more useful for end-users. Traditional fine-tuning converts a model from general language modeling to accomplishing a specific task that leverages a model's pre-trained language capabilities. Most LLMs are now instruction-tuned to not do any specific task but be generally capable of accomplishing many types of tasks.[21]

Below, we catalog these fine-tuning tasks with the goal of showing how Wikimedia content can be valuable in post-training and encouraging development of models that are more useful for Wikimedia-relevant tasks. Arguably the most salient usage of Wikimedia content for language modeling is related to Q&A tasks—e.g., SQuAD (Rajpurkar et al., 2016) or WikiQA (Yang et al., 2015). Q&A is a reader-focused task and one that receives plenty of attention in language modeling. Here we choose to focus on the needs of Wikimedia editors. In this domain, we see ample opportunity for LLM developers to make greater use of these Wikimedia-based post-training tasks. This would be beneficial for Wikimedians but should also support the general alignment goals of LLM developers as we will

[17]While this reduced barrier to entry feels appropriate for pre-training given that Wikipedia content is freely-licensed, we do encourage researchers to understand more deeply the content and processing choices that they are making when it comes to post-training.

[18]Over 100,000 downloads in August 2024 per `https://huggingface.co/datasets/wikimedia/wikipedia`.

[19]`https://w.wiki/4Q7z`

[20]Or e.g., audio transcriptions (Gómez et al., 2023)

[21]Though traditional fine-tuning and instruction tuning have important differences in construction, we do not distinguish between the two as we generally believe that the datasets can be converted between the two formats as necessary.

discuss in Section 3.3.

There are many possible transformations of Wikimedia data into post-training tasks. We represent this diversity by selecting a sample of tasks and example datasets for each one. We further split the tasks into three categories (classification, recommendation, and text generation) to provide some basic structure.

Classification

- **Stance detection**: a core part of Wikimedia is reaching consensus through discussions. Kaffee et al. (2023) studied article deletion discussions in English, German, and Turkish and fine-tuned a language model to predict what policies an editor will cite and their stance regarding deletion based on their comments.

- **Vandalism detection**: patrolling recent edits for vandalism that should be removed is a core task in maintaining Wikipedia's reliability. Trokhymovych et al. (2023) fine-tuned language models in 47 languages to predict whether an edit will be reverted.

- **Citation-needed**: the Verifiability policy requires that many statements on Wikipedia be supported with a citation to a reliable source. Redi et al. (2019) trained language models to predict whether a given sentence needs a citation in English, French, and Italian.

- **Readability**: accessibility of content to readers is important on Wikipedia but can be difficult to measure. Trokhymovych et al. (2024) fine-tuned language models in 14 languages to rank content by its readability.

- **NPOV detection**: a core content policy for Wikipedia is that text must adhere to a neutral point of view. Wong et al. (2021) built a dataset from English Wikipedia of edits that violated various policies for training classifiers to detect NPOV violations and other related content reliability issues.

Recommendation

- **Citation recommendation**: finding a source to verify a claim on Wikipedia can be a difficult task for editors. Petroni et al. (2023) trained a retrieval and ranking model to find citations for statements on English Wikipedia.

- **Entity linking**: a key part of Wikipedia is its network of links that connect content and allow readers to go down rabbit holes. Gerlach et al. (2021) trained a model across six language editions of Wikipedia for recommending links to be added to text spans within articles. There are also multimodal variants of this task such as visual entity linking.[22]

- **Grammatical error correction**: Fixing small spelling mistakes or grammatical errors is a common editing task on Wikipedia. Grundkiewicz and Junczys-Dowmunt (2014) used English Wikipedia revision histories to identify these copy-edits in order to train language models for grammatical error correction.

Text Generation

- **Article descriptions**: all articles can be associated with a short phrase that helps readers disambiguate between similarly-named pages. Sakota et al. (2023) fine-tuned a language model to generate these article descriptions based on the first paragraph of Wikipedia articles and descriptions in other languages for 25 different language editions.

- **Edit Summaries**: each edit on Wikipedia should be accompanied by a short summary that explains what the edit did and why (similar to a code commit message). Šakota et al. (2024) fine-tuned a language model to generate these edit summaries based on extracted diffs of a given edit on English Wikipedia.

- **Between Structured and Unstructured**: Facts can be stored in many different ways on the Wikimedia projects ranging from unstructured text in Wikipedia articles to semi-structured text in infoboxes or tables to the structured statements of Wikidata. Likewise, external sources of content to be incorporated can also be found in a variety of formats. Models for converting between these formats help editors in adding content and making it more accessible. For example, Chen et al. (2021) trained language models to produce long-form text from tabular data compiled from English Wikipedia while Luggen et al. (2021) trained language models to recommend Wikidata properties based on Wikipedia text.

[22]https://huggingface.co/datasets/aiintelligentsystems/vel_commons_wikidata

- **Natural language to SPARQL**: Wikidata contains a wealth of information but querying that content via what's known as SPARQL can be difficult. Liu et al. (2024) compile a dataset of English-language requests for SPARQL queries and the resulting query to evaluate LLM-based approaches for generating SPARQL queries.

- **Simplification**: Entire language editions (Simple English) and namespaces (Txikipedia) have been created on Wikipedia to provide simpler-language versions of content. Sun et al. (2021) use this correspondence between English and Simple English Wikipedia to build a dataset of article leads and their simpler equivalents to train language models to simplify text.

- **Summarization**: summarization has many potential use-cases on the wikis from helping editors understand long discussions on-wiki such as RFCs (Im et al., 2018) or the information across multiple external sources. Ghalandari et al. (2020) compile a dataset from the English Wikipedia Current Events portal of multi-document summaries.

- **Machine translation**: translation plays an increasing role in assisting in content creation on Wikipedia and making the 300+ language editions accessible to all readers.[23] There are both datasets of published translations[24] for all languages and datasets of aligned text across languages like Schwenk et al. (2021).

- **Article writing**: Wikipedia is a tertiary source whose content is a consolidation of other sources as reflected in the citations. Shao et al. (2024) prompted LLMs to write English Wikipedia articles by gathering and summarizing sources related to a given topic.

This catalog of tasks demonstrates the diversity of NLP post-training tasks that already exist that could be beneficial to Wikimedia editors—ranging from simple binary classification to natural language generation, from short-form texts to long-form articles, and from models that must reflect Wikimedia-specific policies to more generic tasks like translation or summarization. This catalog also reveals large language gaps: despite the over 300 language editions of Wikipedia, most example datasets leverage English Wikipedia alone. This sometimes seems to be purely about precedent and familiarity—e.g., edit summaries exist in all language editions so expanding a dataset of them is largely trivial, but many language modeling tasks start with English. Other times, this stems from structural challenges on the Wikimedia projects that would take more extensive work to overcome—e.g., many language editions use various content reliability templates to flag NPOV issues but the templates and norms around them can vary language-to-language, making it difficult to scale datasets to more languages (Johnson and Lescak, 2022).

We focused here on language as the most salient facet of these datasets, but as identified in Section 2.1, open-source licensing and compactness are also important to assessing the value of models to the Wikimedia projects. This is especially true in models that touch on privacy-sensitive areas such as search queries (e.g., natural language to SPARQL) where depending on 3rd-party models would open up individuals to surveillance. The NLP community has made important strides in both of these spaces in recent years but cataloging which tasks are lacking in good open-source models would be beneficial for considering future research.

3.3 Evaluation: from tasks to benchmarks

Paraphrasing Bowman and Dahl (2021), benchmarks for natural-language understanding are datasets that have the following characteristics: 1) they are representative of the task in question, 2) their data are accurate and unambiguous, 3) they can accurately rank models, and, 4) they disincentivize biased or harmful models. While the existence of many Wikimedia-focused tasks in Section 3.2 is heartening, few of these meet the standards of benchmarks. Trivially, many datasets that are derived from Wikimedia data can be found in the pre-training data used by many LLMs and thus are not accurate evaluations of these model's ability to generalize to new examples. This lack of Wikimedia benchmarks means that editors do not have easy or effective means of evaluating models (especially LLMs) for their usefulness to Wikimedia. Additionally, many LLMs are not open-source or are too large to be trained (or even fine-tuned in some cases) by Wikimedia developers. Developing core Wikimedia benchmarks could provide an important means of nudging NLP practitioners to

[23] https://www.mediawiki.org/wiki/MinT

[24] https://www.mediawiki.org/wiki/Content_translation/Published_translations

develop models that are more beneficial out-of-the-box for the Wikimedia projects.

When it comes to evaluation of language models, it is less clear that the needs of the Wikimedia projects and NLP practitioners are currently well-aligned. Instruction-tuned LLMs are generally designed for a few purposes as demonstrated by the benchmarks that the model developers choose to test their models on. For example, the Llama 3 models (Dubey et al., 2024) are described as being benchmarked in eight top-level categories: (1) commonsense reasoning; (2) knowledge; (3) reading comprehension; (4) math, reasoning, and problem solving; (5) long context; (6) code; (7) adversarial evaluations; and (8) aggregate evaluations. Most of these categories are relevant for chat-bots to better answer questions but only incidentally tell us how these models might handle tasks related to applying Wikimedia content policies when editing or performing content moderation tasks.

The core content policies of Wikipedia that guide many of the post-training tasks in Section 3.2 have clear corollaries with the intentions of LLMs developers. Neutral Point-of-View aligns well with training models that are not biased or harmful.[25] No Original Research aligns well with the goal of reducing hallucinations. Verifiability is perhaps less clear as a stated goal of many LLM models—i.e. the ability to cite sources for answers. However, we are witnessing a shift towards attribution of sources in LLM-backed products via retrieval-augmented generation, and Verifiability has nice overlap with chain-of-thought approaches (Khalifa et al., 2024) that have been demonstrated to improve model performance in many reasoning tasks (Wei et al., 2022). In all, LLMs that are more useful for Wikimedia-related tasks should also be more useful for many tasks outside of Wikimedia. In Table 2, we focus on these core content policies and examine the state of benchmarks for following these policies when creating content[26] as well as evaluating existing content for whether it adheres to the policy.

Table 2 shows that there are existing benchmarks for evaluating the Verifiability and No Original Research policies. While citation-needed was developed with Wikipedia in mind, ALCE, FEVER, and WildHallucinations[27] were developed with Wikipedia content but are oriented towards standard NLP tasks such as Q&A or textual entailment. Work is still required to raise the quality of these benchmarks to ensure their freshness akin to FreshWiki's approach of only extracting content that was extensively edited after a given knowledge cut-off. And as with post-training tasks, these benchmarks are still heavily English-focused and do not cover the many other languages of Wikipedia.

Neutral Point-of-View has more mixed coverage. The NPOV policy contains multiple facets, of which two core components are the issue of biased language and the issue of biased coverage (due weight). Benchmarks do currently exist for the biased language facet based on editor activity from English Wikipedia. Biased coverage is harder to assess. WikiContradict(Hou et al., 2024) assesses a particular case where two reliable sources present contradictory information but there is a need for benchmarks that could e.g., determine whether content produced via multi-document summarization gives appropriate weight to different claims based on the level of their support across the documents. A core challenge here is not giving undue weight to fringe theories that may be mentioned by sources but are not well-supported.

We focused in this paper on the core content policies as an important first step for capturing facets important to the Wikimedia community and the basic existence of reasonable benchmarks in these areas. Moving forward, this framework could be extended to include more Wikimedia policies and guidelines and explore the fourth criteria asserted by Bowman and Dahl (2021) of disincentivizing bias through these benchmarks.

We recommend a few additional policies to consider for extending this framework.[28] The policy on Copyright Violations[29] touches on the importance of summarizing sources instead of copying them. Notability[30] is a major guideline for determining whether an article should exist or not for a topic. Benchmarks might focus on evaluating sources for

[25]Longpre et al. (2024) showed that including Wikipedia in pre-training data greatly decreases model toxicity.

[26]Editing existing content is a different task but we also consider it under content creation.

[27]WildHallucinations also covers content outside of Wikipedia but a related benchmark FActScore (Min et al., 2023) is extracted purely from English Wikipedia.

[28]We have linked to English Wikipedia policies and guidelines here but other language editions have developed their own policies and guidelines (Hwang and Shaw, 2022).

[29]https://en.wikipedia.org/wiki/Wikipedia:Copyright_violations

[30]https://en.wikipedia.org/wiki/Wikipedia:Notability

Content Policy	Context	Benchmark
Verifiability	Creating content: given a topic to generate content, does the model appropriate cite its sources?	FreshWiki for English, which uses the citation quality metrics from ALCE (Gao et al., 2023)
	Evaluating content: given a statement, does it require a citation?	Citation Needed (Redi et al., 2019) for English, French, and Italian
No Original Research	Creating content: given a topic to generate content, does the model hallucinate any claims?	WildHallucinations (Zhao et al., 2024) which covers English Wikipedia and English non-Wikipedia topics.
	Evaluating content: given a claim and source, is the claim supported?	FEVER (Thorne et al., 2018) for English
Neutral Point-of-View (biased language)	Creating content: given a topic or sentence, can the model remove biased language?	(Pryzant et al., 2020) and then (Ashkinaze et al., 2024) for a more recent evaluation of LLMs and English Wikipedia.
	Evaluating content: given a sentence, can the model identify if it uses biased language?	
Neutral Point-of-View (due weight)	Creating content: given a topic, can a model fairly represent all reliable sources?	WikiContradict (Hou et al., 2024) is the closest analog, which evaluates how well models handle the summarization of contradictory information.
	Evaluating content: given an article, can a model determine if the content is fairly represented?	None

Table 2: Benchmark tasks for Wikipedia's core content policies.

whether there is significant coverage of a given topic. There are also many style-related guidelines such as the Manual of Style[31] which touch on how to structure and format content such as capitalization, abbreviations, and mixing of dialects. One gap that is unlikely to be filled is assessing source reliability (a core component of all three core content policies). English Wikipedia, for example, tracks sources whose reliability is often questioned in a list known as Perennial Sources[32]. These assessments can change as sources themselves evolve and reflect consensus from long discussions about these sources. It is both hard to imagine LLMs making these assessments (except perhaps as a support for summarizing discussions) and undesirable to leave this complex sense-making to AI.

For disincentivizing bias through benchmarks, there is a long history of research on biases on the Wikimedia projects to pull from (Redi et al., 2020). One key step is expanding benchmarks to cover more languages but researchers might also develop benchmarks that only use articles that comprise a more balanced representation of the world. Datasets like Merity et al. (2016) that filter articles to only those deemed to be of the highest quality by Wikimedians would be another way to ensure that benchmark data is maximally likely to e.g., fully meet the expectations of the NPOV policy.

4 Conclusion

We present a summary of how Wikimedia data is curated to support the different stages of model training with a focus on NLP. At each stage, we highlight data that could be converted into more useful forms for training language models and identify ways in which these models could be more useful for Wikimedia editors. This shows that while Wikimedia content has been hugely influential and important to the development of AI as a source of language data, the field still has gaps in developing benchmarks and models that reflect the needs of Wikimedia editors. We hope that the opportunities that we highlight in this space encourage a more mutualistic relationship between NLP and the Wikimedia communities.

[31] https://en.wikipedia.org/wiki/Wikipedia:Manual_of_Style

[32] https://en.wikipedia.org/wiki/Wikipedia:Reliable_sources/Perennial_sources

References

Joshua Ashkinaze, Ruijia Guan, Laura Kurek, Eytan Adar, Ceren Budak, and Eric Gilbert. 2024. Seeing like an ai: How llms apply (and misapply) wikipedia neutrality norms. *arXiv preprint arXiv:2407.04183*.

Samuel Bowman and George Dahl. 2021. What will it take to fix benchmarking in natural language understanding? In *Proceedings of the 2021 Conference of the North American Chapter of the Association for Computational Linguistics: Human Language Technologies*, pages 4843–4855.

Tom B Brown. 2020. Language models are few-shot learners. *arXiv preprint arXiv:2005.14165*.

Mingda Chen, Sam Wiseman, and Kevin Gimpel. 2021. Wikitablet: A large-scale data-to-text dataset for generating wikipedia article sections. In *Findings of the Association for Computational Linguistics: ACL-IJCNLP 2021*, pages 193–209.

Creative Commons. 2023. Making AI Work for Creators and the Commons - Creative Commons — creativecommons.org. https://creativecommons.org/2023/10/07/making-ai-work-for-creators-and-the-commons/.

Marta R Costa-jussà, James Cross, Onur Çelebi, Maha Elbayad, Kenneth Heafield, Kevin Heffernan, Elahe Kalbassi, Janice Lam, Daniel Licht, Jean Maillard, et al. 2022. No language left behind: Scaling human-centered machine translation. *arXiv preprint arXiv:2207.04672*.

Jacob Devlin. 2018. Bert: Pre-training of deep bidirectional transformers for language understanding. *arXiv preprint arXiv:1810.04805*.

Abhimanyu Dubey, Abhinav Jauhri, Abhinav Pandey, Abhishek Kadian, Ahmad Al-Dahle, Aiesha Letman, Akhil Mathur, Alan Schelten, Amy Yang, Angela Fan, et al. 2024. The llama 3 herd of models. *arXiv preprint arXiv:2407.21783*.

Wikimedia Foundation. 2024. Artificial intelligence/Bellagio 2024. https://meta.wikimedia.org/w/index.php?title=Artificial_intelligence/Bellagio_2024&oldid=26436782.

Leo Gao, Stella Biderman, Sid Black, Laurence Golding, Travis Hoppe, Charles Foster, Jason Phang, Horace He, Anish Thite, Noa Nabeshima, et al. 2020. The pile: An 800gb dataset of diverse text for language modeling. *arXiv preprint arXiv:2101.00027*.

Tianyu Gao, Howard Yen, Jiatong Yu, and Danqi Chen. 2023. Enabling large language models to generate text with citations. In *Proceedings of the 2023 Conference on Empirical Methods in Natural Language Processing*, pages 6465–6488.

Martin Gerlach, Marshall Miller, Rita Ho, Kosta Harlan, and Djellel Difallah. 2021. Multilingual entity linking system for wikipedia with a machine-in-the-loop approach. In *Proceedings of the 30th ACM International Conference on Information & Knowledge Management*, pages 3818–3827.

Demian Gholipour Ghalandari, Chris Hokamp, John Glover, Georgiana Ifrim, et al. 2020. A large-scale multi-document summarization dataset from the wikipedia current events portal. In *Proceedings of the 58th Annual Meeting of the Association for Computational Linguistics*, pages 1302–1308.

Rafael Mosquera Gómez, Julián Eusse, Juan Ciro, Daniel Galvez, Ryan Hileman, Kurt Bollacker, and David Kanter. 2023. Speech wikimedia: A 77 language multilingual speech dataset. *arXiv preprint arXiv:2308.15710*.

Roman Grundkiewicz and Marcin Junczys-Dowmunt. 2014. The wiked error corpus: A corpus of corrective wikipedia edits and its application to grammatical error correction. In *Advances in Natural Language Processing: 9th International Conference on NLP, PolTAL 2014, Warsaw, Poland, September 17-19, 2014. Proceedings 9*, pages 478–490. Springer.

Mandy Guo, Zihang Dai, Denny Vrandečić, and Rami Al-Rfou. 2020. Wiki-40b: Multilingual language model dataset. In *Proceedings of the Twelfth Language Resources and Evaluation Conference*, pages 2440–2452.

Yufang Hou, Alessandra Pascale, Javier Carnerero-Cano, Tigran Tchrakian, Radu Marinescu, Elizabeth Daly, Inkit Padhi, and Prasanna Sattigeri. 2024. Wikicontradict: A benchmark for evaluating llms on real-world knowledge conflicts from wikipedia. *arXiv preprint arXiv:2406.13805*.

Yiqing Hua, Cristian Danescu-Niculescu-Mizil, Dario Taraborelli, Nithum Thain, Jeffery Sorensen, and Lucas Dixon. 2018. Wikiconv: A corpus of the complete conversational history of a large online collaborative community. In *Proceedings of the 2018 Conference on Empirical Methods in Natural Language Processing*, pages 2818–2823.

Sohyeon Hwang and Aaron Shaw. 2022. Rules and rule-making in the five largest wikipedias. In *Proceedings of the International AAAI Conference on Web and Social Media*, volume 16, pages 347–357.

Jane Im, Amy X Zhang, Christopher J Schilling, and David Karger. 2018. Deliberation and resolution on wikipedia: A case study of requests for comments. *Proceedings of the ACM on Human-Computer Interaction*, 2(CSCW):1–24.

Isaac Johnson and Emily Lescak. 2022. Considerations for multilingual wikipedia research. *arXiv preprint arXiv:2204.02483*.

Lucie-Aimée Kaffee, Arnav Arora, and Isabelle Augenstein. 2023. Why should this article be deleted? transparent stance detection in multilingual wikipedia editor discussions. In *Proceedings of the 2023 Conference on Empirical Methods in Natural Language Processing*, pages 5891–5909.

Muhammad Khalifa, David Wadden, Emma Strubell, Honglak Lee, Lu Wang, Iz Beltagy, and Hao Peng. 2024. Source-aware training enables knowledge attribution in language models. In *ICLR 2024 Workshop on Secure and Trustworthy Large Language Models*.

Elisa Kreiss, Fei Fang, Noah Goodman, and Christopher Potts. 2022. Concadia: Towards image-based text generation with a purpose. In *Proceedings of the 2022 Conference on Empirical Methods in Natural Language Processing*, pages 4667–4684.

Shicheng Liu, Sina J Semnani, Harold Triedman, Jialiang Xu, Isaac Dan Zhao, and Monica S Lam. 2024. Spinach: Sparql-based information navigation for challenging real-world questions. *arXiv preprint arXiv:2407.11417*.

Shayne Longpre, Gregory Yauney, Emily Reif, Katherine Lee, Adam Roberts, Barret Zoph, Denny Zhou, Jason Wei, Kevin Robinson, David Mimno, et al. 2024. A pretrainer's guide to training data: Measuring the effects of data age, domain coverage, quality, & toxicity. In *Proceedings of the 2024 Conference of the North American Chapter of the Association for Computational Linguistics: Human Language Technologies (Volume 1: Long Papers)*, pages 3245–3276.

Michael Luggen, Julien Audiffren, Djellel Difallah, and Philippe Cudré-Mauroux. 2021. Wiki2prop: A multimodal approach for predicting wikidata properties from wikipedia. In *Proceedings of the Web Conference 2021*, pages 2357–2366.

Stephen Merity, Caiming Xiong, James Bradbury, and Richard Socher. 2016. Pointer sentinel mixture models. *arXiv preprint arXiv:1609.07843*.

Sewon Min, Kalpesh Krishna, Xinxi Lyu, Mike Lewis, Wen-tau Yih, Pang Koh, Mohit Iyyer, Luke Zettlemoyer, and Hannaneh Hajishirzi. 2023. Factscore: Fine-grained atomic evaluation of factual precision in long form text generation. In *Proceedings of the 2023 Conference on Empirical Methods in Natural Language Processing*, pages 12076–12100.

Fabio Petroni, Samuel Broscheit, Aleksandra Piktus, Patrick Lewis, Gautier Izacard, Lucas Hosseini, Jane Dwivedi-Yu, Maria Lomeli, Timo Schick, Michele Bevilacqua, et al. 2023. Improving wikipedia verifiability with ai. *Nature Machine Intelligence*, 5(10):1142–1148.

Reid Pryzant, Richard Diehl Martinez, Nathan Dass, Sadao Kurohashi, Dan Jurafsky, and Diyi Yang. 2020. Automatically neutralizing subjective bias in text. In *Proceedings of the aaai conference on artificial intelligence*, volume 34, pages 480–489.

Hongjing Qian, Yutao Zhu, Zhicheng Dou, Haoqi Gu, Xinyu Zhang, Zheng Liu, Ruofei Lai, Zhao Cao, Jian-Yun Nie, and Ji-Rong Wen. 2023. Webbrain: Learning to generate factually correct articles for queries by grounding on large web corpus. *arXiv preprint arXiv:2304.04358*.

Pranav Rajpurkar, Jian Zhang, Konstantin Lopyrev, and Percy Liang. 2016. Squad: 100,000+ questions for machine comprehension of text. In *Proceedings of the 2016 Conference on Empirical Methods in Natural Language Processing*, pages 2383–2392.

Miriam Redi, Besnik Fetahu, Jonathan Morgan, and Dario Taraborelli. 2019. Citation needed: A taxonomy and algorithmic assessment of wikipedia's verifiability. In *The World Wide Web Conference*, pages 1567–1578.

Miriam Redi, Martin Gerlach, Isaac Johnson, Jonathan Morgan, and Leila Zia. 2020. A taxonomy of knowledge gaps for wikimedia projects (second draft). *arXiv preprint arXiv:2008.12314*.

Marija Šakota, Isaac Johnson, Guosheng Feng, and Robert West. 2024. Edisum: Summarizing and explaining wikipedia edits at scale. *arXiv preprint arXiv:2404.03428*.

Marija Sakota, Maxime Peyrard, and Robert West. 2023. Descartes: generating short descriptions of wikipedia articles. In *Proceedings of the ACM Web Conference 2023*, pages 1446–1456.

Holger Schwenk, Vishrav Chaudhary, Shuo Sun, Hongyu Gong, and Francisco Guzmán. 2021. Wikimatrix: Mining 135m parallel sentences in 1620 language pairs from wikipedia. In *Proceedings of the 16th Conference of the European Chapter of the Association for Computational Linguistics: Main Volume*, pages 1351–1361.

Yijia Shao, Yucheng Jiang, Theodore Kanell, Peter Xu, Omar Khattab, and Monica Lam. 2024. Assisting in writing wikipedia-like articles from scratch with large language models. In *Proceedings of the 2024 Conference of the North American Chapter of the Association for Computational Linguistics: Human Language Technologies (Volume 1: Long Papers)*, pages 6252–6278.

Krishna Srinivasan, Karthik Raman, Jiecao Chen, Michael Bendersky, and Marc Najork. 2021. Wit: Wikipedia-based image text dataset for multimodal multilingual machine learning. *arXiv preprint arXiv:2103.01913*.

Renliang Sun, Hanqi Jin, and Xiaojun Wan. 2021. Document-level text simplification: Dataset, criteria and baseline. In *Proceedings of the 2021 Conference on Empirical Methods in Natural Language Processing*, pages 7997–8013.

James Thorne, Andreas Vlachos, Christos Christodoulopoulos, and Arpit Mittal. 2018. Fever: a large-scale dataset for fact extraction and verification. In *Proceedings of the 2018 Conference of the North American Chapter of the Association for Computational Linguistics: Human Language Technologies, Volume 1 (Long Papers)*, pages 809–819.

Mykola Trokhymovych, Muniza Aslam, Ai-Jou Chou, Ricardo Baeza-Yates, and Diego Saez-Trumper. 2023. Fair multilingual vandalism detection system for wikipedia. In *Proceedings of the 29th ACM SIGKDD Conference on Knowledge Discovery and Data Mining*, pages 4981–4990.

Mykola Trokhymovych, Indira Sen, and Martin Gerlach. 2024. An open multilingual system for scoring readability of wikipedia. *arXiv preprint arXiv:2406.01835*.

Jason Wei, Xuezhi Wang, Dale Schuurmans, Maarten Bosma, Fei Xia, Ed Chi, Quoc V Le, Denny Zhou, et al. 2022. Chain-of-thought prompting elicits reasoning in large language models. *Advances in neural information processing systems*, 35:24824–24837.

KayYen Wong, Miriam Redi, and Diego Saez-Trumper. 2021. Wiki-reliability: A large scale dataset for content reliability on wikipedia. In *Proceedings of the 44th International ACM SIGIR Conference on Research and Development in Information Retrieval*, pages 2437–2442.

Yi Yang, Wen-tau Yih, and Christopher Meek. 2015. Wikiqa: A challenge dataset for open-domain question answering. In *Proceedings of the 2015 conference on empirical methods in natural language processing*, pages 2013–2018.

Wenting Zhao, Tanya Goyal, Yu Ying Chiu, Liwei Jiang, Benjamin Newman, Abhilasha Ravichander, Khyathi Chandu, Ronan Le Bras, Claire Cardie, Yuntian Deng, et al. 2024. Wildhallucinations: Evaluating long-form factuality in llms with real-world entity queries. *arXiv preprint arXiv:2407.17468*.

Blocks Architecture (BloArk): Efficient, Cost-Effective, and Incremental Dataset Architecture for Wikipedia Revision History

Lingxi Li[1] Zonghai Yao[1] Sunjae Kwon[1] Hong Yu[1,2,3,4]
[1]Manning College of Information and Computer Sciences, University of Massachusetts Amherst
[2]Department of Medicine, University of Massachusetts Medical School
[3]Miner School of Computer and Information Sciences, University of Massachusetts Lowell
[4]Center for Healthcare Organization and Implementation Research, VA Bedford Health Care
{lingxili,zonghaiyao,sunjaekwon}@umass.edu, hong_yu@uml.edu

Abstract

Wikipedia (Wiki) is one of the most widely used and publicly available resources for natural language processing (NLP) applications. Wikipedia Revision History (WikiRevHist)[1] shows the order in which edits were made to any Wiki page since its first modification. While the most up-to-date Wiki has been widely used as a training source, WikiRevHist can also be valuable resources for NLP applications. However, there are insufficient tools available to process WikiRevHist without having substantial computing resources, making additional customization, and spending extra time adapting others' works. Therefore, we report Blocks Architecture (BloArk), an efficiency-focused data processing architecture that reduces running time, computing resource requirements, and repeated works in processing WikiRevHist dataset. BloArk consists of three parts in its infrastructure: blocks, segments, and warehouses. On top of that, we build the core data processing pipeline: builder and modifier. The BloArk builder transforms the original WikiRevHist dataset from XML syntax into JSON Lines (JSONL) format for improving the concurrent and storage efficiency. The BloArk modifier takes previously-built warehouses to operate incremental modifications for improving the utilization of existing databases and reducing the cost of reusing others' works. In the end, BloArk can scale up easily in both processing Wikipedia Revision History and incrementally modifying existing dataset for downstream NLP use cases. The source code[2], documentations[3], and example usages[4] are publicly available online and open-sourced under GPL-2.0 license.

[1]https://meta.wikimedia.org/wiki/Data_dumps
[2]GitHub: https://github.com/lilingxi01/bloark
[3]Documentations: https://bloark.lingxi.li/
[4]Example usages: https://wikidata.lingxi.li/

1 Introduction

Wikipedia has played an important role in natural language processing (NLP) areas, such as information extraction (Kwon et al., 2022; Tran et al., 2014; Fisichella and Ceroni, 2021; Althoff et al., 2015; Liu et al., 2020), rephrasing (Botha et al., 2018; Martínez et al., 2024), and relationship graphs (Gonzalez-Hevia and Gayo-Avello, 2022; Piscopo et al., 2017; Schmelzeisen et al., 2021; Pellissier Tanon et al., 2019). As most researchers embrace informative large language models (LLMs) trained on the latest snapshot of Wikipedia (Naveed et al., 2023), the value of the WikiRevHist dataset has been underrated. WikiRevHist is valuable for its nature of human editing records, which roots the human reasoning on how to create and revise documents in decades. However, existing methods for pre-processing complex NLP data like Pandas (Thiébaut et al., 2011; Pivarski et al., 2020) are either requiring complicated setup or incompatible with the scale of WikiRevHist. While researchers have a lot of concurrent approaches to do batch processing of Wikipedia XML data dumps (Thiébaut et al., 2011), those approaches require complex configurations and an extensive amount of computing resources online (Rawat et al., 2019). In addition, popular Python data processing libraries like Pandas have difficulties working with nested data structures (Pivarski et al., 2020) and do not have multiprocessing out of the box, which takes time to setup and overcome hardware bottlenecks. And finally, none of the data processing libraries provide an easy way to handle large-sized dataset, such as checking unit data structures, extracting metadata for faster queries, and limiting maximum disk space usage. This often results in the overuse of shared disk space on computing clusters and the failure of processing jobs. Therefore, a high-performing, cost-effective, and convenient

Proceedings of the First Workshop on Advancing Natural Language Processing for Wikipedia, pages 102–111
November 16, 2024

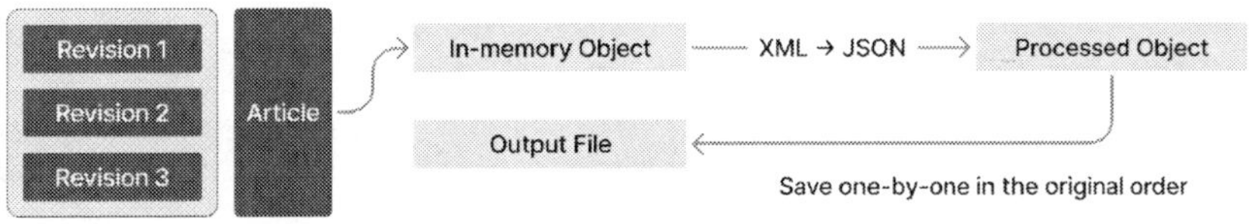

Figure 1: Traditional single-process multi-thread Python script for processing WikiRevHist. It needs to have the entire XML file decompressed into disk space before parsing, load revisions one-by-one, transform to JSON objects, apply changes, then store to JSON files.

solution for handling downstream works on the WikiRevHist dataset becomes significant.

To address this, we propose Blocks Architecture (BloArk), a new dataset architecture designed for processing WikiRevHist and building downstream datasets conveniently. To the best of our knowledge, this work is the first data architecture for processing WikiRevHist in an efficient, cost-effective, and incremental way.

To improve the computing resource utilization, BloArk uses multiprocessing, which divides a dataset building task into unit processing items and applies onto CPU cores in parallel. Unlike traditional single-process Python scripts in processing WikiRevHist as Figure 1, BloArk improves the processing speed by distributing the load onto multiple independent workers. From our experiment, parsing 50 dump files that have a total compressed size of 90 GB from the WikiRevHist took 12 hours 43 min using an Apple M1 chip with only one process, while the same process took 5 hours 19 min with four processes. As the extracted size of the entire WikiRevHist dump is more than 30 TB, researchers will spend days waiting for the process without using frameworks like Hadoop. Therefore, the ability to do parallel processing is what we consider first when designing this architecture.

To improve querying speed and dataset structure clarity, BloArk embeds metadata along with each warehouse. For example, article title and tags are saved in metadata to help filtering based on related categories. The byte offsets for each article in associated warehouse file are also saved to bring article-level concurrency into data processing.

Furthermore, to reduce the cost of reusing processed datasets, BloArk introduces a standardized protocol for all datasets created by BloArk. Researchers and prospective users can save a significant amount of time spent on adapting the dataset format of others' works on WikiRevHist. Users can easily access a preview of the dataset structure and make incremental modifications without the need for additional customization.

2 Similar Frameworks

While large-scale data analytics frameworks like Hadoop and Spark are convenient to use, they do not offer end-to-end toolkit such as data structure preview and row-level modifier defined as a Python function. While BloArk is not powerful and extensible comparing with enterprise-level data frameworks, BloArk is straightforward out-of-box, and does not require any complicated setup to run.

Furthermore, researchers can benefit from both BloArk and Spark. While Spark does not natively support XML dumps, it does support JSONL formats. Researchers can use BloArk to convert XML to JSONL and modify the row-level data structure through a straightforward definition. Subsequently, researchers can analyze the data stored in BloArk warehouses utilizing Spark.

3 Background

3.1 File Format

One of the most critical factors of efficiency is concurrency. We decided to use JSONL as the base file format for expanding the possibility of concurrency. JSONL is similar to JSON (JavaScript Object Notation) structure, which uses curly brackets for embracing an object with key-value pairs. JSON Lines (as known as JSONL format) have one JSON at a line, where the root of the file represents a list of objects. The benefit of using JSONL structure is that the processing of a file does not have to be linear. It is possible only to read the third object of a JSONL file without reading the first two objects. File formats like JSON and XML require linear parsing, which is not feasible for parallel processing within a file.

In general cases, the parallel processing will stay at the file level, such that one file would only be as-

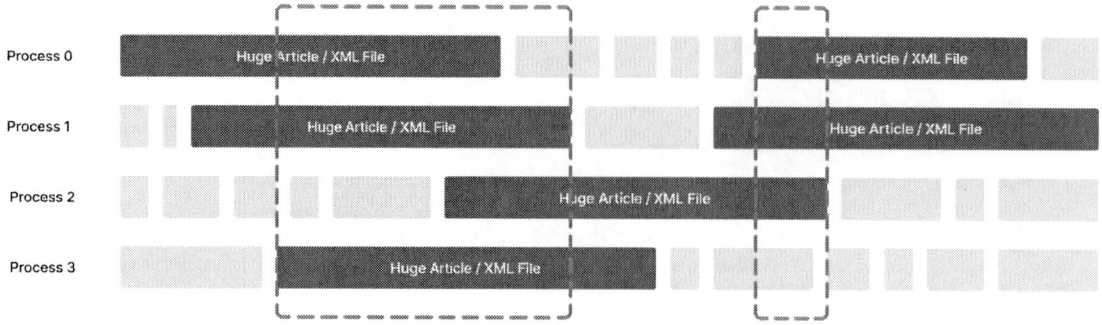

Figure 2: Understanding the congestion problem from a scheduling perspective. When we process huge articles or XML files at the same time, we also need to keep their decompressed files simultaneously, which increases the storage space bottleneck. Besides that, since large items take longer to process, disk space usage can easily accumulate because large articles are more likely to collide than smaller articles.

signed to one process. In contrast, BloArk expands the parallelism to article-level. When transforming JSONL files, BloArk assigns the same JSONL file into multiple processes, where each process knows the starting and ending byte offset that corresponds to an article. In this way, only certain bytes of data is loaded for one process, which avoids memory overhead and I/O bottleneck.

3.2 Unit Independence

First, one XML file from the original WikiRevHist dataset contains many articles that are independent of each other, which could be sent to different processes for improving running efficiency. However, in the given flow, there are two steps that require a linear processing: XML reading and JSONL writing. In the raw WikiRevHist dataset, the structure of one XML file looks like this:

```
<mediawiki>
  <siteinfo>...</siteinfo>
  <!-- First article -->
  <page>
    <title>...</title>
    <id>...</id>
    <!-- First revision -->
    <revision>
      <id>...</id>
      <parentid>...</parentid>
      <timestamp>...</timestamp>
      <text>...</text>
    </revision>
    <!-- Second revision -->
    <revision>
      ...
    </revision>
  </page>
  <!-- Second article -->
  <page>
    ...
  </page>
</mediawiki>
```

XML needs to be read line-by-line because each object consists of a starting tag and an ending tag. Without finding the ending tag, we cannot finalize the current object and cannot start accepting the next object. Besides that, we need to read XML into objects at revision level instead of article level because some articles with a few thousands of revisions can easily exceed the memory limit. Therefore, within one XML file, this reading process is forced to be linear. Although there exists an approach (Zhang, 2022) to parallelize the XML parsing process for speeding up, this approach requires chunking XML files and eventually loading the entire XML file into memory, which is not feasible for dataset having large individual files, such as WikiRevHist.

The same situation happens in writing JSONL file as well, where each line of a JSONL file is a complete JSON object. Even though we have independence between lines, we cannot write the next line efficiently until the current line is completed. There are also potential writing conflicts between processes without locking, so it is best practice to only allow one process to write a JSONL file.

Ultimately, most researchers end up utilizing only one CPU per XML file, which leads to a potential issue: the necessity for an excessive amount of storage space on shared clusters to accommodate decompressed XML files concurrently.

3.3 Unit Processing Item and Resource Congestion

The unit processing item, such as all revisions of one article, is an important factor in dealing with large-sized datasets like WikiRevHist. Loading all revisions of an article as a unit processing item

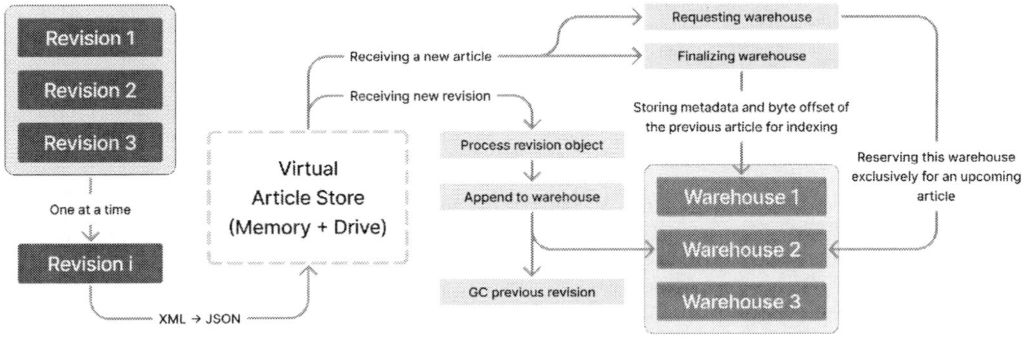

Figure 3: BloArk execution diagram of the "building process" in a single-process perspective. BloArk reads each XML file from top to bottom and at the third depth. When a revision is received, we store each revision as one JSON object in the warehouse file (JSONL format) and store the metadata in a separate, uncompressed JSONL file. When a new article is detected, we finalize the previous article and assign a new warehouse for storage.

can be oversized for the memory when the revision size is large, especially in a concurrent scenario where all processes share the same memory. For instance, some articles that have 300K revisions could easily take up to 60 GB of memory when we are loading from a raw XML file, making changes, and outputting to a JSON file.

In addition, due to the nature of Python multiprocessing, no exception will be thrown from the child process if it runs out of memory, such as when all revisions of a long article are loaded into memory at once. The unhandling scenario like this increases the engineering complexity and failure rate especially on large datasets like WikiRevHist. In our experiments, resource congestion problem as described in Figure 2 can be observed frequently.

To resolve this, we define the unit processing item to be per revision instead of per article, which reduces the amount of data loaded into memory at the same time, and improves the concurrency. We will discuss this in detail in a later section.

3.4 Reusability

When conducting research using WikiRevHist, a significant challenge arises. Researchers often encounter the need for extensive additional work to adapt and utilize others' works effectively. Decompression and recompression processes were configured repeatedly, and dataset structures varied. To improve reusability and downstream research collaborations, BloArk standardizes the data structure for revision-based dataset such as WikiRevHist and embeds repeated works within a unified data pipeline. Any dataset built from BloArk should be

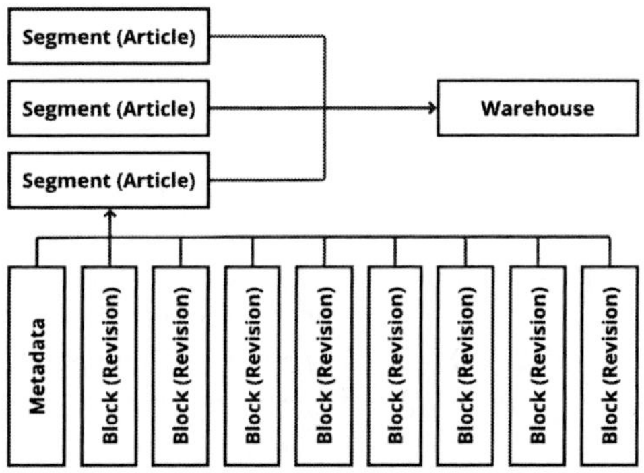

Figure 4: BloArk's data structure has three components: blocks, segments, and warehouses. In the mapping to WikiRevHist, a block represents a revision, a segment consists of a metadata object and all revisions on a timely basis, and a warehouse contains multiple segments (articles) until exceeding the size limit.

effortlessly imported, viewed, and updated without the need of heavy engineering configurations. Details of our approach will be described in the "modifying process" below.

4 Architecture and Usage

One goal of this research is to build a highly reusable architecture for supporting a wide range of downstream research in exploring the potential value of WikiRevHist. Since Wikipedia XML dumps are difficult to handle and expensive to process (Thiébaut et al., 2011), BloArk transforms the XML dumps into JSONL format before any data processing for easier storage and handling. This is called the "building process". This pro-

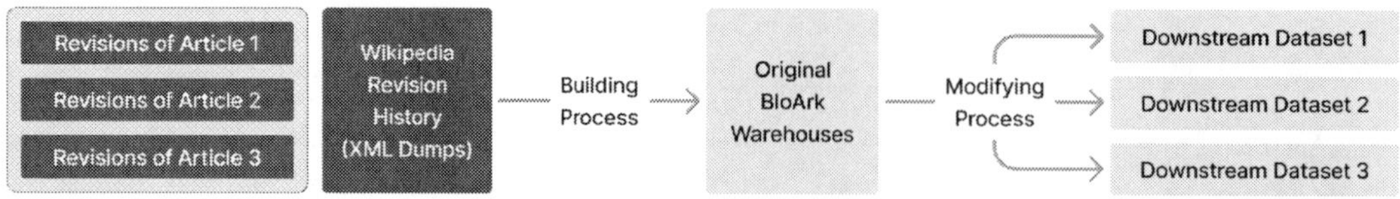

Figure 5: BloArk's data flow reduces the processing cost by making all downstream datasets on top of an original processed BloArk warehouses, which transforms XML data into JSON format. Under this setting, the most time-consuming process, the "building process", will only be executed once for an entire WikiRevHist dump of a month.

cess is used for overcoming the high cost of processing XML files by only executing it once. After the "building process", researchers can create downstream datasets based on a modifier that tells BloArk how to transform each unit processing item in the dataset. This is called the "modifying process".

4.1 Building Process

In the building process, we use parallel CPU cores to decompress raw XML dumps of WikiRevHist and transform revision objects from XML syntax into JSON format before storing into the disk, as illustrated in Figure 3. Due to the independence reason mentioned in Section 3.2, the optimal approach is to process one XML file per CPU core, which makes this step harder to scale.

As described in Figure 4, BloArk consists of three parts: blocks, segments, and warehouses. These three components are shared across two processes. In the mapping to the WikiRevHist, a block corresponds to a single revision, a segment represents an article comprising multiple revisions, and a warehouse consists of a specified number of articles, defined by a size limit. Each block represents an JSON object equivalent to the structure below:

```
{
  "article_id": "...",
  "revision_id": "...",
  "timestamp": "...",
  "contributor": {
    "username": "...",
    "id": "..."
  },
  "comment": "...",
  "format": "...",
  "text": {
    "@bytes": "...",
    "#text": "..."
  },
  "sha1": "..."
}
```

4.2 Modifying Process

After building the raw dataset from XML dumps into BloArk warehouses, we can make batch changes to the existing dataset. To configure the modifying process, researchers need to define a BloArk modifier that takes revision information in each step, and outputs the target block that should be stored. Article-level computations can also be done through segment metadata, such as word counts and article URL extractions. This step is similar to MapReduce (Dean and Ghemawat, 2008), which applies batch changes to the dataset, but BloArk modifier is simpler to define and easier to use on smaller-sized machines. We will describe the example usage and process setup in Section 5. To avoid overflowing the memory in subprocesses, BloArk loads blocks only when it is requested, and discards the loaded variable once the modification of a block has been done. For example, if we are trying to extract link differences between adjacent revisions from WikiRevHist while discarding all irrelevant information, the modified block will be structured like this:

```
{
  "article_id": "...",
  "revision_id": "...",
  "timestamp": "...",
  "added_urls": ["...", "...", "..."],
  "removed_urls": ["...", "...", "..."]
}
```

4.3 Parallelization

In order to deliver a similar performance as Hadoop while keeping usability and convenience on smaller machines, we specify the unit processing item for all BloArk jobs. Unit processing item is the minimum unit that its peer can be safely processed in other CPU cores without duplicating efforts. In the "building process", a unit processing item is one XML file. Even though articles are independent from each other on Wikipedia, they are stored in a way that has a linear dependency in the XML dumps. For example, we cannot get the second article in a certain way without going through the first article. After building the warehouses, BloArk stores the file offset for a segment, so it is fast and convenient to locate the revisions of an article without needing to go through the articles stored before it. Therefore, in the "modifying process", it is possible to process articles from the same warehouse across multiple CPU cores. This increases the computing resource utilization when processing size is small.

5 Example Usages

In this section, we demonstrate the complete usage of BloArk library from downloading the source dataset, building original warehouses, to modifying previously-built warehouses based on specific research needs. The complete data flow for WikiRevHist downstream datasets is illustrated in Figure 5.

Please note that Python snippets in this section are simplified for demonstration purposes. They are designed to be run in Jupyter Notebooks. Additional code and type verification might be needed to run them directly as a Python script, such as:

```
if __name__ == '__main__':
    # Your code snippet goes to here
```

5.1 Download the Source Data

Before building the original warehouses, the source WikiRevHist data dump is required, such as English Wikipedia (enwiki)[5] hosted on Wikimedia Foundation. It can be downloaded efficiently using WikiDL library[6] and with a maximum of 3 processes for a fair use of public resources[7]. The code sample for downloading WikiRevHist is demonstrated below. Downloading may require a significant amount of time.

```
from wikidl import WikiDL

downloader = WikiDL(
    # Specify parallel downloading (max 3).
    num_proc=3,
    # Update this to the latest dump date.
    snapshot_date='20240801',
    # This means: Edit History Dump (EHD).
    select_pattern='ehd',
)
```

[5]https://dumps.wikimedia.org/enwiki/

[6]WikiDL Docs: https://wikidl.lingxi.li/

[7]This 3-process limit is observed from Wikimedia gateway rules. HTTP Error 503 will be returned if having more than 3 parallel downloads.

```
# Process starts.
downloaded_files = downloader.start(
    # Save all compressed dumps into `/input`.
    output_dir='./input',
)
```

5.2 Build Original Warehouses from the Source Data

The "building process" of BloArk should be applied to transform original XML dumps of WikiRevHist dataset into BloArk warehouses in JSONL format. As described in Section 4, the "building process" is required for any downstream dataset and expected to only run once.

For better system reliability, it is recommended to reserve at least 1 GB of memory per CPU in this long-running job. This memory limit depends on the largest size of an article. Memory overflow is generally difficult to identify in Python, and it leads to a CPU process that never joins back to the main process. As the WikiRevHist is updated every month, larger memory budget per CPU is recommended to avoid losing long-running progress.

```
import bloark

builder = bloark.Builder(
    # Define the output location for warehouses.
    output_dir='./warehouses',
    # Use 8 processes (CPUs) in parallel.
    num_proc=8,
)

# Load all compressed XML dump file names.
# It does not load files into memory yet.
builder.preload('./input')

# Optional: if you want to test with the first 10
# compressed XML dumps, use following line.
# builder.files = builder.files[:10]

# This command will take a long time.
builder.build()
```

5.3 Example Dataset: Clean Text and Links

All WikiRevHist contents use Wikitext, a markup language for all Wikipedia documents. To extract clean text that does not include any markup syntax for better downstream training, we propose a new dataset that can be easily built using BloArk. In the "modifying process", we define the block-level modifier function using Grimm package[8] and store texts, links, and images as new blocks into new warehouses.

Cleaned WikiRevHist data has been widely used in training editing models, such as in modeling

[8]Grimm Package Docs: https://twiki.lingxi.li/docs/grimm/get-started

editing processes (Reid and Neubig, 2022) task. BloArk can improve the efficiency of data preparation by simplifying the implementation and enhancing the processing speed.

```
import bloark
from grimm import clean_syntax

class CleanModifier(bloark.ModifierProfile):
    def block(
        self, content: dict, metadata: dict
    ):
        text_content = content['text']['#text']
        output = clean_syntax(text_content)
        text, ext_urls, int_urls, imgs = output

        new_content = {
            "revision_id": content['revision_id']
            "clean_text": text,
            "external_links": ext_urls,
            "internal_links": int_urls,
            "images": imgs,
        }
        return new_content, metadata

modifier = bloark.Modifier(
    output_dir='./output',
    num_proc=8,
)

# Load original warehouses.
modifier.preload('./warehouses')

# Tips: you can add more than one profile.
modifier.add_profile(CleanModifier())

# This command will take a long time.
modifier.start()
```

The original input of this process shapes as described in Section 4.1. After running the "modifying process", outputted blocks in new warehouses will be structured like this:

```
{
  "revision_id": "...",
  "clean_text": "...",
  "external_links": ["...", "...", "..."],
  "internal_links": ["...", "...", "..."],
  "images": ["...", "...", "..."]
}
```

5.4 Example Dataset: 6-Month Snapshots

One way to modify original warehouses is by filtering, such as keeping only revisions that meet specific criteria. This can also help reduce the size of the dataset and the cost of future processing. In the past, significant efforts have focused on generating the next revision of an article based on previous revision histories. In those NLP tasks, WikiRevHist can conveniently provide article snapshots every six months within the past decade. Therefore, we propose a new dataset based on BloArk that has revision snapshots of an article for every 6 month. The block-level structure of this dataset should remain the same as described in Section 4.1, but have less blocks.

There are two benefits. First, it is easier to observe apparent changes in snapshots every 6 months than continuous editing histories. When using all editing revisions to train the model, some revisions might not help generalize the pattern of changes for the actual event, as those are simply replacing some unnecessary words or fine-tuning paragraphs. Second, WikiRevHist data hosting platforms like Wikimedia Foundation does not keep latest revision data dumps that are older than 3 months, which makes it very hard to find the snapshot at a specific time frame from the internet without accessing the full revision history.

The following is a simplified example code for modifying this dataset from original warehouses.

```
from datetime import datetime, timedelta
import bloark

class SnapshotModifier(bloark.ModifierProfile):
    last_date: datetime = None

    def block(
        self, content: dict, metadata: dict
    ):
        timestamp = content['timestamp']
        curr_date = datetime \
            .fromisoformat(timestamp)

        if self.last_date and curr_date < (
            self.last_date + timedelta(days=180)
        ):
            # `None` for not saving this block.
            # `metadata` is still needed.
            return None, metadata

        self.last_date = curr_date
        return content, metadata

modifier = bloark.Modifier(
    output_dir='./output',
    num_proc=8,
)
modifier.preload('./warehouses')
modifier.add_profile(SnapshotModifier())
modifier.start()
```

5.5 Example Dataset: 6-Month Edit Summaries

In the task of summarizing human edits, we need a dataset that contains the edit differences and a generated summary on those differences. Original WikiRevHist dump kept all revisions, which is too frequent for this dataset and is not cost-effective to have a large amount of generation works. Therefore, we propose a new dataset based on BloArk to extract the summary of edits from each article in a 6-month time frame. For every adjacent revisions in an article, we compare their text, get a list of differences, and use LLM to generate a summary.

With the incremental modification by BloArk, the creation process of this dataset could be based on the 6-month snapshot dataset mentioned in Section 5.4. It saves time on re-filtering revisions from the source, and it is convenient to reuse works that had already been done by BloArk.

```
import bloark

class SummaryModifier(bloark.ModifierProfile):
    last_text: str = None

    def block(
        self, content: dict, metadata: dict
    ):
        if not last_text:
            last_text = curr_text
            return None, metadata

        curr_text = content['text']['#text']

        # TODO: Implement this function.
        changes = diff_function(...)

        # TODO: Implement this function.
        summary = summarize_changes(...)

        last_text = curr_text
        new_data = {
            "changes": changes,
            "summary": summary,
            "timestamp": content['timestamp'],
        }
        return new_data, metadata

modifier = bloark.Modifier(
    output_dir='./output',
    num_proc=8,
)

# Load the previously-built snapshot dataset.
# This saves the time to filter from source.
modifier.preload('./6-month-snapshots')
modifier.add_profile(SummaryModifier())
modifier.start()
```

The modified block will have differences for every 6 month, and be structured as below. The actual format of edit differences will be based on the implementation of difference function.

```
{
  "changes": [
    { "type": "add", "content": "..." },
    { "type": "remove", "content": "..." },
  ],
  "summary": "...",
  "timestamp": "..."
}
```

6 Limitations and Future Works

First, current BloArk does not have a way to incrementally sync changes when the source XML dumps are updated. WikiRevHist dumps update once a month. Therefore, users need to rebuild from the source every month in order to get the most up-to-date dataset. In the future, the "building process" of BloArk can be expanded with a feature to extract differences between two XML dumps and update previously-built warehouses from the differences.

Second, raw WikiRevHist XML dumps store each revision in full text. To improve storage efficiency, users can extract differences between adjacent revisions using libraries like difflib or ergodiff, and only store the differences. This extraction process can be achieved with a BloArk modifier applied after the "building process".

Third, current BloArk does not support the separation of blocks. This can be improved by designing a new API for modifiers, which allows returning multiple blocks instead of requiring one-on-one mapping. This future work can be widely used on tasks like expanding a single revision into multiple knowledge entries where each block is a tuple for knowledge graph.

Lastly, this work currently lacks a benchmark or evaluation. Establishing an empirical benchmark to evaluate the efficiency of data processing frameworks on WikiRevHist would be beneficial for comparing the performance and usability among similar frameworks. Additionally, it would serve as a measuring guideline for future research in this area.

7 Conclusion

In this work, we introduce BloArk, an efficient, cost-effective, and incremental dataset architecture for processing WikiRevHist. BloArk provides two different processes, the "building process" and the "modifying process", for resolving two main issues: high cost of handling XML dumps, and inconvenience of querying and modifying existing datasets built upon XML dumps. Since all datasets built by BloArk can be easily imported and modified further, the cost of doing research on WikiRevHist will be decreased. With BloArk, prospective users can save their time when exploring the potential value of WikiRevHist and other downstream datasets.

References

Tim Althoff, Xin Luna Dong, Kevin Murphy, Safa Alai, Van Dang, and Wei Zhang. 2015. Timemachine: Timeline generation for knowledge-base entities. In *Proceedings of the 21th ACM SIGKDD International Conference on Knowledge Discovery and Data Mining*, pages 19–28.

Jan A Botha, Manaal Faruqui, John Alex, Jason Baldridge, and Dipanjan Das. 2018. Learning to split and rephrase from wikipedia edit history. *arXiv preprint arXiv:1808.09468*.

Jeffrey Dean and Sanjay Ghemawat. 2008. Mapreduce: simplified data processing on large clusters. *Communications of the ACM*, 51(1):107–113.

Marco Fisichella and Andrea Ceroni. 2021. Event detection in wikipedia edit history improved by documents web based automatic assessment. *Big Data and Cognitive Computing*, 5(3):34.

Alejandro Gonzalez-Hevia and Daniel Gayo-Avello. 2022. Leveraging wikidata's edit history in knowledge graph refinement tasks. *arXiv preprint arXiv:2210.15495*.

Sunjae Kwon, Zonghai Yao, Harmon S Jordan, David A Levy, Brian Corner, and Hong Yu. 2022. Medjex: A medical jargon extraction model with wiki's hyperlink span and contextualized masked language model score. In *Proceedings of the Conference on Empirical Methods in Natural Language Processing. Conference on Empirical Methods in Natural Language Processing*, volume 2022, page 11733. NIH Public Access.

Yinan Liu, Wei Shen, Zonghai Yao, Jianyong Wang, Zhenglu Yang, and Xiaojie Yuan. 2020. Named entity location prediction combining twitter and web. *IEEE Transactions on Knowledge and Data Engineering*, 33(11):3618–3633.

Antonio David Ponce Martínez, Thierry Etchegoyhen, Jesus Javier Calleja Perez, and Harritxu Gete. 2024. Split and rephrase with large language models. In *Proceedings of the 62nd Annual Meeting of the Association for Computational Linguistics (Volume 1: Long Papers)*, pages 11588–11607.

Humza Naveed, Asad Ullah Khan, Shi Qiu, Muhammad Saqib, Saeed Anwar, Muhammad Usman, Naveed Akhtar, Nick Barnes, and Ajmal Mian. 2023. A comprehensive overview of large language models. *arXiv preprint arXiv:2307.06435*.

Thomas Pellissier Tanon, Camille Bourgaux, and Fabian Suchanek. 2019. Learning how to correct a knowledge base from the edit history. In *The World Wide Web Conference*, pages 1465–1475.

Alessandro Piscopo, Chris Phethean, and Elena Simperl. 2017. What makes a good collaborative knowledge graph: group composition and quality in wikidata. In *Social Informatics: 9th International Conference, SocInfo 2017, Oxford, UK, September 13-15, 2017, Proceedings, Part I 9*, pages 305–322. Springer.

Jim Pivarski, David Lange, and Peter Elmer. 2020. Nested data structures in array frameworks. In *Journal of Physics: Conference Series*, volume 1525, page 012053. IOP Publishing.

Charu Rawat, Arnab Sarkar, Sameer Singh, Rafael Alvarado, and Lane Rasberry. 2019. Automatic detection of online abuse and analysis of problematic users in wikipedia. In *2019 Systems and Information Engineering Design Symposium (SIEDS)*, pages 1–6. IEEE.

Machel Reid and Graham Neubig. 2022. Learning to model editing processes. *arXiv preprint arXiv:2205.12374*.

Lukas Schmelzeisen, Corina Dima, and Steffen Staab. 2021. Wikidated 1.0: An evolving knowledge graph dataset of wikidata's revision history. *arXiv preprint arXiv:2112.05003*.

Dominique Thiébaut, Yang Li, Diana Jaunzeikare, Alexandra Cheng, Ellysha Raelen Recto, Gillian Riggs, Xia Ting Zhao, Tonje Stolpestad, and Cam Le T Nguyen. 2011. Processing wikipedia dumps-a case-study comparing the xgrid and mapreduce approaches. In *CLOSER*, pages 391–396. Citeseer.

Tuan Tran, Andrea Ceroni, Mihai Georgescu, Kaweh Djafari Naini, and Marco Fisichella. 2014. Wikipevent: Leveraging wikipedia edit history for event detection. In *International Conference on Web Information Systems Engineering*, pages 90–108. Springer.

Yunsong Zhang. 2022. A parallel xml parsing algorithm based on nem-xml. In *2022 8th Annual International Conference on Network and Information Systems for Computers (ICNISC)*, pages 437–439. IEEE.

A Distribution and Maintenance

- **Will the source code of BloArk be open sourced on public platforms? Will it be published?**
  Yes. BloArk is open sourced on GitHub under GPL-2.0 license. Everyone is welcomed to submit issues/pull requests (PRs) on BloArk's GitHub public repository. BloArk package is published on PyPI and free to download for everyone using Python package manager.

- **When will the source code be distributed?**
  The source code is immediately available on our GitHub public repository.

- **Who will be supporting/maintaining the BloArk?**
  Lingxi Li will maintain the BloArk code base

on GitHub and publish version changes to PyPI periodically. Bug reports can be opened on GitHub issues and Lingxi Li will address them by severity.

- **How can the owner/curator/manager of the dataset architecture be contacted (e.g., email address)?**
  Lingxi Li, the creator/maintainer of BloArk, can be contacted at: *research@lingxi.li*.

- **Will downstream datasets be distributed publicly?**
  No. BloArk is a data processing architecture that can be used to build datasets. It is not a dataset. Downstream datasets will be built, distributed, and owned by prospective users.

- **Will original warehouses be distributed to third parties outside of the entity (e.g., company, institution, organization) on behalf of which the dataset was created?**
  Yes, but for sample access only. Users can use BloArk package and example code provided above to replicate the "building process" and build original warehouses on their own resources. We may consider releasing one version of original warehouses built from WikiRevHist XML dumps to Hugging Face for public sample access.

- **Is there an erratum?**
  BloArk has changelogs recorded in its official website[9]. This information will also be available on GitHub publishes.

- **Will BloArk be updated (e.g., bug fixes, performance improvements, feature requests)?**
  Lingxi Li will fix severe bugs and monitor GitHub issues for bug reports and questions. Feature requests and performance improvements will be made by maintainers' decisions. Since BloArk is open sourced, everyone can contribute to the code base, and Lingxi Li will review the contribution to ensure the quality and safety of BloArk.

- **Has BloArk been used for any tasks already?**
  BloArk has already been used in tasks given in example datasets described in Section 5.

- **Will older versions of BloArk continue to be hosted?**
  All previous versions of BloArk package will always be available to download through Python package manager from PyPI.

- **If others want to extend/augment/build on/contribute to this dataset architecture, is there a mechanism for them to do so?**
  Yes. BloArk's GitHub repository is public and opened to everyone for contributions through PR. Lingxi Li will review submitted code to ensure quality and safety of BloArk package.

- **Will BloArk be distributed under a copyright or other intellectual property (IP) license, and/or under applicable terms of use (ToU)?**
  BloArk is open sourced under GPL-2.0 license. The copyright of WikiRevHist dataset belongs to its original license from Wikipedia. All downstream datasets will not have ownership connection to BloArk.

[9]https://bloark.lingxi.li/resources/changelog

ARMADA: Attribute-Based Multimodal Data Augmentation

Xiaomeng Jin [†] **Jeonghwan Kim**[†] **Yu Zhou**[¶] **Kuan-Hao Huang**[§]
Te-Lin Wu[‡] **Nanyun Peng**[‡] **Heng Ji**[†]

[†]University of Illinois, Urbana Champaign [¶,‡]University of California, Los Angeles
[§]Texas A&M University
{xjin17, jk100, hengji}@illinois.edu, yu.zhou@ucla.edu
{telinwu, violetpeng}@cs.ucla.edu, khhuang@tamu.edu

Abstract

In Multimodal Language Models (MLMs), the cost of manually annotating high-quality image-text pair data for fine-tuning and alignment is extremely high. While existing multimodal data augmentation frameworks propose ways to augment image-text pairs, they either suffer from *semantic inconsistency* between texts and images, or generate unrealistic images, causing *knowledge gap* with real world examples. To address these issues, we propose **A**tt**r**ibute-based **M**ultimod**a**l **D**ata **A**ugmentation (ARMADA), a novel multimodal data augmentation method via knowledge-guided manipulation of visual attributes of the mentioned entities. Specifically, we extract entities and their visual attributes from the original text data, then search for alternative values for the visual attributes under the guidance of knowledge bases (KBs) and large language models (LLMs). We then utilize an image-editing model to edit the images with the extracted attributes. ARMADA is a novel multimodal data generation framework that: (i) extracts knowledge-grounded attributes from symbolic KBs for semantically consistent yet *distinctive* image-text pair generation, (ii) generates visually similar images of disparate categories using neighboring entities in the KB hierarchy, and (iii) uses the commonsense knowledge of LLMs to modulate auxiliary visual attributes such as backgrounds for more robust representation of original entities. Our empirical results over four downstream tasks demonstrate the efficacy of our framework to produce high-quality data and enhance the model performance. This also highlights the need to leverage external knowledge proxies for enhanced interpretability and real-world grounding.

1 Introduction

Multimodal Language Models (MLMs) exhibit remarkable abilities in comprehending and integrating various modalities, encompassing texts, images, and videos. Recently, many MLMs have been proposed by researchers in both academic and industrial communities (Li et al., 2020; Radford et al., 2021; Li et al., 2022a,b; Liu et al., 2023b; Dai et al., 2023; Achiam et al., 2023), demonstrating significant achievements across various downstream tasks, such as image-text retrieval (Radford et al., 2021; Li et al., 2022a) and visual question answering (VQA) (Liu et al., 2023b,a; Dai et al., 2023). Training MLMs for downstream tasks, which usually involves fine-tuning and alignment stages, requires substantial amounts of annotated data. However, collecting and annotating such datasets demand considerable human effort and are notorious for their expense and time-consuming nature. A common strategy to overcome this problem is leveraging data augmentation techniques, which automatically synthesize new data instances from existing datasets, relieving the need to rely on manually annotated datasets to train these models.

Existing multimodal data augmentation methods, which require the perturbation of both the visual and textual modalities in tandem, can generally be classified into the following two groups: (i) latent space-based methods that perturb the latent representations of existing data instances (Liu et al., 2022) via adversarially trained augmentation networks, and (ii) surface form-based methods (Müller and Hutter, 2021; Hao et al., 2023) that simply perturb superficial representations such as orientations/pixel-level mixture of images. Latent space-based methods such as LeMDA (Liu et al., 2022) generate augmented multimodal latent features aligned with the training data distribution, but are inherently confined by their lack of interpretability and controllability. While surface form-based methods partly provide interpretable and controllable alternative, their simple augmentation schemes such as random solarization and pixel-level interpolation lead to *semantic inconsistency*. For instance, Figure 1 shows that random cropping or image interpolation cause semantic

Proceedings of the First Workshop on Advancing Natural Language Processing for Wikipedia, pages 112–125
November 16, 2024 ©2024 Association for Computational Linguistics

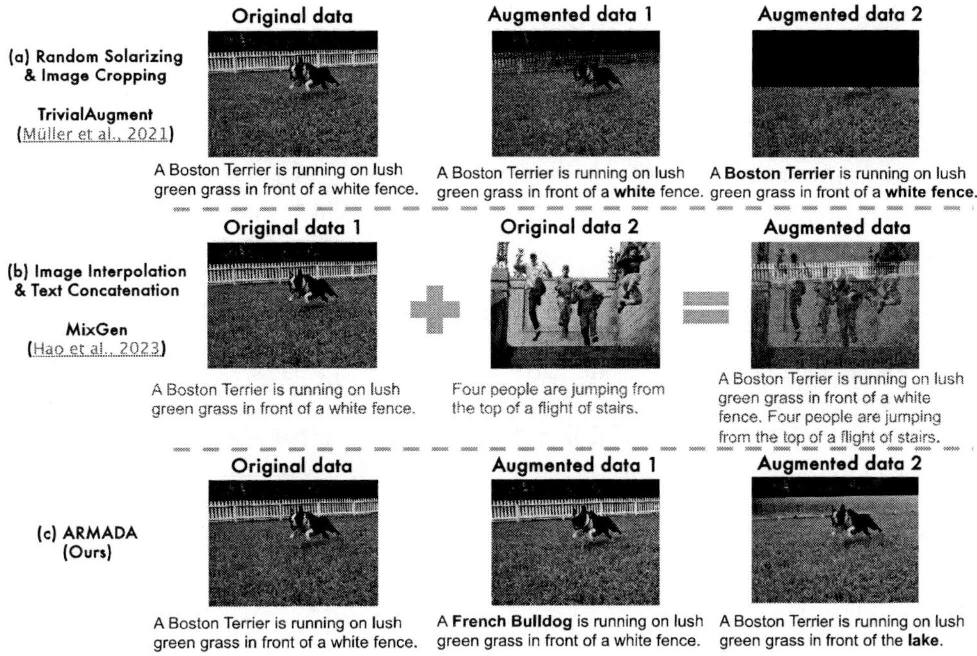

Figure 1: Generated examples using two previous data augmentation methods and our approach. **(a)** is generated by TrivialAugment (Müller and Hutter, 2021), showing the altered images from randomly solarizing or cropping the dog and the fence out from the original image, demonstrating semantic inconsistency. **(b)** shows the output image from MixGen (Hao et al., 2023), demonstrating the unrealistic output from simple image interpolation and text concatenation. **(c)** shows the augmented data from our method *ARMADA*, which are semantically consistent.

gaps between paired images and texts, leading to images far from realistic. Moreover, such perturbations cannot deal with variable entity categories that appear in a similar background, or same entities with variable physical attributes, since they disregard attribute-level details. Our work aims to address these issues by leveraging a rich bank of attributes from a hierarchical knowledge base for interpretable and controllable multimodal data augmentation that guarantees semantic consistency and knowledge-grounding of generated entities.

In this paper, we introduce a novel *attribute-based*, multimodal data augmentation framework, *ARMADA*, that extracts the entities and visual attributes, then modifies the visual attributes of entities in images by building an entity-attribute multimodal knowledge base (KB). We perform entity-related knowledge extraction through entity linking using Spacy Entity Linker on Wikidata KB to: (i) generate augmented images and texts that faithfully reflect knowledge-grounded, entity-related attributes, and (ii) exploit the neighboring entities, e.g., a Boston Terrier and French Bulldog in Figure 1, for generating similar yet distinguished entity categories. Our work also leverages LLMs as additional knowledge proxy as they can generate alternatives to any textual attributes without related entities in KB. We then modify images based on revised texts by employing an off-the-shelf image editing model, InstructPix2Pix (Brooks et al., 2023). Our framework produces semantically consistent, knowledge-grounded multimodal data instances. In-depth experiments across four different image-text downstream tasks against five different baselines demonstrate the significance of augmenting multimodal data instances guided by entity-related attribute knowledge. Our contributions can be summarized as follows:

- We propose a knowledge-guided multimodal data augmentation framework that is guided by entity-centric KBs to generate entities that are of the same type yet differing attributes, or of similar yet disparate categories.
- The proposed augmentation pipeline in this work demonstrates semantically consistent and knowledge-grounded multimodal data, addressing the limitations of previous multimodal data augmentation methods.
- Our empirical results demonstrate that our

proposed data augmentation strategy leads to substantial gains in various image-text downstream tasks such as image-text retrieval, VQA, image captioning, and especially in fine-grained image classification tasks that rely on attribute-centric information.

2 Related Work

External Knowledge Proxies. External symbolic knowledge bases (KBs) like Wikidata (Vrandečić and Krötzsch, 2014) and real-world knowledge proxies like large language models (LLMs) (Achiam et al., 2023; Touvron et al., 2023; Almazrouei et al., 2023) contain ample amount of real-world, entity-centric knowledge. While symbolic KBs have frequently been used in various domains of natural language processing for augmentation (LUO et al., 2023; Sun et al., 2023; Pan et al., 2024), the use of symbolic KBs in the multimodal domain is yet to be explored. LLMs, while they may suffer from hallucinatory outputs, contain rich world knowledge that enables them to generalize to attributes of various kinds. Our work reaps the benefits of the both worlds by exploiting the relational knowledge of KBs and generalization abilities of LLMs to perform knowledge-guided multimodal data augmentation.

Vision Language Models. Vision Language Models (VLMs) have achieved new state-of-the-art performances across various downstream tasks such as image-to-text retrieval and visual question answering (VQA) (Radford et al., 2021; Li et al., 2022a; Dai et al., 2023; Liu et al., 2023b,a). CLIP (Radford et al., 2021) is a widely used VLM for image-text retrieval and image classification. InstructBLIP (Dai et al., 2023) and LLaVA (Liu et al., 2023b) are instruction-tuned multimodal models that combine vision encoders and LLMs. The major drawback of these models is that they require an extensive amount of image-text pair datasets to either pre-train or fine-tune the models. Such shortcomings call for the need of a new, robust augmentation method, which our work aims to offer.

Data Augmentation. Existing work on data augmentation mainly focuses on augmenting a single modality, e.g., text (Thakur et al., 2021; Yoo et al., 2021; Chen et al., 2023; Jin and Ji, 2024) or image (Luo et al., 2023; Trabucco et al., 2023; Müller and Hutter, 2021). Most recently in the multimodal domain, several augmentation methods have been proposed to augment multiple modalities at the same time. MixGen (Hao et al., 2023) generates new data instances by interpolating images and concatenating their accompanying texts. As discussed in Figure 1, one potential issue is the low quality of the generated data. LeMDA (Liu et al., 2022), another augmentation method that jointly augments multimodal data in the feature space, is limited in terms of interpretability and controllability since the generation occurs in latent space. BiAug (Wu et al., 2023) augments multimodal data in a similar manner as our approach by decoupling entities and their attributes. However, BiAug heavily relies on LLMs to generate the attributes, which are susceptible to hallucinatory outputs. Our proposed approach, in contrast, leverages entity-related attributes from knowledge base and delegates entity independent perturbations to LLMs.

3 Our Approach

Suppose we have a set of image-text pairs $\mathcal{D} = \{(I_1, T_1), \cdots\}$ as the training dataset. T_i is a task-dependent text that is paired with its corresponding image, I_i. For example, T_i can be the label of image I_i in image classification task, a caption that describes I_i in image-text retrieval task, or a question-answer pair if the image I_i appears in a VQA task. Given that the training dataset with gold-standard annotations $\mathcal{D}$ is usually too small to train the vision language model sufficiently well, we aim to augment the original training dataset and generate additional image-text pairs $\mathcal{D}' = \{(I'_1, T'_1), \cdots\}$. The augmented dataset $\mathcal{D}'$ can be used in conjunction with the original dataset $\mathcal{D}$ to train the VLMs and further improve their performance.

3.1 Extracting Entities and Visual Attributes from Text

The primary goal of our proposed data augmentation framework is to generate new images by modifying the value of visual attributes of the mentioned entities. For example, as shown in Figure 2, our data augmentation method changes the *color* (visual attribute) of a *linckia laevigata* (entity) from *blue* (attribute value) to *orange* (attribute value). The first step of text modification is to identify the mentioned entities and visual attributes of mentioned entities within a given piece of text. To this end, we use large language models (LLMs) to extract entities, visual attributes and attribute values given an input text, T, as they demonstrate exceptional capabilities in text comprehension and

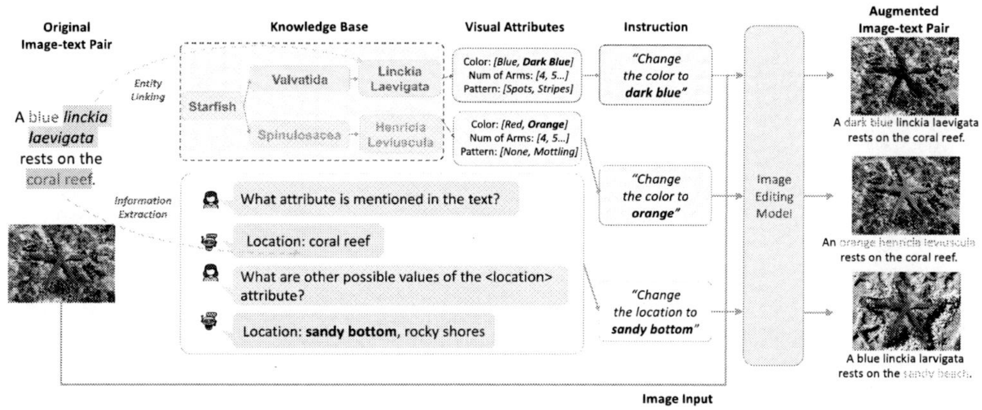

Figure 2: The overall framework of our data augmentation method. Given an image-text pair as input, we first extract entities and their corresponding visual attributes from text. If the object can be linked to an entity in our pre-defined attribute knowledge base, then we collect all possible attribute values from the information of the linked entity. If the object cannot be linked to the knowledge base, then we utilize Large Language Models (LLMs) to extract other possible values. After selecting which visual attribute to modify, we rewrite the original text and use an image editing model to generate new images based on the new text. Finally, we rank the augmented data and output data based on the similarity scores.

generation. Given an original image-text pair (I, T), we input the text T into an LLM along with the prompt "`Extract the mentioned objects, their visual attributes, and values of visual attributes from the sentence:` T". For example, as illustrated in Figure 2, we can extract from the sentence "*A blue linckia laevigata rests on the coral reef*" that the *entity* is *linckia laevigata*, the *visual attributes* are *color* and *location*, and the *attribute values* are *blue* and *coral reef*, respectively. The entities, visual attributes and their values serve as candidates for subsequent visual attribute value substitution.

3.2 KB-based Visual Attribute Substitution

Knowledge Base Construction. After identifying visual attributes mentioned in text T we determine potential substitutions for their attribute values. We leverage attributes from entity-centric KBs to provide accurate and reliable knowledge for substituting visual attribute values. We first parse the information from Wikidata and Wikipedia, and construct an attribute-level KB consisting of entities and their attributes, which consists of two steps: (1) *Graph topology*: We collect entities from Wikidata and use a node in the KB to represent an entity. Each node has an outgoing edge to its parent category node. For instance, as illustrated in Figure 3, both *linckia laevigata* and *linckia guildingi* belong to the parent category *valvatida*, thus resulting in two directed edges from these nodes to *valvatida*. (2) *Node attributes*: The visual information for each node in the KB is derived from its corresponding Wikipedia articles. We collect the textual content of each Wikipedia page, then employ LLMs to extract all visual attributes and their possible values described within the article. For instance, the entity *linckia laevigata* may have *color* of *blue* and *dark blue*, with the *number of arms* starting from four.

After building the KB, we link each entity extracted from T to a node N in the KB using the Spacy Entity Linker (Honnibal et al., 2020). To generate a new augmented data sample, we use the following two attribute value substitution methods.

Attribute Substitution within Single Entity. A single entity may possess multiple plausible attributes, which are identifiable through entity linking to KB. Some of these extracted entities with specific attributes may occur less frequently in the original training dataset than those with more frequently occurring attributes. Therefore, we aim to augment the data to increase the coverage of such long-tail entity instances, so that the model is better fine-tuned to recognize these rare cases well. To elaborate, we randomly choose a visual attribute connected to the entity node N and then sample an attribute value to substitute the current attribute value of N. In this case, the entity stays the same while only its one attribute value is changed. For example, *blue linckia laevigata* $\rightarrow$ *dark blue linckia laevigata* as illustrated in Figure 2.

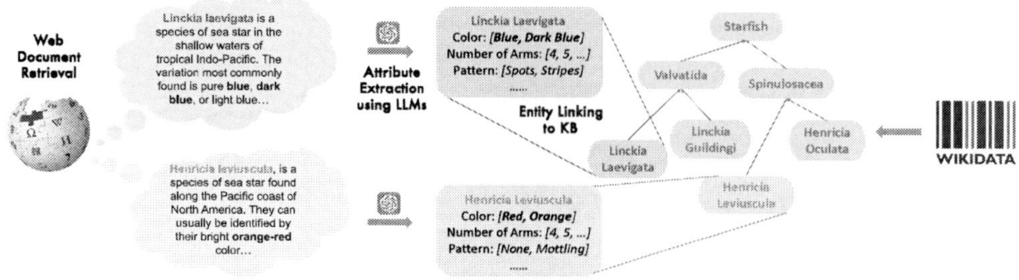

Figure 3: An example from the our pre-defined attribute library. Each node represents an entity collected from Wikidata. An outgoing edge is connected from a node to its parent category. Each node has its visual attributes extracted from the Wikipedia articles.

Attribute Substitution across Sibling Entities. In addition to substituting attributes within a single entity, we notice that there are many entities in KBs that belong to the same parent category and share many visual attributes in common, e.g., the *linckia laevigata* and *henricia leviuscula* in Figure 2. This inspires us to substitute attributes across these sibling entities to introduce similar but different concepts as augmented training data. In this way, the model will contrastively learn from these confusing entities, thereby increasing its robustnesss to visually similar but different entity concepts. Specifically, we consider changing the entity node n_i to its sibling entity node n_s who share the most visual attributes with n_i. For example, in Figure 3, *linckia laevigata* and *henricia leviuscula* have many attributes in common, so it is feasible to change the original entity to the new entity. We therefore substitute the entity *linckia laevigata* with *henricia leviuscula*, and then change its *color* for *henricia leviuscula* (e.g., *orange*). The resulting substitution is therefore *blue linckia laevigata* $\rightarrow$ *orange henricia leviuscula*.

3.3 LLM-based Visual Attribute Substitution

In some cases, the extracted entity or visual attribute is too general and cannot be linked to any node in the KB (e.g., *coral reef* serving as a background in Figure 2). Therefore, in addition to KBs, we also use LLMs to obtain new values for auxiliary visual attributes such as background, as they are broadly trained on a large amount of data and thus have acquired commonsense knowledge to provide alternative attribute values for such cases. For example, in Figure 2, after we extract that the *location* is *coral reef*, we use the prompt "`What are other possible values for the <location> attribute in this sentence?`" to generate new location value substitutions, such as *sandy bottom* and *rocky shores*. It is worth noting that LLMs may not consistently produce valid substitute attribute values, as they may lack adequate knowledge regarding specialized fields or long-tail concepts. This deficiency may lead to LLMs generating inaccurate responses, i.e., hallucination. For instance, when prompt the LLMs for all possible colors of *linckia laevigata*, LLMs may provide incorrect answers such as "*orange*" and "*yellow*", which are implausible colors for *linckia laevigata*. Therefore, we rely on KBs to extract accurate, knowledge-grounded attributes for substitution.

It is worth noting that the models we utilize in each component may not be perfect, which can affect the performance of the proposed approach. Our experimental results in Section 4.6 indicate that the error rates of the information extraction, entity linking, and visual attribute substitutions are relatively low, which do not significantly impact the quality of the generated data.

3.4 Image Editing

After modifying an image-text pair (I, T) to (I, T') with a new text T', we edit the image I according to T'. We employ an image editing model InstructPix2Pix (Brooks et al., 2023), which can take as input an image and instruction on how to modify the image, and output the modified image following the instruction. The instruction here is "`Change the [attribute] of the [entity] to [value]`", where `[entity]` and `[attribute]` are the mentioned entity and selected attribute type, respectively, and `[value]` is the new attribute value output by the KB or LLM. As illustrated in Figure 2, starting with the original image on the left, we generate three new images on the right using InstructPix2Pix with different instructions. The first image keeps the entity *linckia laevigata* unchanged while changing its color to *dark blue*, whereas the second image changes the color to *orange*, updating the entity category to *henricia leviuscula* and its corresponding text description accordingly. The third one is the result of changing the attribute of *location* to *sandy beach* by querying LLMs; this leaves the central entity of the image unperturbed, providing a robust way to leverage LLMs only for attributes that are not entity-related.

3.5 Augmented Data Selection

Our method transforms an image-text pair (I, T) to a modified image-text pair (I', T'). However, not all modified image-text pairs are suitable as augmented data; some image I' being too similar to their original counterpart I, thereby providing minimal new signal for subsequent model training. Conversely, other generated image I' diverging too much from their original counterpart I may significantly drift the image away from the original data distribution and mislead the model training. To determine the validity of the augmented data, we calculate the similarity between a generated image I' and its original image I using the Fréchet Inception Distance (FID) score (Heusel et al., 2018). FID calculates the Fréchet distance between feature vectors of the original and generated images, which aligns closely with human judgment and is frequently utilized to assess the quality of generated data. Ideally, we aim to empirically maintain the similarity score within a specific range to ensure that I' exhibit *a reasonable amount* of difference from I as indicated in the ablation study. The experimental results on selecting the similarity range is presented in Appendix A.3.

4 Experiments

To assess the effectiveness of data augmentation methods, we select four evaluation tasks: *image classification*, *visual question answering*, *image-text retrieval*, and *image captioning*.

4.1 Foundation Models and Baseline Methods

We use CLIP (Radford et al., 2021) and LLaVA-1.5 (7B) (Liu et al., 2023a) model as the foundation models in this work. CLIP is a multimodal model that uses contrastive learning to jointly align the visual and textual representations. LLaVA-1.5 is an open-source, auto-regressive multimodal vision-language model (VLM) trained by fine-tuning Vicuna-v1.5 (Chiang et al., 2023) on GPT-4-generated multimodal instruction-following data. Given an image input and text instruction, LLaVA-1.5 generates output texts based on its reasoning upon the two modalities. We use GPT-4 (OpenAI, 2023) as the LLMs in each component.

We compare our proposed method against five different baseline methods to demonstrate its effectiveness (we do not include BiAug (Wu et al., 2023) since the code has not been released yet): (1) *Zero-shot*: Models are evaluated without fine-tuning on any data. This setting is established to examine the initial ability of the models on all four downstream tasks. (2) *NoAug*: Only the original training data is used to fine-tune the models without any augmented data. (3) *NaiveAug*: Two naive augmentation methods are applied to texts and images independently as follows. We use AEDA (Karimi et al., 2021) to randomly insert punctuation marks into original text, and we use TrivialAugment (Müller and Hutter, 2021) to randomly apply center cropping, rotation, or invert, to images. (4) *MixGen* (Hao et al., 2023): Generates new data instance by interpolating images on the pixel-level and concatenating texts. This is state-of-the-art augmentation method. Specifically, given two image-text pairs (I_i, T_i) and (I_j, T_j), a new image-text pair (I'_k, T'_k) is generated by $I'_k = \lambda I_i + (1 - \lambda) I_j$ and $T'_k = concat(T_i, T_j)$, where λ is a hyper-parameter. (5) *LeMDA* (Liu et al., 2022): Generates augmented data in the latent feature space. We use CLIP to encode the original training data into embeddings, then feed them to LeMDA to generate new latent embeddings; these embeddings are used as augmented data to fine-tune an MLP module in the image classification task. Note that LeMDA cannot be used for LLaVA-1.5 and cannot be used in tasks other than image classification.

4.2 Image Classification

Dataset. We use *iNaturalist 2021* (Horn et al., 2018) as the dataset for image classification. The iNaturalist dataset consists of large scale species of plants and animals in the natural world. It contains 10,000 species with a training set of 2.7M images. To better mimic the scenario of annotated data scarcity, we sample from a mini dataset with all 246 species of Mammalia. Each class has 30/15/15 images for training/validation/inference.

Experimental Setup. For CLIP, we transform the class labels in iNaturalist dataset into natural language descriptions: "[label]" $\rightarrow$ "*a photo of* [label]", following caption formats in CLIP (Radford et al., 2021). CLIP takes as input an image and all class labels, then outputs logit scores for these classes. The label with the highest logit score is taken as the predicted result of CLIP model. For LLaVA-1.5, we evaluate its performance by asking the model what is included in the image, and then verify whether the true labels are presented in the generated responses. The evaluation prompt is: "`What is the name of the mammal that appears in this image? For example, if it's a picture of a bengal tiger, output a fine-grained label 'Bengal Tiger' or use its binomial nomenclature 'Panthera tigris tigris'. Provide your answer:`". This allows us to assess model's classification ability based on the provided images.

Results. The results of *Precision*, *Recall*, and F_1 for image classification task are presented in the left part of Table 1. As shown from the zero-shot results, the pretrained foundation models have poor performance on fine-grained concept recognition, with F_1 scores of 0.090 and 0.041 on CLIP and LLaVA, respectively. After fine-tuning with the original training data, both models have a much better performance, with a 24.9% and 47.6% absolute gain on F_1 scores. While both NaiveAug and LeMDA demonstrate some improvement in model performance, our method achieves the best results among all existing methods. It is worth noting that the F_1 score of MixGen is worse than NoAug. This is because the interpolation of images distorts the visual attribute of the fine-grained concepts, thereby adversely affects model training. Conversely, our method is able to generate new images by modifying the visual attributes of entities. This facilitates a more comprehensive learning of fine-grained concepts by foundation models.

4.3 Visual Question Answering

Datasets. Visual Question Answering (VQA) v2.0 (Goyal et al., 2017) dataset consists of open-ended questions to images. These questions require understanding vision, language, and commonsense knowledge to provide answers. VQA-2.0 has 265,015 images and each image has at least 3 related questions.

Experimental Setup. We consider the VQA task as an answer generation task. We utilize LLaVA as the foundation model. Given the open-ended nature of the task, we let the model generate free-form answers without any constraints. Then we compute the textual similarity between the output of LLaVA and the true answer.

Results. The results of VQA task are shown in the right part of Table 1. We evaluate the performance on the test-dev dataset via textual similarities using Universal Sentence Encoder (USE) (Cer et al., 2018) and BERTScore (Zhang et al., 2020).. It is clear that, compared with Zero-shot, the performance of LLaVA improves greatly after fine-tuning. This is probably because the ground truth answers to the questions are typically simple and short, which makes the task relatively easier. As demonstrated in the table, the textual similarity achieved by our method surpasses the best baseline method MixGen by 1.1% on USE and 1.4% on BERTScore.

4.4 Image-Text Retrieval

Dataset. *Flickr30k* (Young et al., 2014) contains 31,000 images, each with 5 human-annotated referenced sentences that describe the image. This dataset is widely used in image-text retrieval task. Similar to iNaturalist, we sample 5k images from the training set and use the entire 1k test set for evaluation.

Experimental Setup. Image-text retrieval includes two subtasks: text-to-image and image-to-text retrieval. We use CLIP to calculate the embedding of the given image, as well as the embeddings of all candidate captions in the test set. We compare the cosine similarity between the image embedding and each text embedding, and output top K captions with the highest similarity scores as the retrieved results. We follow existing work and use $Recall@K$ as evaluation metric.

Results. The results of image-text retrieval are shown in the left part of Table 2. The zero-shot performance of the pretrained CLIP is already very good on both image retrieval and text retrieval, because it is originally trained using the contrastive loss between image and text embeddings. After fine-tuning, the performance on both subtasks can be further improved in most cases. Note that the improvement of our method over baseline methods in this task appears less significant compared to other tasks. This is primarily due to the already high zero-shot performance of CLIP, leaving limited room for further improvement.

4.5 Image Captioning

Experimental Setup. Image captioning task aims to generate natural language descriptions of an image. We use LLaVA-1.5 as the foundation model, and Flickr30k as the evaluation dataset as intro-

Method	Image Classification (CLIP)			Image Classification (LLaVA)		VQA	
	$Precision$	$Recall$	F_1	F_1	$ExactMatch$	USE	$BERTScore$
Zero-shot	0.074	0.113	0.090	0.041	0.002	0.221	0.825
NoAug	0.332	0.347	0.339	0.517	0.557	0.815	0.949
NaiveAug	0.386	0.336	0.359	0.192	0.241	0.821	0.961
MixGen	0.343	0.318	0.330	0.314	0.357	0.824	0.959
LeMDA	0.368	0.354	0.361	-	-	-	-
ARMADA	**0.391**	**0.386**	**0.389**	**0.588**	**0.621**	**0.835**	**0.975**

Table 1: Results of Precision, Recall, and F_1 on iNaturalist dataset for image classification (left part) and results of textual similarity on VQA v2.0 dataset for visual question answering (right part). The foundation model is LLaVA-1.5 for VQA.

Method	Image Retrieval			Text Retrieval			Image Captioning	
	$R@1$	$R@3$	$R@5$	$R@1$	$R@3$	$R@5$	*USE*	*BERTScore*
Zero-shot	0.589	0.765	0.824	0.612	0.775	0.836	0.422	0.896
NoAug	0.619	0.785	0.830	0.645	0.807	0.854	0.642	0.907
NaiveAug	0.631	0.788	0.838	0.641	0.804	0.862	0.648	0.911
MixGen	0.626	0.786	0.838	0.592	0.770	0.826	0.659	0.903
ARMADA	**0.646**	**0.797**	**0.847**	**0.646**	**0.811**	**0.872**	**0.682**	**0.918**

Table 2: Results of Recall@K for image-text retrieval (left part) and results of textual similarity for image captioning (right part). We use Flickr30k dataset for both tasks. The foundation model is CLIP for image-text retrieval and LLaVA-1.5 for image captioning.

duced in Section 4.4. Specifically, given an image as input, we use the prompt "`Describe this image using one simple sentence`" to ask LLaVA-1.5 to generate a caption.

To evaluate the quality of generated captions, we compare the textual similarity between the generated caption and the gold-standard annotation for a given image using USE and BERTScore. Since there may be multiple gold-standard captions for an image, we calculate the similarity score of a generated caption with each gold-standard caption, and return the maximum as the final score for this generated caption.

Results. The results of image captioning task are presented in the right part of Table 2. Our method *ARMADA* achieves the best performance over all baseline methods. Specifically, the performance gain of our method on USE score is 4.0% over NoAug, and 2.3% over the best baseline augmentation method MixGen. We provide detailed case analysis of the generated captions by our method and by baseline methods in Appendix B.

4.6 Error Analysis

We investigate the error rate of each component in the data augmentation process and how they affect our model. Specifically, we manually check the correctness of attribute extraction and the visual attribute substitution. It turns out that the percentage of incorrect attributes that are extracted is quite low (4 / 113 = 3.5%). The percentage of inappropriate substitution by LLMs is also very low (1 / 73 = 2.7%). The visual attribute substitutions from KBs are template-based substitutions from possible attribute values, which will not incur any error aggregation issues.

5 Conclusions and Future Work

We propose a novel data augmentation method that utilizes KBs and LLMs to generate multimodal data. The proposed framework is able to generate semantically consistent data that solves the potential issues of the existing methods. Our method significantly improves the MLM' performance on various downstream tasks, without the need of high-cost annotated data. Experiment results also demonstrate the effectiveness of our proposed method compared to the baseline methods.

In the future, we aim to incorporate more modalities into our framework such as video and audio. We also plan to rank visual attributes and select the most influential attributes for augmentation. Moreover, existing image editing tools our framework relies on do not perform consistently well. Designing a new visual attribute editing model to further enhance the quality of the augmented data is also a promising research direction.

6 Limitations

Our proposed method demonstrates the effectiveness only on image-text data. However, to enhance the practical utility of our method, it would be advantageous to expand our data augmentation method to include more modalities, such as video and audio. Furthermore, as discussed earlier, although the error rate in each component is low and will not affect the performance much, we still aim to incorporate better attribute extraction and visual attribute substitution models into the framework to further improve our method.

7 Ethical Consideration

We acknowledge that our word is aligned with the *ACL Code of the Ethics* (Gotterbarn et al., 2018) and will not raise ethical concerns. We do not use sensitive datasets/models that may cause any potential issues.

References

Josh Achiam, Steven Adler, Sandhini Agarwal, Lama Ahmad, Ilge Akkaya, Florencia Leoni Aleman, Diogo Almeida, Janko Altenschmidt, Sam Altman, Shyamal Anadkat, et al. 2023. Gpt-4 technical report. *arXiv preprint arXiv:2303.08774*.

Ebtesam Almazrouei, Hamza Alobeidli, Abdulaziz Alshamsi, Alessandro Cappelli, Ruxandra Cojocaru, Merouane Debbah, Etienne Goffinet, Daniel Heslow, Julien Launay, Quentin Malartic, Badreddine Noune, Baptiste Pannier, and Guilherme Penedo. 2023. Falcon-40B: an open large language model with state-of-the-art performance.

Tim Brooks, Aleksander Holynski, and Alexei A. Efros. 2023. Instructpix2pix: Learning to follow image editing instructions. *Preprint*, arXiv:2211.09800.

Daniel Cer, Yinfei Yang, Sheng yi Kong, Nan Hua, Nicole Limtiaco, Rhomni St. John, Noah Constant, Mario Guajardo-Cespedes, Steve Yuan, Chris Tar, Yun-Hsuan Sung, Brian Strope, and Ray Kurzweil. 2018. Universal sentence encoder. *Preprint*, arXiv:1803.11175.

Xiusi Chen, Jyun-Yu Jiang, Wei-Cheng Chang, Cho-Jui Hsieh, Hsiang-Fu Yu, and Wei Wang. 2023. Minprompt: Graph-based minimal prompt data augmentation for few-shot question answering. *Preprint*, arXiv:2310.05007.

Wei-Lin Chiang, Zhuohan Li, Zi Lin, Ying Sheng, Zhanghao Wu, Hao Zhang, Lianmin Zheng, Siyuan Zhuang, Yonghao Zhuang, Joseph E. Gonzalez, Ion Stoica, and Eric P. Xing. 2023. Vicuna: An open-source chatbot impressing gpt-4 with 90%* chatgpt quality.

W Dai, J Li, D Li, AMH Tiong, J Zhao, W Wang, B Li, P Fung, and S Hoi. 2023. Instructblip: Towards general-purpose vision-language models with instruction tuning. arxiv 2023. *arXiv preprint arXiv:2305.06500*.

DW Gotterbarn, Bo Brinkman, Catherine Flick, Michael S Kirkpatrick, Keith Miller, Kate Vazansky, and Marty J Wolf. 2018. Acm code of ethics and professional conduct.

Yash Goyal, Tejas Khot, Douglas Summers-Stay, Dhruv Batra, and Devi Parikh. 2017. Making the V in VQA matter: Elevating the role of image understanding in Visual Question Answering. In *Conference on Computer Vision and Pattern Recognition (CVPR)*.

Xiaoshuai Hao, Yi Zhu, Srikar Appalaraju, Aston Zhang, Wanqian Zhang, Bo Li, and Mu Li. 2023. Mixgen: A new multi-modal data augmentation. *Preprint*, arXiv:2206.08358.

Martin Heusel, Hubert Ramsauer, Thomas Unterthiner, Bernhard Nessler, and Sepp Hochreiter. 2018. Gans trained by a two time-scale update rule converge to a local nash equilibrium. *Preprint*, arXiv:1706.08500.

Matthew Honnibal, Ines Montani, Sofie Van Landeghem, and Adriane Boyd. 2020. spaCy: Industrial-strength Natural Language Processing in Python.

Grant Van Horn, Oisin Mac Aodha, Yang Song, Yin Cui, Chen Sun, Alex Shepard, Hartwig Adam, Pietro Perona, and Serge Belongie. 2018. The inaturalist species classification and detection dataset. *Preprint*, arXiv:1707.06642.

Xiaomeng Jin and Heng Ji. 2024. Schema-based data augmentation for event extraction. In *Proceedings of the 2024 Joint International Conference on Computational Linguistics, Language Resources and Evaluation (LREC-COLING 2024)*, pages 14382–14392, Torino, Italia. ELRA and ICCL.

Akbar Karimi, Leonardo Rossi, and Andrea Prati. 2021. Aeda: An easier data augmentation technique for text classification. *Preprint*, arXiv:2108.13230.

Junnan Li, Dongxu Li, Caiming Xiong, and Steven Hoi. 2022a. Blip: Bootstrapping language-image pre-training for unified vision-language understanding and generation. *Preprint*, arXiv:2201.12086.

Manling Li, Ruochen Xu, Shuohang Wang, Luowei Zhou, Xudong Lin, Chenguang Zhu, Michael Zeng, Heng Ji, and Shih-Fu Chang. 2022b. Clip-event: Connecting text and images with event structures. In *Proc. Conference on Computer Vision and Pattern Recognition (CVPR2022)*.

Manling Li, Alireza Zareian, Qi Zeng, Spencer Whitehead, Di Lu, Heng Ji, and Shih-Fu Chang. 2020. Cross-media structured common space for multimedia event extraction. In *Proc. The 58th Annual Meeting of the Association for Computational Linguistics (ACL2020)*.

Haotian Liu, Chunyuan Li, Yuheng Li, and Yong Jae Lee. 2023a. Improved baselines with visual instruction tuning. *Preprint*, arXiv:2310.03744.

Haotian Liu, Chunyuan Li, Qingyang Wu, and Yong Jae Lee. 2023b. Visual instruction tuning. *Preprint*, arXiv:2304.08485.

Zichang Liu, Zhiqiang Tang, Xingjian Shi, Aston Zhang, Mu Li, Anshumali Shrivastava, and Andrew Gordon Wilson. 2022. Learning multimodal data augmentation in feature space. *arXiv preprint arXiv:2212.14453*.

LINHAO LUO, Yuan-Fang Li, Reza Haf, and Shirui Pan. 2023. Reasoning on graphs: Faithful and interpretable large language model reasoning. In *The Twelfth International Conference on Learning Representations*.

Xue-Jing Luo, Shuo Wang, Zongwei Wu, Christos Sakaridis, Yun Cheng, Deng-Ping Fan, and Luc Van Gool. 2023. Camdiff: Camouflage image augmentation via diffusion model. *Preprint*, arXiv:2304.05469.

Samuel G Müller and Frank Hutter. 2021. Trivialaugment: Tuning-free yet state-of-the-art data augmentation. In *Proceedings of the IEEE/CVF international conference on computer vision*, pages 774–782.

Samuel G. Müller and Frank Hutter. 2021. Trivialaugment: Tuning-free yet state-of-the-art data augmentation. *Preprint*, arXiv:2103.10158.

R OpenAI. 2023. Gpt-4 technical report. *ArXiv*, 2303.

Shirui Pan, Linhao Luo, Yufei Wang, Chen Chen, Jiapu Wang, and Xindong Wu. 2024. Unifying large language models and knowledge graphs: A roadmap. *IEEE Transactions on Knowledge and Data Engineering*.

Alec Radford, Jong Wook Kim, Chris Hallacy, Aditya Ramesh, Gabriel Goh, Sandhini Agarwal, Girish Sastry, Amanda Askell, Pamela Mishkin, Jack Clark, Gretchen Krueger, and Ilya Sutskever. 2021. Learning transferable visual models from natural language supervision. *Preprint*, arXiv:2103.00020.

Jiashuo Sun, Chengjin Xu, Lumingyuan Tang, Saizhuo Wang, Chen Lin, Yeyun Gong, Lionel Ni, Heung-Yeung Shum, and Jian Guo. 2023. Think-on-graph: Deep and responsible reasoning of large language model on knowledge graph. In *The Twelfth International Conference on Learning Representations*.

Nandan Thakur, Nils Reimers, Johannes Daxenberger, and Iryna Gurevych. 2021. Augmented sbert: Data augmentation method for improving bi-encoders for pairwise sentence scoring tasks. *Preprint*, arXiv:2010.08240.

Hugo Touvron, Thibaut Lavril, Gautier Izacard, Xavier Martinet, Marie-Anne Lachaux, Timothée Lacroix, Baptiste Rozière, Naman Goyal, Eric Hambro, Faisal Azhar, Aurelien Rodriguez, Armand Joulin, Edouard Grave, and Guillaume Lample. 2023. Llama: Open and efficient foundation language models. *Preprint*, arXiv:2302.13971.

Brandon Trabucco, Kyle Doherty, Max Gurinas, and Ruslan Salakhutdinov. 2023. Effective data augmentation with diffusion models. *Preprint*, arXiv:2302.07944.

Denny Vrandečić and Markus Krötzsch. 2014. Wikidata: a free collaborative knowledgebase. *Commun. ACM*, 57(10):78–85.

Qiyu Wu, Mengjie Zhao, Yutong He, Lang Huang, Junya Ono, Hiromi Wakaki, and Yuki Mitsufuji. 2023. Towards reporting bias in visual-language datasets: bimodal augmentation by decoupling object-attribute association. *Preprint*, arXiv:2310.01330.

Kang Min Yoo, Dongju Park, Jaewook Kang, Sang-Woo Lee, and Woomyeong Park. 2021. Gpt3mix: Leveraging large-scale language models for text augmentation. *Preprint*, arXiv:2104.08826.

Peter Young, Alice Lai, Micah Hodosh, and Julia Hockenmaier. 2014. From image descriptions to visual denotations: New similarity metrics for semantic inference over event descriptions. *Transactions of the Association for Computational Linguistics*, 2:67–78.

Tianyi Zhang, Varsha Kishore, Felix Wu, Kilian Q. Weinberger, and Yoav Artzi. 2020. Bertscore: Evaluating text generation with bert. *Preprint*, arXiv:1904.09675.

A Ablation Study

A.1 Impact of the Size of the Generated Data

To investigate the impact of the amount of the augmented data, we conduct experiments by varying the size of the augmented data relative to the size of the original training data, ranging from 0% to 300%. The results in Table 3 show a decline in model performance when the augmented data size significantly surpassed the original training data size (exceeding 100% to 200%), potentially due to excessive noise introduced by the augmented data. Our findings suggest that, the augmented data size should approximate that of the original training data for best performance.

A.2 Impact of Using KBs

To assess the importance of utilizing KBs, we conduct additional experiments on the image classification task by solely relying on LLMs to do attribute value substitution. Following the aforementioned experimental setup, we fine-tune a CLIP model on the iNaturalist dataset. The F_1 score exhibits a 2.5% decline (from 38.9% to 36.4%) without using KBs. This suggests that though LLMs are able to provide answers for attribute value substitution, the hallucination issue on fine-grained or rare entities can still introduce noise to the training data, thereby impacting the model performance.

A.3 Impact of Similarity Range for Selecting Augmented Data

We conduct experiments to investigate how the similarity between augmented and original data impact the model performance. In the image classification task, we split the augmented dataset into four groups of equal size according to the similarity of the edited image with its original image. Then we use each group as the augmented data to train CLIP. The F_1 scores of the four groups are 0.377, 0.389, 0.383, and 0.364, respectively, from most-similar to most-dissimilar. The results support our claim in Section 3.5 that maintaining similarity scores within a reasonable range achieves the best performance.

B Case Analysis on the Results of Image Captioning

We perform a case analysis to illustrate the effectiveness of our method. In Figure 4, we present two image-caption pairs from the Flickr30k dataset, including both the human-annotated captions and the captions generated by Zero-shot, NoAug, and *ARMADA* (using LLaVA as the foundation model). For the image on the left, our method is able to identify the fine-grained concept *karate* whereas the zero-shot and NoAug methods generate a more generalized concept *martial arts*. For the image on the right, the caption generated by our method provides a more detailed and accurate description of the hat, which specifies its *knit* pattern and the *beer logo* pattern. These examples suggest that LLaVA can effectively learn the visual attributes and identifies the fine-grained concepts through our method.

C Human Survey

We design a human evaluation and evaluate our generated augmented data based on two metrics: (1) Realism of the augmented images (2) Semantic consistency between the modified image and text. Since the baseline method LeMDA is augmenting data in the feature space and not possible for visualization, we compare our results with another SOTA method MixGen. We randomly selected 140 images and augmented them using our method and MixGen. We asked 7 people to take the questionnaire and each person evaluated 20 images from our method and 20 images from MixGen (randomly shuffled). For each augmented image, assessors are required to give a score within [0, 1, 2, 3, 4, 5] for each metric and higher score suggests better quality. The average scores for the metrics are shown in Table 4. Compared to MixGen where an augmented image is a pixel-level mixture from two original images and the text is the concatenation of the text pairs, the results show that our augmented data are more realistic and consistent.

D Performance on ImageNet1K Dataset

For image classification, we perform an additional experiment with the ImageNet1K dataset. We use the CLIP model and finetune with 10 images from each class in the training set to mimic the scenario of annotated data scarcity. The experimental results for ImageNet1K are shown in Table 5. Results demonstrate that ARMADA still outperforms the other baseline method on datasets with less concepts.

E Ethical Consideration

We acknowledge that our word is aligned with the *ACL Code of the Ethics* (Gotterbarn et al., 2018)

Dataset	Metric	Size of the augmented data			
		0%	100%	200%	300%
iNaturalist	F_1	0.339	**0.389**	0.360	0.328
Flickr30k	$TextSim$	0.642	**0.682**	0.660	0.659
VQA v2.0	$TextSim$	0.815	0.825	**0.835**	0.816

Table 3: The impact of the size of the generated data on the performance of multiple tasks.

Metric	Realism	Consistency
MixGen	1.29	2.86
ARMADA	3.87	4.23

Table 4: Results of Human Survey.

Method	Accuracy
Zero-shot	0.586
NoAug	0.638
NaiveAug	0.642
MixGen	0.451
ARMADA	0.668

Table 5: Results of image classification task on the ImageNet1K dataset.

and will not raise ethical concerns. We do not use sensitive datasets/models that may cause any potential issues.

Annotation	A girl breaking boards by using **karate**.
Zero-shot	Two people are practicing **martial arts** on a mat.
NoAug	Two **martial artists** are practicing their moves.
AttributeAug	A man and a girl are practicing **karate**.

Annotation	A man with gauges and glasses is wearing a Blitz hat.
Zero-shot	A man wearing a beer hat and glasses is looking at the camera.
NoAug	A man wearing a beer hat.
AttributeAug	A man wearing a **knit** hat with a **beer logo** on it.

Figure 4: A case analysis that shows sample outputs on Flickr30k dataset for image captioning task. We select two images from the test set, the human-annotated captions, and the generated captions from each method. For the image on the left, our method is able to recognize the fine-grained concept *karate*. The image on the right demonstrates that the model is able to provide an accurate description of the *hat*, specifying its *knit* texture and *beer logo* pattern.

Summarization-Based Document IDs for Generative Retrieval with Language Models

Alan Li[1] **Daniel Cheng**[1] **Phillip Keung**[3] **Jungo Kasai**[1] **Noah A. Smith**[1,2]
[1]Paul G. Allen School of Computer Science & Engineering, University of Washington, USA
[2]Allen Institute for Artificial Intelligence, USA
[3]Department of Statistics, University of Washington, USA
{lihaoxin,d0,jkasai,nasmith}@cs.washington.edu, pkeung@uw.edu

Abstract

Generative retrieval (Wang et al., 2022; Tay et al., 2022) is a popular approach for end-to-end document retrieval that directly generates document identifiers given an input query. We introduce *summarization-based document IDs*, in which each document's ID is composed of an extractive summary or abstractive keyphrases generated by a language model, rather than an integer ID sequence or bags of n-grams as proposed in past work. We find that abstractive, content-based IDs (ACID) and an ID based on the first 30 tokens are very effective in direct comparisons with previous approaches to ID creation. We show that using ACID improves top-10 and top-20 recall by 15.6% and 14.4% (relative) respectively versus the cluster-based integer ID baseline on the MSMARCO 100k retrieval task, and 9.8% and 9.9% respectively on the Wikipedia-based NQ 100k retrieval task. Our results demonstrate the effectiveness of human-readable, natural-language IDs created through summarization for generative retrieval. We also observed that extractive IDs outperformed abstractive IDs on Wikipedia articles in NQ but not the snippets in MSMARCO, which suggests that document characteristics affect generative retrieval performance.

1 Introduction

Wikipedia-based corpora have long been an important part of NLP research and form a natural benchmark for studying new techniques in text-based recommender and information retrieval systems. In this work, we examine how *generative retrieval* behaves on short-form and long-form documents drawn from Wikipedia and non-Wikipedia sources. We also propose a new type of document ID for generative retrieval based on *document summarization*, which demonstrably improves retrieval performance across the tasks that we examined.

Large language models (LMs) are now widely used across many NLP tasks, and extensions of generative models to document retrieval tasks have recently been proposed (Wang et al., 2022; Tay et al., 2022), in contrast to vector-based approaches like dense passage retrieval (DPR; Karpukhin et al., 2020). DPR is a widely-used technique for training document retrieval models, where queries and documents are mapped to dense vector representations with a transformer encoder (e.g., BERT; Devlin et al., 2019). By increasing the cosine similarity between positive query-document pairs and decreasing it between negative pairs, DPR performs metric learning over the space of queries and the set of documents to be indexed.

Generative alternatives to document retrieval address certain limitations of dense, vector-based approaches to retrieval. For example, query and document representations are constructed separately in DPR, which precludes complex query-document interactions. Using a single dense vector to represent an entire document limits the amount of information that can be stored; indeed, Tay et al. (2022) observed that increasing the number of parameters in the encoder does not significantly enhance DPR performance. Furthermore, the rich sequence generation capabilities of language models (LMs) cannot be used directly in dense retrieval. Tay et al. (2022) and Wang et al. (2022) therefore proposed a new direction called *generative retrieval*, where LMs learn to directly map queries to an identifier that is unique to each document. We illustrate the differences in Figure 1.

Instead of retrieving documents based on cosine similarity, generative retrieval uses an LM to produce a sequence of tokens encoding the relevant document's ID, conditional on the query. Decoding constraints are applied to ensure that only document IDs that exist in the corpus are generated. Tay et al. (2022) and Wang et al. (2022) showed that generative retrieval outperformed DPR on information retrieval benchmarks like Natural Questions (Kwiatkowski et al., 2019) and TriviaQA (Joshi

Proceedings of the First Workshop on Advancing Natural Language Processing for Wikipedia, pages 126–135
November 16, 2024

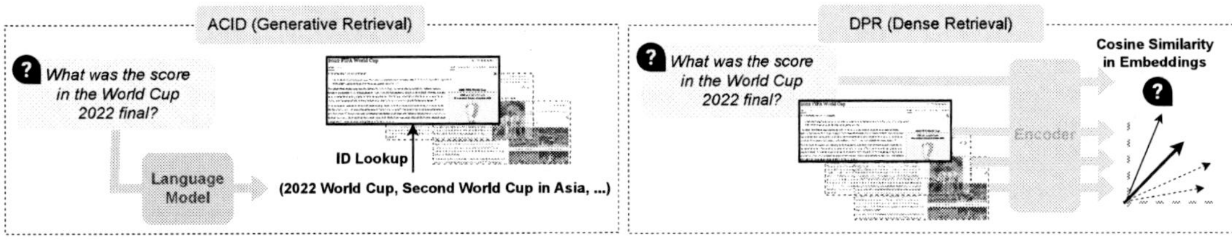

Figure 1: Generative retrieval vs. dense retrieval. In dense retrieval (right), both the query and the documents are encoded into *dense* vectors (i.e., embeddings). Nearest-neighbor search is then applied to find the most relevant documents. Generative retrieval (left) trains a language model to generate the relevant document ID conditional on the query. The ID is tied to a unique document, allowing for direct lookup. We propose summarization-based document IDs like ACID, which uses GPT-3.5 to create a sequence of abstractive keyphrases to serve as the document ID.

et al., 2017), and subsequent publications have corroborated their findings on other retrieval tasks like multilingual retrieval (Zhuang et al., 2023).

State-of-the-art generative retrieval models rely on document clustering to create document IDs, following the work of both Wang et al. (2022) and Tay et al. (2022), and the resulting document ID is an integer sequence corresponding to the clusters that the document belongs to. However, generating arbitrary sequences of integers is very different from what LMs are designed to do, since LMs are pretrained to generate natural language. In addition to negatively impacting LM generation performance, cluster-based integer IDs are not human-readable and require re-clustering if a substantial number of new documents are added to the index.

To address the issues with cluster-based IDs, we consider *summarization-based document IDs*, which are human-readable, natural-language document IDs. We propose **ACID**, an **A**bstractive, **C**ontent-based **ID** assignment method for documents, alongside simpler IDs based on extractive summarization. ACID uses a language model (GPT-3.5 in our experiments) to generate a short sequence of *abstractive keyphrases* from the document's contents to serve as the document ID, rather than a hierarchical clustering ID or an arbitrary integer sequence. We also consider creating content-based IDs extractively: taking the first 30 tokens of each document as its ID or choosing the top-30 keywords with respect to BM25 scores. We find that ACID generally outperforms the cluster-based IDs for generative retrieval (as well as the extractive methods) in direct comparisons on standard retrieval benchmarks. We also observe that longer extractive document IDs are helpful for retrieving long documents, such as the Wikipedia articles in the NQ benchmark, versus the shorter document fragments from the MSMARCO dataset.

Finally, we examine the effect of hyperparameters like model size and beam width on retrieval performance, and compare how cluster-based IDs and summarization-based IDs behave under different settings.

The code for reproducing our results and the keyword-augmented datasets can be found at `https://github.com/lihaoxin2020/Summarization-Based-Document-IDs-for-Generative-Retrieval`, and the data can be found at `https://huggingface.co/datasets/lihaoxin2020/abstractive-content-based-IDs`.

2 IDs for Generative Retrieval

Since generative retrieval is a comparatively new approach for document retrieval, there is significant variation in the literature on how language models are trained to map queries to document IDs. Tay et al. (2022) distinguish between the 'indexing' step (where the LM is trained to link spans from the training, development, and test documents to their document IDs) and the 'finetuning' step (where the training query-document pairs are used to finetune the LM for retrieval). Note that generative retrieval models must index all documents, including the development and test documents, in order for the language model to be aware of their document IDs at inference time. Additionally, Wang et al. (2022) and Zhuang et al. (2023) perform data augmentation in the indexing and finetuning steps by introducing 'synthetic' queries, where a query generation model (Nogueira et al., 2019) based on T5 (Raffel et al., 2020) generates additional queries for each document.

In the three subsections that follow, we elaborate on each of the steps for generative retrieval. Figure 2 depicts the steps needed to create our

Document Text		
List of engineering branches Engineering is the discipline and profession that applies scientific theories , mathematical methods , and empirical evidence to design , create , and analyze technological solutions cognizant of safety , human factors , physical laws , regulations , practicality , and cost . In the contemporary era , engineering is generally considered to consist of the major primary branches of chemical engineering , civil engineering , electrical engineering , and mechanical engineering...		
Cluster-based Document ID		
9, 5, 1, 9, 6, 1, 0, 4, 8, 1, 3, 1, 2, 9, 0		
Summarization-based Document IDs		
First k Tokens	*BM25 Scoring*	*ACID*
List of engineering branches Engineering is the discipline and profession that applies scientific theories , mathematical...	teletraffic optomechanical nanoengineering subdiscipline eegs biotechnical bioprocess mechatronics metallics crazing...	(1) Major engineering branches: chemical, civil, electrical, mechanical (2) Chemical engineering: conversion of raw materials with varied specialties (3) Civil engineering: design...

Table 1: An example of a document, its cluster-based ID (where each level of the clustering has 10 clusters), and its associated natural language, content-based IDs. 'First k tokens' sets the ID to be the document's first k tokens. BM25 scoring uses the top-k highest-scoring tokens from the document as the ID, where scores are based on Okapi BM25. ACID uses an LM (e.g., GPT-3.5) to generate 5 keyphrases as the ID.

summarization-based document IDs, perform data augmentation, index the documents with the LM, and finetune the LM for generative retrieval.

2.1 Document ID Creation

In Table 1, we provide an example of a document about engineering sub-disciplines and the cluster-based and content-based IDs that would be derived from it. From the example, it is clear why we would expect ACID to outperform cluster IDs, since it is straightforward for LMs to generate the keyphrase sequence given an engineering-related query. The cluster ID, on the other hand, resembles an integer hash of the document (with some semantic information carried over from the clustering).

Abstractive, Content-based IDs. We create natural language IDs for every document to be indexed by generating keyphrases. Tokens from the document (up to the maximum context size of 4000 tokens) are used as part of a prompt to an LM to generate 5 keyphrases. The keyphrases are a brief abstractive summary of the topics in the document. The keyphrases are concatenated together to form the ACID for each document. We create IDs for every document in the training, development, and test sets.

We chose the GPT-3.5 API provided by OpenAI to generate keyphrases, though any reasonable pretrained LM can be used instead. The prompt that we used was:

> Generate no more than 5 key phrases describing the topics in this document. Do not include things like the Wikipedia terms and conditions, licenses, or references section in the list: (document body here)

Extractive Summary IDs. We consider two types of extractive summary IDs: a bag of unigrams selected based on BM25 scores, and the first k tokens of the document. For many types of documents (e.g., news articles, Wikipedia articles, scientific papers), the first few sentences would generally provide an overview of the contents of the document, which motivates our choice of the first k tokens as a kind of extractive document ID.

Cluster-based IDs. By way of comparison with our proposed IDs, cluster-based IDs are integer sequences. An encoder creates an embedding vector for each document in the dataset, and the document embeddings are clustered using the k-means algorithm. If the number of documents in a cluster exceeds a predefined maximum, then subclusters are created recursively, until all subclusters contain fewer documents than the maximum. Each document's ID is a sequence of integers, corresponding to the path to the document through the tree of hierarchical clusters. The number of clusters at each level and the maximum number of documents in each cluster are hyperparameters. (For example, the values reported by Wang et al., 2022, were 10 and 100 respectively, which we also use in our experiments.)

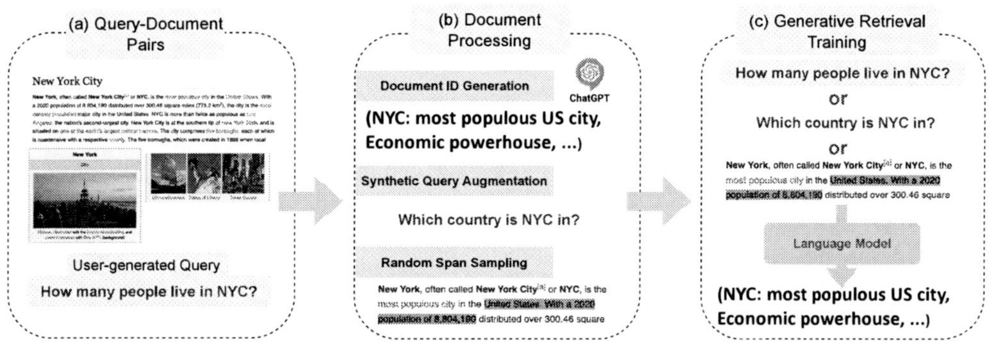

Figure 2: Data processing and model training. (a) Each document-query pair from the training corpus will be converted into inputs and outputs for finetuning the pretrained transformer decoder, which serves as the generative retrieval model. (b) GPT-3.5 is used to generate a sequence of keyphrases, which is used as the document ID. (c) Given a user query or a synthetic query, the generative retrieval model learns to generate the ID of the relevant document. We use a doc2query model to generate synthetic queries as additional inputs. Randomly sampled spans of 64 tokens can also be used as inputs to ensure that the model associates the contents of each document with its ID.

2.2 Document Indexing and Supervised Finetuning

We first index all of the documents in the training, development, and test sets. For indexing purposes, we consider input/output pairs of the form

- (synthetic query, document ID).

In other words, the LM is trained to generate the relevant document ID, given a randomly selected document span or a synthetic query, as part of the indexing task. We use a T5-based query generation model to provide synthetic queries given the body of each document, which serves as a form of data augmentation independent of the queries in the training data. Note that, in our experiments, only synthetic queries are used during the indexing step. Although random document spans are used in other generative retrieval papers, we did not observe an improvement by doing so.

After document indexing, we finetune the model on the retrieval training data:

- (user-generated query, document ID)

In other words, the LM is trained to generate the document ID, given a real, user-generated query.

2.3 Retrieving Documents

At inference time, the LM generates a document ID via beam search, given a user-generated query from the test set. We use a constrained decoder at inference time, which is constrained by a prefix tree such that it can only generate document IDs that exist in the corpus. Since each document ID maps to a unique document, it is straightforward to compute the proportion of queries for which the model retrieved the correct document. Model performance is measured based on the recall of relevant documents retrieved within the top-1, top-10, and top-20 results in our experiments.

3 Experiments

In the experiments below, we demonstrate that summarization-based IDs outperform cluster-based IDs on the NQ and MSMARCO retrieval benchmarks. Simple extractive IDs, like using the first 30 tokens of the document or BM25-based keyword selection, can outperform the cluster-based approach in most cases. We also compare our IDs with another keyword-based document ID method that constructs IDs using learned relevance scores (Zhang et al., 2024). We then show that summarization-based IDs work well across a range of language model sizes (as measured by the total number of parameters). Finally, we show that widening the beam improves retrieval performance meaningfully for ACID, whereas cluster-based IDs benefit from beam width to a lesser degree (or not at all, in the case of the widest beam widths).

The BM25-based IDs were created by ranking all of the unique terms in each document by their BM25 scores, and taking the top 30 terms as the document ID. We used Anserini (Yang et al., 2017) to compute BM25 scores for the documents in each corpus. To avoid selecting very rare terms as part of each document's BM25-based document ID, we required that each term either appear at least 2 times in the document itself, or appear at least 5 times in the corpus.

We use the Natural Questions (NQ; Kwiatkowski et al., 2019) and MSMARCO (Bajaj et al., 2016) datasets. For each dataset, we finetune a pretrained language model for retrieval on 1k, 10k, and 100k random samples of the training split. Note that MSMARCO and NQ do not disclose their test sets publicly, and our results are reported on the provided development sets. Since we did not use the entirety of the training data that was available for NQ and MSMARCO, we created separate development sets for them by taking a random sample of each dataset's training data. We provide the details of each corpus in Table 2. Document length is highly variable, and we truncate all documents after 4k tokens.

We use the Pythia LMs (Biderman et al., 2023) to initialize the retrieval model in our experiments. All of our models are trained on AWS g5 instances equipped with Nvidia A10G GPUs. Models are optimized using AdamW (Loshchilov and Hutter, 2017). We provide the model hyperparameters that were used in the Appendix. The beam width for all experiments is 20, unless stated otherwise.

In Table 2, we provide the basic statistics for the NQ and MSMARCO datasets that we used. We deduplicate documents based on the first 512 tokens of each document, and documents with ≥95% token overlap are considered duplicates.

Note that there is a substantial difference in the average document length between NQ and MSMARCO datasets. While NQ and MSMARCO have queries of similar lengths, their document lengths are very different, since NQ documents are complete Wikipedia articles while MSMARCO passages are a few sentences long, excerpted from a longer document.

	# Pairs	Ave. Query Length	Ave. Doc. Length
NQ-100k	100,000		
NQ-Dev	1,968	49.2	36,379.4
NQ-Test	7,830		
MSMARCO-100k	100,000		
MSMARCO-Dev	2,000	32.8	334.4
MSMARCO-Test	6,980		

Table 2: Dataset characteristics. '# Pairs' refers to the number of query-document pairs. Average lengths refer to the average length in characters.

4 Results

There is substantial variation in the reported results on the NQ dataset among papers that use cluster-based IDs for generative retrieval. In Tay et al. (2022) and Wang et al. (2022), the top-1 recall with the NQ 320k dataset were 27.4% and 65.86% respectively, despite both groups using the same T5-Base model initialization and cluster-based ID approach. There are many possible explanations for the discrepancy (e.g., use of synthetic queries, computational budget, etc.), but at the time of writing, neither paper has made the code or processed data publicly available, which makes replication difficult. For this reason, we focus on internal comparisons rather than external ones, where we control the relevant experimental settings to ensure that the comparisons are fair and the differences in results are meaningful.

4.1 MSMARCO

We begin by examining the performance of our implementations of various types of document IDs on the MSMARCO task. We present the results in Table 3, and all results are based on a 160M-parameter pretrained Pythia LM. Across all training set sizes, the ACIDs offer better retrieval performance compared to the other ID generation techniques, and summarization-based IDs clearly outperform the cluster integer IDs.

4.2 Natural Questions

In Table 4, we compare sparse and dense retrieval techniques against generative retrieval on the NQ dataset. We used the 160M-parameter Pythia LM as our base model to obtain the results in the table. Across the NQ 1k, 10k, and 100k tasks, summarization-based document IDs generally outperform cluster-based integer IDs and TSGen (Zhang et al., 2024). (TSGen learns a scoring function that identifies relevant terms from the document to use as the ID.) As we saw with MSMARCO, the simple approach of using the first 30 tokens from each document to create IDs also outperforms the cluster-based approach.

We further improve the performance of the finetuned 160M-parameter model by performing joint decoding with the 12-billion parameter Pythia LM. We provide 8 query-document ID pairs from the training data to the 12B Pythia model for in-context learning. For a given query, we use both the small model and the large model (with the in-context

	MSMARCO 1k			MSMARCO 10k			MSMARCO 100k		
	Rec@1	@10	@20	Rec@1	@10	@20	Rec@1	@10	@20
Baseline									
Cluster Integer IDs	41.1	59.5	64.2	42.4	62.3	67.1	46.8	68.8	73.4
Extractive Summarization IDs									
BM25 Top-30	48.7	74.3	79.4	49.1	75.7	80.1	52.0	79.2	82.9
First 30 Tokens	49.0	73.0	77.8	48.7	72.8	77.9	51.8	76.0	79.6
Abstractive Summarization IDs									
ACID	**49.1**	**74.3**	**80.1**	**50.4**	**76.3**	**80.4**	**52.9**	**79.5**	**84.0**

Table 3: Recall for MSMARCO. Recall refers to the percentage of queries in the evaluation set for which the ground-truth document ID was produced in the top-1, top-10, and top-20 candidates from constrained beam search decoding. MSMARCO 1k, 10k, and 100k refer to the number of training query-document pairs used to finetune the LM.

	NQ 1k			NQ 10k			NQ 100k		
	Rec@1	@10	@20	Rec@1	@10	@20	Rec@1	@10	@20
Baselines									
BM25	20.9	53.8	62.7	20.9	53.8	62.7	20.9	53.8	62.7
Dense Passage Retrieval	25.8	62.6	70.9	32.8	74.9	82.6	35.5	78.7	86.1
Cluster Integer IDs	38.4	64.2	69.4	40.2	67.5	72.7	40.8	68.2	73.0
TSGen (Zhang et al., 2024)	28.8	67.1	73.6	29.2	67.6	74.4	30.3	71.8	78.3
Summarization-based IDs									
BM25 Top-30	36.5	66.1	70.9	36.8	66.1	71.1	37.0	68.2	72.8
First 30 Tokens	41.9	66.0	69.9	43.3	67.6	71.6	47.7	71.2	74.4
ACID	39.2	69.2	74.0	40.5	70.7	75.2	40.9	74.9	80.2
Summarization-based IDs with Joint Decoding									
First 30 Tokens w/ Joint Dec	**49.1**	**78.7**	**82.6**	**49.7**	**79.2**	**83.1**	**55.3**	**83.0**	**86.4**
ACID w/ Joint Dec	41.3	77.3	82.5	41.3	77.0	82.9	42.3	78.0	84.0

Table 4: Recall for Natural Questions. Recall refers to the percentage of queries in the evaluation set for which the ground-truth document ID was produced in the top-1, top-10, and top-20 candidates from constrained beam search decoding. NQ 1k, 10k, and 100k refer to the number of training query-document pairs used to finetune the LM. 'Joint Dec' refers to joint decoding with the small, task-specific 160M parameter LM and a large 12B parameter LM with in-context learning.

examples) to generate the relevant document ID. The output probabilities from the small and large models are combined using a mixture weight of $\alpha = 0.85$ on the small model.

When we applied joint decoding, the extractive summarization-based document ID that uses the first 30 tokens outperformed all of the other techniques that we examined.

We emphasize that this is one of the major advantages of using generative retrieval with natural-language IDs: we can use a pretrained LLM with in-context learning to significantly boost the performance of a smaller finetuned LM. In contrast, generative retrieval that uses integer IDs does not benefit from joint decoding with an LLM, since the integer ID sequences are far from the pretraining distribution and in-context learning provides no benefit.

We observed that the top-1 recall with the first 30 tokens as the ID is quite high. This may be due to the structure of the NQ documents, which are Wikipedia articles. The first tokens of every document are the title of the Wikipedia page, and so the first 30 tokens represent a very effective ID for retrieval purposes. Nonetheless, without joint decoding, ACID outperforms the first 30 token IDs at top-10 and top-20 recall.

4.3 Model Size

We examine whether the relative outperformance of ACIDs versus cluster integer IDs on MSMARCO is affected by the number of parameters in the generative model. Our default experiments in the previous sections used 160M-parameter Pythia models, and

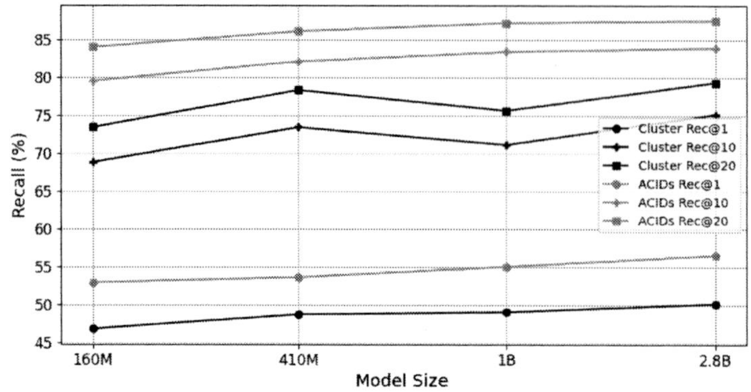

Figure 3: Recall versus the number of parameters in the LM on the MSMARCO 100k dataset.

in Figure 3 we conduct experiments going up to 2.8B-parameter models.

We observe that ACIDs continue to outperform cluster integer IDs, even as we vary the model size. In general, increasing the size of the model leads to an improvement in retrieval performance, regardless of the ID type.

4.4 Beam Width

From Table 5, we see that larger beam widths generally improve recall on MSMARCO, though with rapidly diminishing returns. The top-1 recall does not benefit past a beam width of 8, and the recall rapidly plateaus as beam width increases from 1 to 16. This is true for both cluster integer IDs and ACID, though ACID does benefit more in absolute terms than cluster IDs from a wider beam (when comparing a beam width of 1 to a beam width of 16).

In the same table, we also examine the effect of very wide beams on recall at 10 and 20 for the MSMARCO dataset. Some benefit is observed when ACID is the document ID, but no improvement is observed for cluster IDs.

As discussed previously, the cluster integer ID is typically restricted to a small number of clusters per level (the digits 0 through 9, for example), and so a wide beam in excess of that number doesn't yield any improvements, whereas ACID does benefit from wider beams, since it is a natural-language ID with access to the full vocabulary of the LM.

4.5 ID Length

In Table 6, we present the change in recall on the NQ and MSMARCO tasks depending on the length of the document ID. We use the extractive document ID based on the first 10, 20, 30, and 40 tokens. On MSMARCO 100k, we observe very little change in top-k recall. On NQ 100k, we saw a larger benefit with longer IDs, with the highest recall corresponding to the longest document ID. We speculate that the differences in document length between MSMARCO and NQ ($\sim$334 tokens versus $\sim$36k tokens per document) means that longer IDs tend to benefit the NQ retrieval task more.

5 Related Work

Tay et al. (2022) explore a number of techniques for creating document IDs for generative retrieval, including atomic document IDs, randomly assigned integer IDs, and semantic IDs based on hierarchical clustering. The last technique was found to be the most effective, where the document IDs with were formed via hierarchical k-means clustering on BERT-based document vectors. The main difference between that approach and ours is that, during finetuning, their approach requires learning the "semantics" of the cluster IDs, while ours uses natural language phrases that are already in some sense familiar to the pretrained model. Wang et al. (2022) also used IDs based on hierarchical clustering with BERT embeddings and proposed the prefix-aware weight-adaptor (PAWA) modification, where a separate decoder was trained to produce level-specific linear projections to modify the ID decoder's outputs at each timestep. The authors also incorporated synthetic queries from a doc2query model to augment the user-generated queries in the dataset. Pradeep et al. (2023) scale the cluster ID-based approach to generative retrieval to millions of documents, and explore the impact of adding synthetic queries for documents that do not have a query sourced from a user.

The aforementioned papers used IDs that were

	Cluster IDs			ACIDs		
	Rec@1	@10	@20	Rec@1	@10	@20
Beam width 1	47.6	–	–	54.0	–	–
2	48.7	–	–	56.0	–	–
4	49.0	–	–	55.7	–	–
8	48.8	–	–	56.5	–	–
16	49.0	71.0	–	56.6	84.1	–
20	49.0	71.1	75.6	55.0	83.4	87.2
30	49.0	70.9	75.6	56.4	84.1	88.3
40	49.0	70.9	75.6	56.5	84.1	88.3
50	49.0	70.9	75.6	56.5	84.1	88.4

Table 5: Recall of the 1B-parameter model versus beam width on the MSMARCO 100k dataset.

	MSMARCO 100k			NQ 100k		
	Rec@1	@10	@20	Rec@1	@10	@20
First 10	51.1	75.8	79.8	46.9	65.0	67.6
First 20	50.0	77.0	80.4	46.9	69.1	72.3
First 30	51.8	76.0	79.6	47.7	71.2	74.4
First 40	49.8	75.8	79.2	49.9	72.3	75.4

Table 6: Recall on MSMARCO and NQ 100k versus the length of the document ID. Here, we use the extractive summarization ID based on the first 10, 20, 30, or 40 tokens of each document.

not optimized for the retrieval task, but other work has explored creating document IDs in a retrieval-aware manner. In Sun et al. (2024), the document IDs are treated as a sequence of fixed-length latent discrete variables which are learned via a document reconstruction loss and the generative retrieval loss. However, the authors reported that this method does experience collisions, as some documents are assigned to the same latent integer ID sequence, though the collision rate was not reported.

Bevilacqua et al. (2022) proposed a model that, given a query, generates the n-grams that should appear in the relevant documents. All documents that contain the generated n-grams are then retrieved and reranked to produce the final search results. (This is in contrast our approach, which seeks to associate a unique ID to each document for generative retrieval.) The authors propose several methods for reranking based on n-gram scores produced by the LM. However, the n-gram generation and reranking approach does not always outperform the dense retrieval baseline. Zhang et al. (2024) creates document IDs by selecting terms from the document based on relevance scores that are learned using a contrastive loss and BERT embeddings.

In addition, there is a substantial body of work that involves model-generated text and retrieval. De Cao et al. (2020) generate the text representation of entities autoregressively instead of treating entities as atomic labels in a (potentially very large) vocabulary. Nogueira et al. (2019) use an encoder-decoder model to generate synthetic queries for each document in the index and concatenate them together to improve retrieval performance. The expanded documents are indexed using Anserini and BM25. Synthetic queries from these 'doc2query' models are also used for data augmentation in generative retrieval. Mao et al. (2020) use pretrained language models to expand queries with relevant contexts (e.g., appending the title of a relevant passage to the query, etc.) for retrieval and open-domain question answering.

6 Conclusion

We have demonstrated that summarization-based document IDs are highly effective for generative retrieval. Our results show a clear improvement in retrieval performance on the Natural Questions and MSMARCO datasets versus both cluster-based integer IDs and other keyword-based document IDs. In direct comparisons, abstractive keyphrases work well versus other types of IDs. Surprisingly, we found that the first 30 tokens of a document also works very well among the IDs we tried, but we have not seen this fact documented in the generative retrieval literature. The choice of ID is clearly a major factor in retrieval performance, and we expect that future work will explore other possibilities for creating effective natural-language document IDs.

We also observed that the extractive summarization approach (i.e., first-30 tokens as ID) outperforms the abstractive ACID approach for the long Wikipedia articles in the NQ dataset but not for the shorter snippets in the MSMARCO dataset. Clearly, the characteristics of the documents that are indexed affects generative retrieval, and in the case of Wikipedia documents, the initial sentences tend to be an overview of the rest of the article. As the field of generative retrieval continues to evolve, optimizing document ID generation for specific use cases and document collections may become an important area of study.

Limitations

Due to constraints on our computational budget, the largest dataset that we used contains 100k query-document pairs, which is a subset of the full NQ or MSMARCO datasets, and the largest model that we trained was the 2.8-billion parameter Pythia model, which is not the largest model in the Pythia model family. We expect that the performance characteristics of our method may change as the datasets and models are scaled up to sizes that practitioners in industry settings would typically use.

References

Payal Bajaj, Daniel Campos, Nick Craswell, Li Deng, Jianfeng Gao, Xiaodong Liu, Rangan Majumder, Andrew McNamara, Bhaskar Mitra, Tri Nguyen, et al. 2016. MS MARCO: A human generated machine reading comprehension dataset. In *Proc. of CoCo*.

Michele Bevilacqua, Giuseppe Ottaviano, Patrick Lewis, Scott Yih, Sebastian Riedel, and Fabio Petroni. 2022. Autoregressive search engines: Generating substrings as document identifiers. *Advances in Neural Information Processing Systems*, 35:31668–31683.

Stella Biderman, Hailey Schoelkopf, Quentin Anthony, Herbie Bradley, Kyle O'Brien, Eric Hallahan, Mohammad Aflah Khan, Shivanshu Purohit, USVSN Sai Prashanth, Edward Raff, et al. 2023. Pythia: A suite for analyzing large language models across training and scaling. *arXiv preprint arXiv:2304.01373*.

Nicola De Cao, Gautier Izacard, Sebastian Riedel, and Fabio Petroni. 2020. Autoregressive entity retrieval. *arXiv preprint arXiv:2010.00904*.

Jacob Devlin, Ming-Wei Chang, Kenton Lee, and Kristina Toutanova. 2019. BERT: Pre-training of deep bidirectional transformers for language understanding. In *Proc. of NAACL*.

Mandar Joshi, Eunsol Choi, Daniel S Weld, and Luke Zettlemoyer. 2017. Triviaqa: A large scale distantly supervised challenge dataset for reading comprehension. *arXiv preprint arXiv:1705.03551*.

Vladimir Karpukhin, Barlas Oguz, Sewon Min, Patrick Lewis, Ledell Wu, Sergey Edunov, Danqi Chen, and Wen-tau Yih. 2020. Dense passage retrieval for open-domain question answering. In *Proc. of EMNLP*.

Tom Kwiatkowski, Jennimaria Palomaki, Olivia Redfield, Michael Collins, Ankur Parikh, Chris Alberti, Danielle Epstein, Illia Polosukhin, Jacob Devlin, Kenton Lee, et al. 2019. Natural questions: a benchmark for question answering research. *Transactions of the Association for Computational Linguistics*, 7:453–466.

Ilya Loshchilov and Frank Hutter. 2017. Decoupled weight decay regularization. *arXiv preprint arXiv:1711.05101*.

Yuning Mao, Pengcheng He, Xiaodong Liu, Yelong Shen, Jianfeng Gao, Jiawei Han, and Weizhu Chen. 2020. Generation-augmented retrieval for open-domain question answering. *arXiv preprint arXiv:2009.08553*.

Rodrigo Nogueira, Wei Yang, Jimmy Lin, and Kyunghyun Cho. 2019. Document expansion by query prediction. *arXiv preprint arXiv:1904.08375*.

Ronak Pradeep, Kai Hui, Jai Gupta, Adam D Lelkes, Honglei Zhuang, Jimmy Lin, Donald Metzler, and Vinh Q Tran. 2023. How does generative retrieval scale to millions of passages? *arXiv preprint arXiv:2305.11841*.

Colin Raffel, Noam Shazeer, Adam Roberts, Katherine Lee, Sharan Narang, Michael Matena, Yanqi Zhou, Wei Li, and Peter J. Liu. 2020. Exploring the limits of transfer learning with a unified text-to-text transformer. *JMLR*.

Weiwei Sun, Lingyong Yan, Zheng Chen, Shuaiqiang Wang, Haichao Zhu, Pengjie Ren, Zhumin Chen, Dawei Yin, Maarten Rijke, and Zhaochun Ren. 2024. Learning to tokenize for generative retrieval. *Advances in Neural Information Processing Systems*, 36.

Yi Tay, Vinh Tran, Mostafa Dehghani, Jianmo Ni, Dara Bahri, Harsh Mehta, Zhen Qin, Kai Hui, Zhe Zhao, Jai Gupta, et al. 2022. Transformer memory as a differentiable search index. *Advances in Neural Information Processing Systems*, 35:21831–21843.

Yujing Wang, Yingyan Hou, Haonan Wang, Ziming Miao, Shibin Wu, Qi Chen, Yuqing Xia, Chengmin Chi, Guoshuai Zhao, Zheng Liu, et al. 2022. A neural corpus indexer for document retrieval. *Advances in Neural Information Processing Systems*, 35:25600–25614.

Peilin Yang, Hui Fang, and Jimmy Lin. 2017. Anserini: Enabling the use of lucene for information retrieval research. In *Proceedings of the 40th international ACM SIGIR conference on research and development in information retrieval*, pages 1253–1256.

Peitian Zhang, Zheng Liu, Yujia Zhou, Zhicheng Dou, Fangchao Liu, and Zhao Cao. 2024. Generative retrieval via term set generation. *arXiv preprint arXiv:2305.13859*.

Shengyao Zhuang, Houxing Ren, Linjun Shou, Jian Pei, Ming Gong, Guido Zuccon, and Daxin Jiang. 2023. Bridging the gap between indexing and retrieval for differentiable search index with query generation. *The First Workshop on Generative Information Retrieval at SIGIR*.

Author Index

Association for Computational Linguistics
209 N. Eighth Street
Stroudsburg, Pennsylvania 18360

ISBN 979-8-3313-0856-8

CURRAN ASSOCIATES INC.
proceedings.com